Doing Something
For Someone Else

A History Of The Wisconsin Lions
by Donald P. Rasmussen

Doing Something For Someone Else
A History of the Wisconsin Lions

Donald P. Rasmussen

Copyright 1995, Wisconsin Lions Foundation and New Past Press, Inc.

Publishing Services
Editing, Design, Pre-Press Production by New Past Press, Inc.
Friendship, Wisconsin

Editing: Michael J. Goc
Publishing Assistant, Page Design: Erika Hall

Cover Design: Art provided by
Security Savings Bank, Milwaukee, Wisconsin

Manufactured in the United States of America

ISBN 0-938-627-27-9

Library of Congress Cataloging in Publication

Rasmussen, Donald P.
  Doing something for someone else: a history of the Wisconsin
Lions/ written by Donald P. Rasmussen; edited by Michael J. Goc.
     p.   cm.
  Includes bibliographical references (p.   ) and index.
  ISBN 0-938627-27-9 (hard)
       1. Lions International. Wisconsin District 27–History. 2. Lions
Internationl–History. 3. Friendly societies–Wisconsin-History. 4. Chari-
ties–Wisconsin–History.   I. Goc, Michael J. II. Title.
HS2724.W6R37   1995
369.5–dc20   95-8804
                                                               CIP

This book has been given to
the Wisconsin Lions Foundation Inc.,
and dedicated to
all the past, present and future
Lions, Lionesses and Leos
of Wisconsin.

We give thanks to their families, neighbors,
and friends, for all their help.

Wisconsin Lionism
can take great pride in its many years
and first, in its long list
of service to others.

P.D.G. Lion Donald P. Rasmussen
Wausau, Wisconsin

Information in this book is attributed exclusively
to Donald Rasmussen and not to the
International Association of Lions Clubs

Contents

The History of the Wisconsin Lions

The Wisconsin Lions Today

The Lions International

Foreword

Doing Something For Someone Else is a book of several parts. It represents the life's work of Don Rasmussen, who spent many years researching the story of Lions International and of the Wisconsin Lions, then publishing it in a series of columns for the Wisconsin Lions Magazine. This book consists of those columns, lightly edited and reorganized.

It also includes a photo essay describing the work of the Wisconsin Lions today, and thereby attempts to do the impossible. A few pages in a book can never do justice to the thousands of Wisconsin Lions who live up to the club's wonderfully straightforward creed of service. This book is not large enough – no book could be – to recount every instance of service performed by the Lions of Wisconsin. We can only attempt, as Don Rasmussen has done, to review the record and humbly present a sampling of it.

The Lions organization is both local and international. Lions act locally to serve their neighbors next door. They also think globally, never forgetting that those who live a continent away are also neighbors. Don Rasmussen takes that approach here. He talks about the work of the Lions for international peace in the years after World War II and about the establishment of the Wisconsin Lions Camp. As in Lionism, so in this book, the global accompanies the local.

This theme is well illustrated by the story of Shafeec Mansour, who served as Wisconsin State Secretary in the 1950s. Mansour was a Palestinian-American, fluent in the languages of the Mideast. He used his skills to establish Lions Clubs in Egypt, Turkey, Iran, India and other seemingly exotic places, then came home to the small towns of Wisconsin and did the same thing – establish Lions Clubs, more than 200 of them. What does Argyle, Wisconsin have in common with Cairo, Egypt? Both have Lions Clubs organized with the help of Shafeec Mansour. Both Clubs share a philosophy of service that works equally well in a tiny Wisconsin village and in a teeming mega-city on the edge of the North African desert.

This is only one of the contributions made by a Wisconsin Lion and only one of the stories told by Don Rasmussen. Like Shafeec Mansour, Don Rasmussen thought globally and acted locally. His work is in the best tradition of Lionism, where men and women serve best by "doing something for someone else."

Introduction

This book is to record and preserve as much of the history of the Wisconsin Lions as possible.

Information used came from state records starting in 1941, from records received from Lions International, newspaper accounts and files found in various archives of libraries throughout Wisconsin, and from many cities and Lions state offices and Clubs located throughout the United States.

There is also information from the files of Dr. W.P. Woods furnished by his youngest daughter, Florence W. Foster, Evansville, Indiana, and information from Walter W. Woods D.D.S., of Clarinda, Iowa, a nephew of William Perry Woods.

The history of Lionism begins on August 18, 1911, when Dr. William Perry Woods incorporated the Royal Order of Lions in Indiana. The second important date is October 25, 1916, when he incorporated the International Association of Lions Clubs, also in Indiana.

These articles will prove that Dr. William Perry Woods was the originator, founder, owner and first president of the International Association of Lions Clubs. He was elected to serve as president of the International Association of Lions Clubs at the convention held in the Adolpus Hotel in Dallas, October 9-10, 1917. He was the founder of the International Association of Lions Clubs, and the actual birth place of the International Association of Lions Clubs was in Evansville, Indiana, not in Chicago.

This is also to prove that Dr. William Perry Woods never attended any meeting, or the meeting of June 7, 1917 which was claimed to have been held in Chicago, Illinois. Dr. William Perry Woods claimed that the first time he ever met Melvin Jones was when Melvin Jones called on Dr. Woods in Evansville, Indiana sometime after June 7, 1917, and after Dr. W.P. Woods called for the first meeting to be held in Dallas, Texas.

It was during this visit in Evansville, Indiana that Melvin Jones asked for, and did receive permission for his club, the Business Circle in

Chicago, to join the Lions. He also asked if he could attend the Dallas meeting in October, 1917 and Dr. Woods agreed. These articles will also tell of the work and dedication that Melvin Jones put into Lionism during and after the early, formative years.

There is a list of all the clubs claiming to be Lions Clubs during the Dallas convention, and they are called Founder Clubs. I have not seen or heard if they gave the representatives any distinction, but I would believe that any Lion representative at this convention could be known as Founder Representatives. Therefore, Melvin Jones could call himself a Founder, but not on the same basis as Dr. William Perry Woods, who started and owned the organization.

The first Club to be organized in Wisconsin was in Milwaukee on June 21, 1921. Wisconsin was granted District status, and became District 27 during the International Convention which was held in Hot Springs, Arkansas, during June 19-24, 1922. In the years since, Lionism has grown in Wisconsin, and now consists of ten sub-districts.

We are very proud of our Lions Camp where visually handicapped children and adults can spend a week or longer on Lions Lake.

We are also proud of our eye bank, organ and tissue transplant program. Each year, new records are reached in the number of enunciation of eyes.

Our used eyeglass program is nearing the mark of six-million-pairs, and still going strong.

Over the years, our clubs have originated many "firsts" in projects, and each year, have come up with new ways to raise funds, and new projects to use the funds on.

My thanks to all the Lions, Lionesses, and others who have helped me secure the information that went into this book.

This history has been written as fully and accurately as possible.

Of course, I could not have done it without the help, patience and encouragement that my good wife Irene has given me over the years.

PDG Lion Donald P. Rasmussen

The History
of the
Wisconsin
Lions

Fond du Lac Lions "Gambol," 1923

Milwaukee Lions Club

The first Lions Club in Wisconsin was organized in Milwaukee on June 10, 1921, with fifty Chartered Members. Then known as the Milwaukee Lions Club, it has evolved into Milwaukee Central. Major Christian J. Otjen was elected President; Dr. Gustave I. Hogue, First Vice President; Omar McMahon, Second Vice President; Herbert M. Kieckhefer, Third Vice President; Carl A. Foster, Treasurer, and E.P. Kirby Hade, Secretary.

On November 9, 1921, the Lions of Milwaukee and the state's second club, organized at Racine, received their Charter. The Charter Night banquet, held at Milwaukee's Republican House, was attended by delegates from Chicago, Detroit, Cleveland, Racine and a number of other nearby clubs. Melvin Jones presented the Charter to the Lions Clubs of Milwaukee and Racine. In his remarks, Jones announced a campaign to increase the number of clubs to 600. By charter night, the total charter membership of the Milwaukee club had increased to sixty business and professional men. The committee in charge of the affair was made up of Allen Chalhoun, H.M. Kieckhefer and K.L. Jacobs.

One of the Charter members was Dr. Gustave Hogue, M.D., a leading Milwaukee eye, nose and throat specialist. He managed one of the club's major activities, its *work amongst the blind*. Dr. Hogue headed a drive for the treatment of eyes of newborn babies with nitrate of silver. Administering this eye treatment soon became law, first in Wisconsin, then throughout the country.

It was only one of many pioneering accomplishments of the Milwaukee Club. The Club also:

> • *Instituted an annual Christmas Party for 300–400 sightless people.*

13

● *Convinced the federal government to allow a news-stand operated by a blind man in the federal court-house.*

● *Prompted the city of Milwaukee to pass an ordinance requiring police and bus drivers to help "Red and White Cane" users cross the streets.*

● *Organized a baby clinic in Milwaukee which sponsored the examination of 1,000 babies by the doctors of the Milwaukee Pediatric Society.*

● *Sponsored the exhibit "Freedom on the March" for the Northwest Territory Celebration in 1937.*

● *Donated a pair of lion cubs to the Milwaukee Zoo.*

● *Supported the Leader Dogs for the Blind School in Rochester, Michigan, the Wisconsin Lions Foundation, and the Wisconsin Eye Bank program.*

In honor of the thousands of dollars it had received over the years, the Milwaukee Children's Hospital dedicated a room to the Milwaukee Club.

By 1937, so many new Lions Clubs had been organized in the Milwaukee area, that the original club agreed to International's request that it be renamed Milwaukee Central (Downtown). Membership was also limited to one hundred.

Over the years, Milwaukee Central helped organize new clubs at Delafield-Summit, Hartland, Oconomowoc, East Troy, Memomonee Falls, Grafton, Watertown, Wauwatosa, West Milwaukee, West Allis, Layton Park, South Milwaukee, Washington Park, Uptown, Midtown, Southwest, Northwest, North Side and South Side Milwaukee.

Milwaukee Central Lions who have served as District Governors include: Robert E. Hine, 1925-26; Frank V. Birch, 1929-30; Rev. J. Olson, 1934-35; Dr. H.J. Watson, 1937-39; Ollie Seegers, 1943-44.

After serving as District Governor, Lion Frank V. Birch was elected and served as an International Director. He moved onto Third, Second and First Vice President and was elected and served as President of the Lions International for 1937-38.

The Lions Club Magazine for March 20, 1920 contained an item worthy of note. It stated that on February 18, 1920, a meeting of Milwaukee business men was held at the Athletic Club for the purpose of forming an Lions' Den in Milwaukee. Seven Lions, including Melvin Jones from Chicago, attended and approximately 70 members were enrolled. Directors included August A. Jones, Herman Fehr, Frank Weyenberg, Albert Friedman, E.A. Reddman, F.W. Fellenz, Louis Essex and Charles E. Walters. This meeting and, presumably, the organization of this club, took place some 16 months before the first meeting of the Milwaukee Lions Club as chartered. There is no further record of what happened to this club.

The Milwaukee Central Club, the oldest in the state, can be very proud of its great record of service.

From the Lions Club Magazine, December, 1921

"Parchment" For Milwaukee Club

The charter night meeting of the Milwaukee, Wisconsin, Lions Club was held with enthusiasm as the dominant feature, Wednesday evening, November 9th.

The banquet room of the Republican House seldom has accommodated a more enthusiastic gathering and the committee had provided plenty of entertainment and a luscious dinner.

President C.J. Otjen opened the speaking program by outlining the progress of the club from the initial meeting last June and offered his idea of the possibilities of the club as a civic organization–and Chris, who has quite a reputation as an after-dinner speaker, was at his best. Every Lion present was inspired to redouble his efforts for the club.

"Tommy" Atkinson, a leading figure in the Rotary Club, then welcomed the Lions into the circle of civic organizations in Milwaukee. "Tommy" together with Fred Schroeder, treasurer of the same club, has been one of the true friends of the Lions during the summer. From time to time these men offered sage advice to the new Clubs, and in an inspiring talk on Lionism, Mr. Atkinson congratulated them on the progress they have made.

The charter, or "old parchment," as the Cream City Clubs called it, was presented by the International Secretary - General, Melvin Jones, and incidentally he gave them a clear idea of their responsibilities as Lions, and told them in a beautiful manner of the ideals and purposes of Lionism.

The club's officers for the year are: President Major Christian J. Otjen; First Vice-President, Dr. Gustavus I. Hogue; Second Vice-President, Herbert M. Kieckhefer; Third Vice-President, Omar T. MacMahon; Treasurer, Carl A. Forster; Secretary, E. P. Kirby Hade.

Early History and Growth of Wisconsin District 27

In 1917, when Lionism began, Wisconsin was not even a district. The state was divided to become part of District Nine and District Two. The eastern portion of Wisconsin joined six other states to form the original Ninth District, later to become known as "The Old Ninth." These states were Illinois, Michigan, Ohio, Nebraska, Indiana and Iowa. The western portion of Wisconsin was attached to District Two, which included Minnesota, North Dakota and South Dakota. The border started where the southwest corner of La Crosse County meets the Mississippi River, across from the northeast corner of Iowa. This line then extended north along county lines to Lake Superior. (Plates One and Two)

At the 2nd annual International Convention held at the Marquette Hotel in St. Louis, Missouri on August 19-21, 1918, George W. Milligan of Chicago, Illinois, was appointed first District Governor of the original Ninth District, and William A. Repke of St. Paul, Minnesota was appointed the District Governor of the original District Two.

The 3rd annual International Convention was held at the Hotel La Salle, Chicago, Illinois, on July 9-11, 1919, and Judge John F. Garner of Quincy, Illinois was appointed as the Second District Governor of the original Ninth District.

The first district convention of the original Ninth District was held at Quincy, Illinois in 1920. It was little more than a conference, for Illinois, with nine clubs, was the only state of the seven with more than one or two Lions Clubs. District Governor John F. Garner was elected by the delegates for a second term, and Peoria, Illinois was selected for the 1921 convention.

The second district convention of the Old Ninth District was held at Peoria, Illinois during June 9-10, 1921. There were no delegates from

Wisconsin at this convention, as the Milwaukee Lions Club was not organized until the second day of that convention. Dr. John W. Scott of Springfield, Illinois was elected District Governor and it was voted to hold the 1922 District Convention at Decatur, Illinois.

During the 5th annual International Convention held in the Hotel Oakland at Oakland, California during July 19-22, 1921, the constitution and bylaws were revised, and the whole country was redistricted. To honor the state which was then considered the birthplace of Lionism, Illinois was named the First District. Also included in the First were Indiana, Missouri, and the eastern portion of Wisconsin. The strip along the western border of Wisconsin remained attached to what was then known as District 5, which was made up of Minnesota and the two Dakotas.

More clubs were organized and chartered in Wisconsin, so by convention time in Decatur, Illinois on May 22, 1922, there was a large delegation of Wisconsin Lions. These delegates went by train or by automobile, singly or in caravans, and in those days, the roads were few, rough and often minus road markers.

It was at this convention that Wisconsin delegates requested District status. This request, along with the requests of the Lions from Indiana and Missouri, was approved at the international convention, held at Hot Springs, Arkansas on July 19-22, 1922. These states then split away from Illinois, (and Wisconsin was split away from both District One, Illinois, and District 5, Minnesota). Illinois remained as District One, Indiana became District 25, Missouri became District 26, and Wisconsin became District 27.

Although Wisconsin was a full District, it was not a full district as we know it today. It took a whole year of effort in 1922 and 1923, on the part of our first District Governor, Rev. J.A Holmes of Appleton, to reclaim that western border strip of Wisconsin, and unite the entire State of Wisconsin, as it is shown in Plate Four. (A record shows that District Five had turned over the western portion of Wisconsin to District One, and District One to Wisconsin when Wisconsin gained District status, but the Lion members in the western portion of Wisconsin resisted being united with the eastern portion of Wisconsin to make District 27 the district as we now know it, because of their close ties with their old District of Minnesota and the Dakotas).

Wisconsin held its first convention as an independent District 27 in Madison on May 15-16, 1923. Wisconsin now had 15 clubs with 712 members in Appleton, Ashland, Eau Claire, Fond du Lac, Green Bay, Janesville, La Crosse, Madison, Manitowoc, Milwaukee, Racine, Superior, Two Rivers, Sheboygan and Wausau.

The following Plates illustrate how the United States was divided in 1917, and later in 1921. The rest of the plates deal with Wisconsin and how it was subdivided since 1922.

Plate One

International records tell that under the first arrangement, the districts were numbered with more or less regularity, eastward from the Pacific Coast.

The districts were:

- **District One** - California, Oregon, Washington, Nevada, and Hawaii

- **District Two** - Minnesota, North Dakota, South Dakota and the western portion of Wisconsin

- **District Three** - Colorado, Wyoming and Montana

- **District Four** - The western portion of Texas, New Mexico and Arizona

- **District Five** - The eastern portion of Texas, Louisiana, Mississippi, Alabama, Georgia and Florida

- **District Six** - Oklahoma and Kansas

- **District Seven** - Arkansas and Missouri

- **District Eight** - Kentucky and Tennessee

- **District Nine** - Illinois, Iowa, Nebraska, Ohio, Michigan and the eastern portion of Wisconsin

NOTE: Because there were no clubs in the other states and no method for organizing or administering Lions Clubs, states not mentioned or shaded on the map, were not included in any of those districts. At times, Mississippi was attached to District Eight with Kentucky and Tennessee.

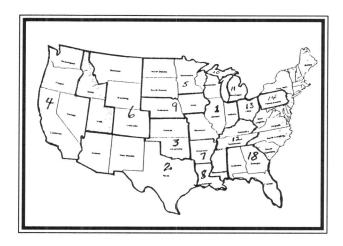

Plate Two

Lionism grew rapidly. Soon there were so many clubs in some districts, that the District Governor could not afford the time to visit and International could not afford the money to properly assist them. Also, Lions Clubs sprang up in states which were outside any district, and it was necessary to direct and control them. Therefore redistricting became an imperative matter.

During the 5th International Convention in Oakland in 1921, delegates redistricted the country. Illinois became District One as an honor, because it was considered the birth place of Lionism, and where the International headquarters was located.

It was noted that following this redistricting, there was confusion over the new numbering system, and the new District Five was using District Six for awhile.

- **District One** - Illinois, Indiana, Missouri and the eastern portion of Wisconsin

- **District Two** - Texas, New Mexico and Arizona

- **District Three** - Oklahoma and Kansas

- **District Four** - California, Oregon, Washington and Nevada

- **District Five** - Minnesota, North Dakota, South Dakota and the western portion of Wisconsin

  Later on this district was changed as listed below:

- **District Five-C** - Saskatchewan

- **District Five-M** - Minnesota, Manitoba and Ontario

- **District Five-N** - North Dakota

- **District Five-S** - South Dakota

- **District Six** - Colorado, Wyoming and Montana

- **District Seven** - Arkansas

20

- **District Eight** - Louisiana and sometimes Mississippi

- **District Nine** - Iowa and Nebraska

- **District Ten** - Upper Michigan

- **District Eleven** - Lower Michigan

- **District Twelve** - Kentucky, Tennessee and Mississippi

- **District Thirteen** - Ohio

- **District Fourteen** - Pennsylvania

Following this redistricting and as soon as any of the states which were either attached or unattached to other districts had enough clubs of their own, they asked for district status, and when district status was granted, it was given the lowest number remaining open.

Plate Three   **Plate Four**

Plate Three: This plate shows where Wisconsin was divided from the northeast corner of Iowa to Lake Superior.

Plate Four: Wisconsin when it became District 27 in 1922-'23.

Plate Five

Plate Six

Plate Seven

Plate Five: By 1936 the number of clubs in Wisconsin had increased so that the District Governor was having trouble making his required visits. During the 1936-37 year, plans were made to subdivide Wisconsin District 27 into smaller districts, each with its own District Governor. This resulted in the creation of Sub Districts A, B, and C.

Plate Six: In 1938, District A had grown so fast that it was divided into two districts. District D was formed by combining parts of District A and C.

Plate Seven: In 1949-'50, District C was divided again and District E created.

Plate Eight   **Plate Nine**

Plate Eight: District B was divided into Districts B1, and B2 during 1966-67.

Plate Nine: In 1968-69, District C was again divided, and became Districts C1 and C2.

Plate Ten   **Plate Eleven**

Plate Ten: In 1971-'72, District A was divided into Districts A1 and A2.

Plate Eleven: District E was divided in 1979-'80 to form E1 and E2.

Plate Twelve

Plate Twelve: In 1980-81, District D was divided, and formed Districts D1 and D2.

Wisconsin then had ten sub-districts. During the past seventy-plus years, the Lions of Wisconsin have worked hard to create a Lionistic record which each Lion, Lioness and Leo member can be very proud of.

Secretary - Treasurers

District Secretary-Treasurer
Albert L. Thuemler

In the early days of Wisconsin Lionism, the state was just one District, with just one District Governor who appointed the District Secretary. The first appointees are listed as follows:

May 22, 1922, E.P. Kirby Hade, Milwaukee

May 15-16, 1923, E.P. Kirby Hade

May 26-27, 1924, *Robert E. Hine, Milwaukee

May 26-27, 1925, H.H. Twose, Milwaukee

May 24-24, 1926, a member of the La Crosse Club

May 20-21, 1927, a member of the New London Club

* An International Lions report for the 1924 Wisconsin State Lions Convention, which was held in Green Bay, reports that the convention chose as its secretary Lion F. Stuart Rodger. Yet, records at International state that Robert E. Hine of Milwaukee was the secretary for the 1924-1925 year.

* At the third convention held at Fond du Lac, a resolution was passed which changed the method of selecting a district secretary. Instead of electing him at the convention, the newly elected District Governor was given the authority to appoint a secretary from his own club. In all the records that I have checked, I cannot find any names of secretaries for the 1926-1927 and the 1927-1928 years.

In 1928, Lion A. L. Thuemler of Sheboygan was appointed to serve as the first District Secretary-Treasurer for District 27.

He joined the Sheboygan Lions Club on February 27th, 1923, and served on various committees before being elected Secretary. He held this position for over twenty-eight years, maintaining a perfect attendance record for every year he was a member.

During his seven years as District Secretary-Treasurer, he served under the following District Governors: Rev. M.S. Weber of Manitowoc, F.V. Birch of Milwaukee, George H. Dobbins of Weyauwega, Lawson E. Lurvey of Fond du Lac, Roman C. Heilman of Madison, Sidney Kaye of Sheboygan, and Rev. Richard Olson of Milwaukee. He rewrote the state constitution and bylaws as adopted at the 1931 Madison Convention. He edited, supervised the printing of, and distributed the "Badger Lion," state bulletin.

While a Deputy District Governor, he also served as a Zone Chairman for three years in the eastern zone of Wisconsin. Meetings were held at Sturgeon Bay, Manitowoc, Washington Island, Fond du Lac, Campbellsport and Sheboygan. In those days, they held two Zone meetings each year. He also attended twenty international conventions and served on various international convention committees. He attended over twenty-five state conventions and served on many state committees. He also found time to inaugurate annual joint meetings with the Manitowoc Lions Club and proposed many successful projects for the Sheboygan Lions Club.

Lion Al was born in Sheboygan, Wisconsin, February 27, 1880. He married Marian Van Ouwerkerk of Sheboygan Falls, August 10, 1910, in Chicago. At the time of the marriage, Mrs. Thuemler was an employee of *The Sheboygan Press.*

After the completion of his education in the Sheboygan grade and high schools in 1899, Al began work as a clerk of the municipal court. In 1902, he was appointed clerk of the Sheboygan County Court and soon after he accepted the post of trust officer of the Citizens State Bank, a position he held until he retired in January, 1951. He became known as "Pa Thuemler" to the employees of the bank. During this time, Lion Al also worked as a reporter for the *Sheboygan Telegram,* covering sports, theatricals, courts and police.

Always interested in local sports activities, particularly basketball, he organized the first Sheboygan amateur basketball team in 1902-03.

In 1915, he organized and coached a local girls basketball team known as the "Sheboygan Kelleys." He formerly served as chairman of the board of appeals for the city, managed the Concordia Hall, and was a trustee of the Fraternal Order of Eagles, and secretary of the Sheboygan Lions Club. Lion Albert L. Thuemler passed away April 10, 1962.

District Secretary-Treasurer
Oliver C. Wordell

In 1935, Lion Oliver (Ollie) C. Wordell of Brillion, Wisconsin became the second Lion to serve Wisconsin District 27 as a District-Secretary-Treasurer. He served through 1939, when he was appointed editor of the *Badger Lion*, where he worked until 1941.

Lion Wordell joined the Brillion Lions Club on June 12, 1929 as a Charter Member and had perfect attendance until March 27, 1979 when poor health forced him to miss a meeting. He received an Honorary Life Time Membership on January 19, 1978 and, on May 6, 1979, the Club's observance of its 50th Anniversary was dedicated to him.

He was Brillion's Chartered Secretary and served as the Club's Secretary (1929-1939), State Secretary-Treasurer (1935-1939), Cabinet Secretary-Treasurer for District Governor F.J. Flanagan (1942-1943), and Club President (1949-1950).

He promoted Brillion's Golden Jubilee in 1935, was instrumental in securing an auditorium for the Brillion High School in 1939-1940, and led a fund drive for a lighted athletic field in 1950. "Ollie" and his wife Irene were religious in their attendance at state and international conventions, as well as at Lions functions in the local, zone and district levels.

He was a great Lion and citizen, in his club and his community. Lion "Ollie" Wordell passed away on March 27, 1979.

State Secretaries

Shafeec A. Mansour

Early in the summer of 1949 the Milwaukee (Central) Lions Club was holding their regular noon meeting in the Milwaukee Sport Club. It was one of those beautiful days in June that could have made this an "eat it and beat it" meeting, even though they had a speaker whose subject was "conditions in Palestine," a topic of great interest and importance during those days. The late George Cashou, a leading oriental rug dealer in Milwaukee and originally from Palestine, had invited and introduced the speaker. The membership was composed of leading business leaders of Milwaukee. Usually, they met at 12:00 noon and adjourned at around 1:00 or 1:30 p.m. Shafeec Mansour stopped his speech at 1:00 p.m., but the members decided to extend the time for adjournment. The Israeli-Palestinian conflict was at its height, and Mansour so intrigued the Lions that his talk and the questions continued until 4:30 p.m. It was the first time in the history of the Milwaukee Central Club that a meeting was in session so long. Reporters from the *Milwaukee Journal* and the *Milwaukee Sentinel* were in attendance and they returned with Mansour to his office in the Central Milwaukee Y.M.C.A. and continued asking questions until long past 6:00 p.m.

During the meeting, Past International President Lion Frank Birch became so impressed with Mansour that he made a special effort to get better acquainted by inviting Shafeec to meet with him in his office the next morning.

Birch learned that Shafeec had been devoted to the welfare and service of his fellows in the Palestinian cities of Jaffa and Jerusalem, where he served for twenty-five years as Secretary of the Y.M.C.A. Mansour was looking for work where he could again serve others and wanted to find out more about Lions Clubs International. At this time the Lions Clubs International was planning to expand outside North

America, so Birch called up Melvin Jones and recommended Shafeec very strongly for the overseas extension.

Jones invited Mansour to come to Chicago. With a letter of introduction from Lion Birch to Secretary-General Jones in his pocket, Shafeec was on the morning train the next day. Jones and his associates quickly recognized the qualities and possibilities that Shafeec had to offer. He was an experienced organizer and an eloquent orator who could speak five languages. They immediately invited him to join their staff, and after summer vacations, he started work on September 6, 1949.

He was given an office right next to Mr. Jones and, for the next three months, Shafeec translated into French and Arabic club constitutions, general information folders, the Jones Law, *The World's Biggest Doers* and other publications of Lions Clubs International. His translations were later used in extension work overseas. Shafeec commuted to Chicago each Monday and returned to his home in Milwaukee on Fridays.

After the translation work was completed, Shafeec devoted all of his time to Extension work with R. Roy Keaton, Director General of Lions Clubs International. On January 1, 1950, he was officially appointed in charge of Extension work in Wisconsin, with its 137 clubs and 6,402 members. A few months later, Upper Michigan was added to his territory. On August 6, 1950, the Mansour family moved to Merrill, Wisconsin, which was more central to his Extension work. By July 1, 1950–six months later–Shafeec had started 32 new Lions Clubs, mostly in District 27-A.

Actually, Lions Clubs Extension work was not new to Shafeec. In the summer of 1949, before he started his work with Lions Clubs International, he worked at the Manitowish Y.M.C.A. summer camp. Acquainted with Lions Clubs International and its work through his meetings with Melvin Jones and Roy Keaton, he promoted, organized and became a Charter Member of his first Lions Club, in nearby Boulder Junction.

At Merrill, Shafeec became acquainted with Lion Raymond A. Galipeau Sr. who later became the fourth Wisconsin Lion to serve as a Director on the International Board of Lions Clubs International. Ray was elected to this position at the 55th International Convention which was held in Mexico City, Mexico, June 28th-July 1st, 1952.

In 1953, Shafeec started his Overseas Extension work and, during six extension and service missions, promoted and organized Lions Clubs in 15 different countries: Greece, India, Pakistan, Iran, Burma, Ceylon, Lebanon, Jordan, Turkey, Cyprus, Egypt, Syria, Sudan, Iraq and Libya.

Shortly, International Director Ray Galipeau became convinced that in order to properly serve the nearly 200 clubs here, Wisconsin would soon require a permanent office. To have a permanent State Secretary, Lions Clubs International required a district or state to have at least 250 clubs.

In November 1958, the Mansours moved to Wausau. That year, former Director General R. Roy Keaton, citing the number of Clubs that he had organized in Wisconsin, agreed to Shafeec's appointment as State Secretary for Multiple District 27-Wisconsin, and International Representative for District 10, Upper Michigan. International Director Ray Galipeau also added his recommendation and Lions Clubs International appointed Shafeec Mansour the first paid State Secretary for Multiple District 27. He held the position until his retirement on September 1, 1969.

Shafeec's wife Eleanor was a great help in taking care of the details of the office work for the two Districts and also during the time of Shafeec's Extension work overseas.

Shafeec Mansour's Overseas Extension Work

August, 1953
- In three months, he founded Lionism in two countries–Lebanon and Jordan–and organized three new Lions Clubs.

1954-55
- Over five months, he organized ten new Lions Clubs and founded Lionism in five countries: Greece, 1; Turkey, 1; Cyprus, 2; Lebanon, 2; Egypt, 1; Jordan, 1; Syria, 2.

1955-56
- In three months, he started six new clubs in three new countries: Egypt, 2; Sudan, 1; India, 2; Pakistan, 1.

1956-57
- In six months, 15 new clubs and 2 new countries: India, 10; Pakistan, 3; Iran, 1; Iraq, 1.

1958

- In four-and-one-half months, 8 new clubs, 3 new countries: India, 5; Libya, 1; Ceylon, 1; Burma, 1.

1961

- In Seven months, he saved 17 clubs in 7 countries; Lebanon, 3; Jordan, 3; Egypt, 3; Sudan, 3; Libya, 1; Syria, 2; Cyprus, 2.

The governments of these countries had ordered their Lions Clubs to sever relations with Lions Clubs International. Lions Clubs had begun in Israel and these countries had declared a boycott on any nation, business or organization that had relations with the Jewish state. A Palestinian himself, Shafeec was able to convince the governments to withdraw their orders and allow these clubs to renew their affiliation with the Lions Clubs International.

In the course of his work, Shafeec met many kings, presidents and other prominent people in the Middle East. On his list were King Hussein II of Jordan; Reza Pahlavi, Shah of Iran; King Faisal II of Iraq; Emperor Haile Selassie of Ethiopia; President Gamel Abdul Nasser of Egypt; President Archbishop Makarios of Cyprus; Prime Minister Jawaharlal Nehru of India; and Pope John XXIII. He also met with the rulers of Sudan, Lebanon, Greece, Syria, Ceylon, Burma, Iraq, Libya and Pakistan.

After traveling to all these exotic places and meeting people who dominated much of the history of their times, Shafeec Mansour came home to the small towns and villages of Wisconsin and Upper Michigan. He promoted and organized a total of 382 Lions Clubs in Wisconsin, Upper Michigan, Africa, Asia and Europe. He didn't stop even after his retirement. He organized one Club and reorganized another in Oregon, pushing his grand total to 384 Clubs.

During his many years of Lionism, Shafeec received many State, District and International Awards, and was one of few Lions to receive the Director General's Award. Shafeec was also presented with the Distinguished Recognition Award by Wisconsin Governor Warren P. Knowles, who acknowledged with grateful appreciation, his dedicated service in the promotion of the state of Wisconsin.

Shafeec, who was born in Nazareth, Palestine, on January 29, 1904, was of Palestinian Arab Christian descent. A citizen of the United States, he could speak, read and write Arabic, English, French, German and Turkish. Shafeec attended English schools in Palestine, graduated with honors from St. Joseph's College in Jaffa and George Williams College in Chicago, where he majored in Y.M.C.A. Administration and Social Sciences. He worked for four years as Inspector of the Department of Customs, Excise and Trade of the Government of Palestine during the British Mandate and for twenty-five years as secretary of the Jaffa and Jerusalem Y.M.C.A.s. Co-founder of the largest orphanage in Palestine, he spent three years broadcasting regular weekly programs for the youth of the Arab world. He was active in and has held offices in many Masonic organizations and has served as superintendent of Sunday schools in Palestine and the United States. He was also a past-president of the United Nations Association of the United States, Wausau, Wisconsin-and listed in the *Midwest Who's Who.*

A student of history and the Bible, Shafeec presented a comprehensive review of Palestine to the United Nations covering the religious, historical, national and humanitarian aspects of Palestine for the 4,500 years from 2,500 BC to 1946 AD. During his 20 years as state secretary of Wisconsin Lions Multiple District 27, he was instrumental in organizing and promoting the Wisconsin Lions Camp.

Eleanor Mansour was born in Pluderhausen, Germany on September 19, 1909 and met Shafeec in Chicago in 1931. They were married in Pluderhausen on November 25, 1933. They had two children: Dr. Nabeel Mansour, who is married and a professor at Oregon State University in Corvallis, Oregon; and Randa who, with her husband Dr. Robert Rice, lives in Turlock, California. Upon retiring, Shafeec and Eleanor moved to Corvallis, Oregon, where he remained a Lion. He became president of the Mid Valley Lions Club, Corvallis, Oregon for the year 1986-87 and a Melvin Jones Fellow.

Shafeec passed away January 31, 1992 in Corvallis, Oregon and was buried in the Oaklawn Memorial Park Cemetery there.

State Secretary James W. Wenzel

The office is now closed and the sign on the door says, "Closed–Gone Fishing."

When he retired, Lion Jim and his wife Ann found it great just to go fishing, and while fishing, they reminiscenced about his many Lionistic years and the mementos which decorated their home.

James Wenzel joined the East Troy Lions Club in 1947, and has held all club offices except Lion Tamer. Jim served as Zone Chairman (1950-60), Deputy District Governor (1960-61), and was a 100 per cent District Governor of District 27-A (1961-62), the year the international convention was held in Nice, France.

On July 1, 1969, upon the retirement of State Secretary Shafeec Mansour, Wenzel was appointed special representative of Lions Clubs International and assigned to Wisconsin. The Wisconsin State Council of Governors then appointed Wenzel as Wisconsin State Secretary and the State Office was located at Stevens Point. Jim transferred his membership to the Stevens Point Noon Lions Club.

On July 1, 1980, the State Secretary and the Extension Representative positions were split, and Jim then spent full time as Extension Representative. He and Ann moved their home and office to St. Germain, where Jim became an active member of the St. Germain Lions. Jim continued his extension work until he retired June 30, 1983.

During his years as State Secretary and Extension Representative, Lionism in Wisconsin grew from 13,000 members in 369 clubs to 24,000 members in 519 clubs.

Lion Jim has attended thirty-one state conventions, twenty-four international conventions, and has served on various state and International committees. During his Lionistic years, he received many state and International awards, including the Ambassador of Good Will Award, two International Presidential Awards, and the Melvin Jones Award of the East Troy Lions Club. For his exceptional work in extension-during which he organized twenty or more clubs per year–he received four International Presidential Extension Awards.

"Jim" was born in Loyal, Wisconsin, May 3, 1917. Ann Anich was born in West Allis, but was raised and lived most of her life in Mukwonago, Wisconsin. Jim and Ann were married May 25, 1946 and have three children Tim, Mary, and John. Ann passed away in 1994.

State Secretary Gary M. Lutz

Our next state secretary was from the Stevens Point area. Gary Lutz joined the Plover-Whiting Lions Club in December 1970, was elected to the Club's Board in 1971 and served as Club President during (1973-74). Lion Gary served as Zone chairman of District 27-C1 (1974-75), Deputy District Governor (1975-77) and as a 100 Per Cent District Governor in 1977-78. In 1979, he was elected to the Wisconsin Lions Foundation and served on the Camp Committee. He applied for and was

selected by the 1978-79 Council to serve as the State Secretary for the Wisconsin Lions, effective July 1, 1980.

Shortly, Lion Gary moved the State Office to 2715 Post Road, and in 1992 to 2809 Post Road. Upon the death of PID Ray Galipeau, he took over the general operations of the *Wisconsin Lions Magazine*. He later assumed responsibility for the State Lions Pin program, established the Research and Long Range Planning Committee and, in 1985, arranged for the purchase of the Lions first computer.

PDG Gary has attended international conventions since 1977 and all the USA FORUMS since the first was held in that same year.

The many awards which Lion Gary has received over the years include the Melvin Jones Fellow Award, presented to him by the Plover-Whiting Lions Club after he completed his year as District Governor.

Gary was born in Stevens Point on December 1, 1937. After receiving a First Class Radio Telephone License from the DeVry Technical Institute in Chicago, he was hired by AT&T at Palmyra, Wisconsin and, in 1963, AT&T transferred him home to Stevens Point.

On June 27, 1959, Gary married his high school sweetheart, Georgia Gountanis. They have three children: Bill, Dan and Judy. Due to health reasons, PDG Gary resigned as State Secretary effective December 31, 1986.

State Secretary Alan B. Becker

On February 7, 1987, Alan B. Becker was appointed State Secretary of the Wisconsin Lions. Lion Al had joined the South Milwaukee Lions Club in 1965, served as club secretary (1967-1968, 1982-1987) and as club president during the 1970-1971 year. On the District A1 level, Lion Al has served in different years as Chair of the Lions Information Committee, L.C.I.F., Public Relations, as Extension Co-chairman (East), Zone Chairman and Deputy District Governor. He has helped to organize three Lions Clubs.

After receiving his Masters Degree from Marquette University, he  spent 12 more years there as a faculty member. He was with Blue Cross and Blue Shield United of Wisconsin from 1970 until February 7, 1987, working with company publications, contracts and promotional literature. He was a product development manager when he left Blue Cross to accept his position with the Lions.

Lion Al is a veteran who has served four years in the US Navy as a part of the Fleet Marine Force and is a life member of the Disabled American Veterans. He is very active in civic organizations, having served on the South Milwaukee School Board (1972-1984) and spent four years on the board of Cooperative Education Service Agency 19.

He has maintained a perfect attendance record since he joined the Lions, is a Melvin Jones Fellow, a Master Key member, holds three Extension Awards and received the International President's Award in 1984. Lion Al and his wife, Marie, have one daughter, Heidi. He resigned as State Secretary effective January 1, 1988.

State Secretary Debi Lutz

Debi Lutz was appointed to serve as the Wisconsin State Lions State Secretary, effective July 1, 1988. Her appointment came after she had served as secretary at the state office for six years and as interim State Secretary since January 1, 1988.

Lioness Debi joined the Plover-Whiting Lioness Club in 1982 where she has maintained perfect attendance and held many offices. During her year as club president she was a 100 Per Cent President.

Debbie resigned as State Secretary in June of 1993. She currently holds the position of Clerk for the Village of Whiting.

At the 67th Wisconsin State Lions Convention in 1990, the Council of Governors honored Lioness Debi as a Melvin Jones Fellow and in 1993 as a Birch Sturm Fellow. Lioness Debi and her husband, Lion David, have two daughters, Sarah and Jennifer.

State Secretary Thomas E. Thorson

Thomas E. Thorson was appointed to serve as the Wisconsin Lions State Executive Secretary June 1, 1993. He has been a member of the Neenah Lions Club since 1978. He has served his club by holding many club offices including president in 1981-82.

The other offices Lion Thorson has held include hearing and Speech Chairman, Diabetes Chairman, Cabinet Secretary-Treasurer, region Chairman and LCIF Chairman. He served as District Governor of 27-B1 and Council Chairman in 1989-90. He has also served as MD #27 LCIF Chairman and Chairman of the State International Convention Committee. He was a 100% District Governor, received two International Presidents Certificates of Appreciation and an International President's Leadership Award. He is a Melvin Jones Fellow. He also served as a Wisconsin Lions Foundation Director prior to being named State Executive Director.

Following a 29 year career, Lion Thorson retired from Aid Association for Lutherans in 1987. Tom is single and lives in Plover.

Wisconsin Lions Serving The International

The 7th Annual International Convention was held on June 27-29, 1923, at the Steel Pier, in Atlantic City, New Jersey. The constitution and bylaws were revised to provide, among other things, for the creation of a board consisting of the Governors elected in the various districts.

The International Board appointed a small group selected from the current District Governors known as the Executive Council of the Board of Governors. While these were honorary appointments, the chairman was an ex-officio member of the International Board and served as a liasion person between the District Governors and the Board. Lions who have represented Wisconsin on the International level are as follows:

1923-24: Rev. J.A Homes, Appleton, Executive Council,
Board of Governors

1924-25: John F. Baker, Milwaukee, Executive Council,
Board of Governors

1926-27: Robert E. Hine, Milwaukee, Executive Council,
Board of Governors

1928-29: Giles H. Putnam, New London, Executive Council,
Board of Governors

1930-31: Frank V. Birch, Milwaukee, Executive Council,
Board of Governors

1931-32: George H. Dobbins, Fremont, Executive Council,
Board of Governors

1931-32: Frank V. Birch, Milwaukee, Director

1932-33: Frank V. Birch, Milwaukee, Director

1934-35: Frank V. Birch, Milwaukee, 3rd Vice President

1935-36: Frank V. Birch, Milwaukee, 2nd Vice President

1936-37: Frank V. Birch, Milwaukee, 1st Vice President

1937-38: Frank V. Birch, Milwaukee, President

1938-39: Frank V. Birch, Milwaukee, Immed. Past President

1940-41: George H. Dobbins, Weyauwega, Director

1941-42: George H. Dobbins, Weyauwega, Director

1944-45: Louis E. Means, Beloit, Executive Council Board
of Governors

1948-49: Clarence L. Sturm, Manawa, Director

1949-50: Clarence L. Sturm, Manawa, Director

1950-51: A.M. Bearder, Lake Geneva, Executive Council,
Board of Directors

1952-53: Ray A. Galipeau, Merrill, Director

1953-54: Ray A. Galipeau, Merrill, Director

1954-55: Clarence L. Sturm, Manawa, Director

1955-56: Clarence L. Sturm, Manawa, Directors

1956-57: Clarence L. Sturm, Manawa, 3rd Vice President

1957-58: Clarence L. Sturm, Manawa, 2nd Vice President

1958-59: Clarence L. Sturm, Manawa, 1st Vice President

1959-60: Clarence L. Sturm, Manawa, President

1960-61: Clarence L. Sturm, Manawa, Immediate Past
President

1963-64: Edward S. Eick, Chilton, Director

1964-65: Edward S. Eick, Chilton, Director

1966-67: Louis W. Sheahan, New London, Executive Council,
Board of Directors

1968-69: James D. Foster, River Falls, Director

1069-70: James D. Foster, River Falls, Director

1971-72: Jerome Radlinger, Dorchester, Director

1972-73: Jerome Radlinger, Dorchester, Director

1976-77: Joseph E. Wimmer, Waukesha, Director

1977-78: Joseph E. Wimmer, Waukesha, Director

1982-83: Dr. Raymond A. Noonan, Waukesha, Director

1983-84: Dr. Raymond A. Noonan, Waukesha, Director

1987-88: Helmer N. Lecy, Arkdale, Director

1988-89: Helmer N. Lecy, Arkdale, Director

1991-92: Harry T. Merriman, Green Bay, Director

1992-93: Harry T. Merriman, Green Bay, Director

1994-95: Phillip J. Ingwell, Deerfield, Director

1995-96: Phillip J. Ingwell, Deerfield, Director

Shafeec Mansour was not yet a Lion member when he was hired by Melvin Jones to do translation work at the International Headquarters. On January 1, 1950 he was put on extension work in Wisconsin and Upper Michigan.

In August 1976, PDG George Hoffmann was assigned to the International Headquarters to be in charge of the District and Club Administration Division and was later put in charge of the Extension and Membership Division.

Past International President Frank V. Birch

The 15th International Convention of Lions Clubs International was held at Toronto, Ontario, July 14-17, 1931. On July 17th, Lion Frank V. Birch became the first Wisconsin Lion to represent Wisconsin's Clubs on the International Board of Lions Clubs International.

Frank joined the Milwaukee (Central) Lions Club in 1924. He served as Lion Tamer, Director, Vice-President and as President for 1927-1928. He was also a life member of the Board of Directors, and headed many of its committees. He was elected to serve as District Governor for 1929-1930. During those days, the District Governor was also Governor for all the Lions Clubs in Wisconsin.

In 1930, he began to move up the ranks of the International Association: Board of Governors, Director, Third, Second and First Vice President and, in 1937-38, President of Lions Clubs International.

Under his capable leadership, Lionism enjoyed one of the most successful years in its history to that point. He traveled extensively, meeting with Lions throughout the world and addressing them with inspirational words. He was the first Lions International President to pay official visits to the Lions Clubs of Hawaii, Alaska and Puerto Rico. While in Cuba, he was made a Knight of the Order of Carlos Manuel de Cespedes, and was decorated with the Medal of that Order by the President of Cuba in a very colorful ceremony. He was an Honorary Citizen of Texas, an Honorary Texas Ranger, a Kentucky Colonel and an Arkansas Traveller. In 1957, Lion Birch was designated Ambassador of GoodWill by International President Jack Stickley and again in 1960 by International President Clarence Sturm. In 1958, he was appointed by International President Dudley L. Simms, to the position of Chairman of the Public Relations Committee of Lions Clubs International, a position he held for life.

Frank Birch was born in Stevens Point, Wisconsin and received his early schooling at Minneapolis, Minnesota and Fond du Lac, Wisconsin. At the University of Wisconsin he was a member of *Beta Gamma Sigma*, the honorary business fraternity; *Sigma Delta Chi*, the honorary journalism fraternity; *Acacia*, the social fraternity; and was editor-in-chief of *The Badger* year book. In 1917, during his junior year, he played on the varsity basketball team which won the Big Ten championship.

After graduation in 1918, Birch was commissioned a lieutenant in the Army Air Service and took his training in Texas, at Cornell University in New York and at Post Field in Oklahoma. After the close of World War I, he entered advertising, first in Chicago, then with Klau-Van Pietersom-Dunlap of Milwaukee. He stayed with the company until he retired as chairman of the board in 1957. His counsel on advertising matters has been sought by many corporations in the United States and overseas. He was also president and treasurer of his own manufacturing company, BirchKraft, Inc.

While a member of the Milwaukee Central Lions Club, Lion Birch was also an active member of the Lions Club of Islamorada, Florida, where he resided for five or six months of the year at the home he called "BirchKraft." Lion Birch had the unique distinction of having attended, as a delegate, more successive Lions International conventions than any other Lion in the entire Association. He attended his first international convention in Miami, Florida, in 1927 and did not miss one until he died. He also attended every State Convention since his first one in 1924. Most importantly, he was one of the founders of the Wisconsin Lions Camp.

Lion Frank was a 32nd Degree Mason, a member of the Tripoli Shrine club, the Alonzo Cudworth Post Number 23 of the American Legion and a member of the Presbyterian Church. He also held a membership in the Milwaukee University Club, the University of Wisconsin Alumni Association, and was a past president of the National *W* Club, the organization of athletic emblem winners at Wisconsin. He was also chairman of the board of directors of the University of Wisconsin Foundation and served as its president for six years. The Foundation raised funds to help provide buildings, scholarships and research facilities for the University. In 1954, he received an award from the Milwaukee Order of Eagles for outstanding civic work. In 1957 and again in 1965, he was honored by the alumni association for his work on behalf of the

University of Wisconsin. He was a past president of the Milwaukee Advertising Club, one of the largest organizations of its kind in the United States. For several years, he had been a member of the Board of Directors of the Green Bay Packers professional football team, as well as of the Greater Milwaukee Committee and the Milwaukee Civic Progress Commission. Lion Birch passed away on August 8, 1973.

When Frank was awarded The American Legion Distinguished Service Award in 1969, he remarked, "Live up to your potential, no matter what that potential may be."

Past International Director
George H. Dobbins

Havana, Cuba, hosted the 24th International Convention on July 23-25, 1940 and during this time, PDG Lion George H. Dobbins became the second Wisconsin Lion to serve on the International Board.

George was a charter Member of the Weyauwega-Fremont Lions Club, chartered on April 2, 1928. He served as a Vice President and was

a key member of his Club. At State Lions Convention in Sheboygan in 1930, he was elected to serve as Governor of District 27 for 1930-31. He was chosen for his willingness to spend time and effort in the interests of Lionism in Wisconsin and for his personal ability to interest and stimulate the clubs in his district. Governor Dobbins visited all the clubs during his year as District Governor. He added 23 new clubs and 412 new members during his term, to bring the state total to 66 clubs with 1,644 members.

At the 15th International Convention in Toronto, Canada, July 14-17, 1931, PDG George was appointed to serve on the Executive Council of the Board of Governors of Lions Clubs International for 1931-32. At the 24th International Convention in Havana, Cuba, July 23-25, 1940, Dobbins was elected to serve as an International Director for 1940-42.

George Dobbins was born on May 24, 1876 in Auroraville, Wisconsin and died December 26, 1964. He is buried in the Lakeside Cemetery at

Fremont, Wisconsin. By 1895, he had finished a three-year course at Ripon College and a post-graduate course at the University of Wisconsin. In 1899, he came to Fremont as a school teacher and after three years, became the principal of Fremont's state graded school.

In the early 1900s, he founded the Fremont Telephone Company, whose first long distance line ran to the potato warehouse in nearby Tustin. Dobbins purchased the Weyauwega Telephone Company in 1926 and later acquired the Rural, the Waupaca and the Poysippi Telephone Companies, which together served portions of Waupaca, Waushara, Portage and Winnebago Counties. He bought, remodeled and operated the Dobbins Hotel in Weyauwega from 1936 to 1949. He also owned and operated the Dobbins Mercantile General Store in Fremont, the Fremont Feed and Seed business and the Fremont Pearl Button Factory. He acted for eighteen years as Supervisor of the Village of Fremont, was a member of the Waupaca County Board for over 29 years, and acted as chairman of the Wisconsin Good Will Tour Train. The Wisconsin Good Will Tours took a train of Wisconsin exhibitions and produce into various sections of the country and to Mexico where the exhibits were viewed by over 50,000 people. In 1929, it was planned so that the special train arrived in Washington for the Inauguration of President Herbert Hoover.

George Dobbins was married to Mae Bergstresser of Fremont on November 14, 1900. She passed away on June 24, 1907 after bearing a son who died in infancy and a daughter, Grace. On June 17, 1913 he and Gertrude Bartlett of Melrose, Wisconsin were married. They had four daughters, Dorothea, Dolores, Jean, and Charlotte.

The Fremont Pearl Button Factory was located on the east side of the Wolf River and the men pulled clams out of the river with hooks. The buttons were cut from the shells, polished and the women of Fremont carded the buttons. George Dobbins was a member of F&AM Lodge No. 182, Weyauwega, Tripoli Shrine of Milwaukee, the First Presbyterian Church of Weyauwega, where he served as an elder and trustee. As active as he was with his family and in community and business organizations, he still found time to go duck hunting and fishing.

Past International President Clarence L. Sturm

New York, New York hosted the 31st International Convention of Lions Clubs International during July 30, 1948. At this convention, Clarence L. Sturm became the third Lion from Wisconsin to serve on the International Board of Lions Clubs International.

Clarence was a charter member of the Manawa, Wisconsin Lions Club, and held nearly all club offices, including Director and President. He served as Zone Chairman and Deputy District Governor of District 27-B, and was elected to serve as District Governor of District 27-B for 1941-42. As a member of the Board of Directors of the Wisconsin Lions Foundation, Clarence helped start and maintain the Children's Camp at Rosholt. In 1948, Clarence was elected to serve a two-year term as an International Director on the International Board of Lions Clubs International. Re-elected in 1954, Lion Clarence became one of the few Lions to serve two terms as an International Director. In 1956, he was elected Third Vice-President and began his ascent to the International presidency in 1959.

Clarence has received many awards over the years, including the 100 Per Cent District Governor's Award, 100 Per Cent Attendance Awards, membership key, and the coveted Lions Ambassador of Good Will. He was awarded Peru's "Order of the Sun, in the degree of Knight Commander," and the Dameao Medal in recognition of the outstanding work performed by Lions to help those suffering from Hansen's Disease in Brazil.

Lion Clarence was born and raised in Manawa, Wisconsin, graduated from the Oshkosh Business College and Northwestern University. A partner in the firm of A. Sturm and Sons wholesale foods, he was a Director of the Farmers State Bank in Manawa since 1953 and President since 1986. He was also a member of the Chicago Mercantile Exchange and the Advisory Council of Valparaiso University. Clarence was an active member of St. Paul Lutheran Church, Manawa, and served as president of the Church Council. He served on the Bishop's Advisory Council for the Green Bay Diocese, and on the National Advisory Council for Valparaiso University. In February 1962, he was elected as a Director of the Aid Association for Lutherans. He also served many years as Vice-President of CARE, the International Welfare organization, and headed the comittee for the collection and distribution of Lions Clubs' funds for assistance to Hungarian refugees.

Lion Clarence married Norma Kasper of Bear Creek in 1930, and they have one daughter, Beverly Carl. Clarence Sturm died and was buried in the Little Wolf Cemetery, in his home town of Manawa on August 15, 1973.

Past International Director
Raymond A. Galipeau, Sr.

Mexico City was the site of the 35th International Convention on June 25-28, 1952 and Lion Ray became the fourth Lion from Wisconsin to serve on the International Board.

Ray joined the Merrill Lions Club in April 1941, served as president during the 1943-1944 year, was Secretary from July 1969 until June 1981 and has held all other club offices and many committee positions during his years as a member. In 1974, he was honored by his club with a Life Time Membership. He served as Zone Chairman of District 27-C (1944-45) and was elected to serve as District Governor of District 27-C (1945-46).

The list of his accomplishments as a Lion on the Club, District, State and International levels is long. He helped found the Past District Governors' Organization and served as its president. He helped organize the Merrill Lady Lionettes, which later became the Merrill Lioness Club, served as Council chairman, founded and served as editor of the *Wisconsin Lion Magazine* from 1956 until he passed away in 1981 and served on the advisory board of the Leader Dog School in Rochester, Michigan. He became known as **Mr. Lion** in Merrill and throughout the Lionistic World.

Ray received many awards, honors and recognitions in the civic, fraternal, community, governmental and business fields. His Lionistic awards included the 100 Per Cent District Governors Award, Good Will Award, Membership Key, Master Key, Senior Master Key, Grand Master Key, Key of the State, Key of Nations, Monarch Key and International Key. He was the fifth Lion to receive the special plaque and medallion for sponsoring 250 members. There are very few Lions in Lions Clubs International who have received this key award. He had forty years of perfect attendance, never missed a State Convention since joining in 1941, and missed only three international conventions during these years. He prized the letter he received from Senator John F. Kennedy after the Senator visited Merrill during his campaign for the presidency in 1960.

Raymond Arthur Galipeau was born on October 28, 1901 in Merrill, Wisconsin. He was raised and attended school in Merrill, graduated from the Business Management School and a Dale Carnegie course. He has worked for a fruit distributing company, as a clerk for the Milwaukee Road Railroad, owned and operated The Gold Arrow Bowling Lanes from 1938 to 1962. Then he and some partners started the Merrill Lincoln Lanes Bowling establishment. He was a member of the National Guard and has served on many civic, church and fraternal committees. As vice chairman of the local Housing Authority he supervised the construction of a 100-unit high rise and later a 102-unit high rise for the elderly as well as nine moderate-income family housing units in Merrill. Ray was also a member of the Fraternal Order of Eagles, and fourth degree Grand Knight of the Knights of Columbus.

Ray and his wife Helene Cecilia Wyss were married on May 9, 1922 in Huntington, Indiana, where Helene was born and raised. They had five children: Bernadette Ann, Mary Lou, Betty Mae, Raymond Jr., and Loretta Ann. Ray passed away on November 21, 1981, Helene on April 23, 1986, and Raymond Jr. July 17, 1984.

Past International Director
Edward S. Eick

The 46th annual convention of Lions Clubs International was held in Miami Beach, Florida on June 19-22, 1963, and the Lions of the world honored the Wisconsin Lions by electing Lion Eddie Eick to represent the Wisconsin Lions on the International Board for the next two years.

Eddie joined the Brillion Lions Club in 1931, held many club offices and committees and served as president in 1953-1954. During 1944-45, he served as Zone chairman of District 27-B and in June, 1945 at a district convention at Appleton, (due to the war restrictions, no International or State Lions Conventions were held that year), he was elected to serve as District Governor of District 27-B for 1945-46.

During his term as Governor, he served as the State Council Secretary and Treasurer. He also Chartered the Mishicot Club with 34 Charter Members, and the Crandon Club with 86 Charter Members, which might be a record for chartered members. District 27-B ended up with a net gain of 292 members in his year. In 1963, Eddie became the fifth Wisconsin Lion to serve on the International Board.

During his many years as a Lion, he served as a member of the State Lions Bowling Committee, June, 1955 to June, 1965, and as Chair of the Bowling Committee in 1959-1960 and 1964-1965. He was also a member of the State Resolution Committee for 10 years as well as Secretary in 1959-1960, Vice President in 1960-1961, and President in 1961-1962 of the Past District Governors Organization. On the International Level, he served as chairman of the State Parade and Delegates Committee to the 1956 International Convention. He also served on the Elections Committee at the international conventions during the years 1966, 1967, 1968 and 1970 and as chairman of the Credentials Committee in 1960.

Eddie has received many awards and citations, including the 100 Per Cent District Governor's Award, Melvin Jones Birthday Program Award, Key Member Award, Extension Award and five International President's Awards. He has maintained a perfect attendance record since becoming a member and is now an Honorary Life Director of the Brillion Lions Club. He received a certificate of award, dated August 23, 1944, signed by President Franklin D. Roosevelt and Administrator Chester Bowles; a certificate of appreciation dated, July 1, 1959, signed by President Dwight D. Eisenhower, and co-signed by Governor Gaylord Nelson for serving for ten years as an uncompensated member of the Selective Service System; the same certificate, dated May 31, 1964, for fifteen years signed by President Lyndon B. Johnson and co-signed by Governor John W. Reynolds; and later the same certificate, dated May 31, 1969, for 20 years signed by President Richard M. Nixon and co-signed by Governor Warren P. Knowles.

As a civic leader in his community, he has served as district attorney of Calumet County (1931-1939); Secretary of the Calumet County Bar Association (1937-1961); President of the Calumet County Bar

Association (1961-64); President of the Fraternal Order of Eagles Aerie 1228 (1941-42); Grand Knight of the Knights of Columbus 2556 (1941-1942); chairman, Calumet County Chapter of Infantile Paralysis, (1939-1954); Chilton city attorney (1947-1963).

Lion Eddie was born in Brillion, Wisconsin October 13, 1905. After graduating from the Marquette University Law School, he became a practicing attorney on August 4, 1930. He is an Elk, Knight of Columbus and a member of the Fraternal Order of Eagles.

Phyllis Luther was born in Chilton, Wisconsin. She and Eddie were married May 27, 1933 and have one daughter, Mary Lee, and two sons, Edward C. and Paul R. Eddie passed away in November, 1992.

Past International Director
James D. Foster

On June 26-29, 1968, the 51st International Convention was held in Dallas, Texas, and Lion Jim Foster was elected to serve a two-year term as an International Director.

Jim joined the River Falls Lions Club in January, 1959, served as President in 1962-63, Zone Chairman for District 27-E in 1963-64, Deputy District Governor in 1964-65, District Governor of District 27-E and Council Treasurer in 1965-66. Jim then served as Foundation Director during the years 1966-68. In l968, he became the sixth International Director from Wisconsin.

During his many years as a Lion, Jim has received many awards, including the 100 Per Cent District Governor's Award, District Governor's Appreciation Award, Master Key Award, three Extension Awards, five International Presidents Awards, River Falls Lion of the Year Award for 1973, and the coveted Ambassador of Good Will Award.

He was President of the Foster Furniture Company from 1955 to 1972, and is now busy in the furniture promotion business throughout the Midwest. Lion Jim and his wife, Mercedes, were married August 26, 1944 and have three sons, Jim, Mike, and Tim.

Past International Director
Jerome L. Radlinger

Our seventh International Director came from Dorchester, Wisconsin, and served during the years 1971-1973.

Jerry became a Lion in 1956 and served as the Charter President of the Dorchester Lions Club. In 1958, he became a Cabinet Member of District 27-C, served as a Zone Chairman for two terms and Deputy District Governor for five terms. In 1965, he was elected to serve as the District Governor of District 27-C. In 1970, PDG Jerry started his campaign for the International Board of Directors in Las Vegas, Nevada. He won in 1971 and served until 1973.

The Dorchester Lions Club worked on many projects over the years. Dorchester Days and Dorchester Park are annual projects, co-sponsored by the Dorchester Lions Club, American Legion and Volunteer Firemen.

During his many years as a Lion, Jerry has received many awards, including the 100 Per Cent District Governor's Award, District Governor's Extension Award for the seven clubs chartered during his year as District Governor, nine International President's Awards, three Extension Awards, Master Key and Senior Master Key awards. Jerry is also a Melvin Jones Fellow.

Lion Jerry was born in Marshfield, Wisconsin, on January 25, 1927. He and his wife Betty Jane were married in Clark county in 1948, have one daughter Julene and three grandchildren. He is a Navy Veteran of World War II and holder of a Purple Heart, a member of the American Legion, Veterans of Foreign Wars, the Elks Lodge, and was a member of the Dorchester Fire Department for many years.

Past International Director Joseph E. Wimmer

Honolulu, Hawaii was the site of the 59th International Convention on June 23-26, 1976. After the voting was over, the Wisconsin Lions learned that our state would be represented on the International Board by Joe Wimmer. It is told that he received more votes than any other previous candidate for the post.

Joe became a Lion when he joined the Waukesha Noon Lions Club

in June 1962, held many club offices and served as president of the Waukesha Noon Lions Club in 1966-67. In 1967, he became a member of the District 27-A Cabinet and served as Zone Chairman for one term, Deputy District Governor one term and was elected to serve District 27-A1 for the year 1972-73. He also served four years on the District Cabinet. He was the eighth Wisconsin Lion to serve on the International Board.

During his Lionistic years, Joe has received many awards, including the 100 Per Cent District Governor's Award, Key Award, Extension Award, Melvin Jones Membership Development Award, eight International President's Awards, and the Ambassador of Good Will Award. He is also a Melvin Jones Fellow.

Joe and his wife Sue received their greatest award in Joe's first year on the International Board when their daughter Jodie was born. She is the only child ever born to a serving Director or officer in the history of Lions Clubs International.

Both Joe Wimmer and Sue Chase were born, raised and married in Watertown, Wisconsin. They have a son, Steve, and three daughters: Nancy Sue, Amy Lynn and Jodie Elizabeth. They also have 7 grandchildren.

Joe was born July 21, 1934 and after graduating from the University of Wisconsin Law School in June 1962, he and Sue moved to Waukesha where he is a partner in the law firm of Wimmer, Evans, Vollmar, Kuchler and Huismann. He is also a former assistant district attorney and past president of the Waukesha County Junior Bar Association. He was elected to represent the 32nd Assembly District in the Wisconsin legislature in November, 1982, where he would serve for 9 years. In September of 1991 he became part of the judiciary when appointed to Circuit Court Branch 1, Waukesha County, by Governor Tommy Thompson. In April of 1992 he was elected to a six year term.

Past International Director Raymond A. Noonan

The 65th International Convention was held in Atlanta, Georgia, June 30-July 3, 1982. It was there that Lion Ray Noonan became the ninth Wisconsin Lion to serve on the International Board.

Ray became a Lion when he joined the Waukesha Noon Lions Club in 1964. He served as club secretary and president. Lion Ray fondly recalls several aspects of his Lionistic service as first chairman of his club's Chicken Bar-B-Que, now a major fund-raiser for the club. Ray served as Cabinet Secretary Treasurer for District Governor Joe Wimmer in 1972-73, Deputy District Governor in 1975-76 and was elected to serve as District Governor for District 27-A1 for 1976-77. Lion Ray has held various committee positions for his club and district and was the Lioness liaison for district 27-A1 when the first Lioness District in Wisconsin was formed.

As an International Director, Ray served on the Service Activities Committee and developed policy concerning the role of our Association and its members in eye banks. He also served on the Executive Committee.

Lion Ray has received numerous awards, including the 100 Per Cent District Governor's Award, Master Key Award, the Ambassador of Good Will Award. He is also a Melvin Jones Fellow.

Ray was born in Mauston, Wisconsin on October 26, 1926, was raised on a small farm near Elroy, Wisconsin and is a World War II Navy veteran. In 1951, Ray graduated from the Wisconsin State University at La Crosse with a B.S. degree in Physical Science. In 1962, he was elected a senior member of the Society of Plastics Engineers. He graduated from Marquette University Dental School in 1964. He is a member of the Waukesha County Dental Society, Wisconsin Dental Association, American Dental Association and *Omicron Kappa Upsilon,* the National Honorary Dental Society. A licensed pilot, Ray also holds the rank of Colonel in the Civil Air Patrol and served as a Commander for the State of Wisconsin from September 1982 to March 1987.

His wife, Roe, is the former Roe Mary Potaracke of La Crosse, Wisconsin. Lioness Roe served as Lioness District President for District 27-A1 in 1986-87. Ray and Roe were married in 1949 and have two daughters, Shannon and Erin.

Past International Director Helmer N. Lecy

Taipei,
An Ancient City
in an Ancient Land-
Taiwan,
a beautiful
banana shaped island
once known as Formosa-
off the coast of China,
tucked in between
the East China Sea,
the South China Sea,
the Formosa Strait,
and the Philippine Sea,
All a half a world away
from Wisconsin.
Chungyung Shanmo-
a forest covered mountain range
on the Philippine Sea side,
like a shield
to the plains and sea shores behind-
all laced together
by the many rivers
which tumble and churn down the slopes
slowing to dampen the many farms,
serving as a highway
between the villages and the cities-
finally becoming fishing bases on the seas
and ports to the world.

During July 1-4, 1987, the Lions of the world held their 70th International Convention at Taipei, Taiwan. They honored the Lions of Wisconsin by electing Past District Governor Helmer Lecy to represent the Wisconsin Lions on the International Board for 1987-89. Lion Lecy was the tenth Lion from Wisconsin to serve as an International Director.

Lion Helmer Lecy, a charter member of the Roche-A-Cri Lions Club, which was chartered during January 1972, served as the Chartered Second Vice President, First Vice President, and as a 100 Per Cent President. He was also a 100 Per Cent Secretary for three terms and Club Bulletin Editor for eleven years. He has eighteen years of perfect attendance, been a delegate to seventeen State and twelve international conventions. On the District 27-C1 level he has served as Zone Chairman for three terms, Cabinet Secretary Treasurer, a 100 Per Cent District Governor for 1979-1980 and Council Chairman during the 1980-81 year.

He also served as Council Representative to the Wisconsin Lions Foundation and as State Convention Chairman for five years. He served the Wisconsin Lions Foundation as Secretary, Camp Committee Chairman, Vice President and President (1981-84). He served on the Public Relations Committee, Chairman of the Kitchen Expansion Project, Co-chairman of the special sewer project and authorized and edited the camp's long-range plan. He was also instrumental in launching the Pine Wood Lodge project.

During all these years, he also found time to serve on many club projects, as District Eye Bank chairman in 1984-85, and attend nine USA/Canada Forums. He was a presenter for the Officer Training School for ten years, for state convention seminars for four years, also for various district conventions. A member of the State Public Relations Committee, he worked as International Convention Coordinator, Wisconsin Representative to International Board Luncheons for five years, chairman for four years of Multiple District Leadership Development. He was a member of the District Convention Committee, Multiple District International Activity Committee for three years, State Convention Credentials Committee, State Convention Rules and Procedures Committee, International Elections Committee, and International Credentials Committee. He was District Lioness Chairman for three years, worked on Multiple District Protocol Development for two years, was the author and editor of a book on protocol, participated in seven

International Parades, presented at the USA/Canada Forum in 1983, and was a USA/Canada Forum Discussion Leader for four years.

Over the years PID Helmer has been awarded the following awards: 100 Per Cent Club President, three 100 Per Cent Secretary Awards, his home club's Lion of the Year Award, Advancement Key Award, Lion of the Year, ten Chairmanships, 100 Per Cent District Governor, District Governor's Extension Award for seven new clubs, five District Governor's Appreciation Awards, three Extension Awards, seven Lioness Extension Awards, Guiding Lion Award, LCIF Honor Roll for 1979-80, a Melvin Jones Lion Fellowship with one diamond, four International President's Certifications of Appreciation, three International President's Awards, the Ambassador of Goodwill Award, and in the past year he has become a Birch-Sturm Fellow. Other honorary awards and recognitions include: a Kentucky Colonel, an Arkansas Traveler, Honorable Mayor of Altus, Oklahoma, Honorable Mayor of Trenton, Ohio, Admiral of the Great Navy of Nebraska, Honorary Deputy Marshal of Dodge City, Kansas, A Screecher of Newfoundland, "Tarnished Brass" of Florida's Multiple District 35. He is also a Distinguished Alumni of the Adams-Friendship High School.

Lion Lecy is presently concluding his service on the International Campaign SightFirst Committee as a National/Multi National coordinator serving the States of Wisconsin, Illinois, Iowa and Missouri. Under his leadership, the four states have raised $5,142,940. He has also coordinated Wisconsin's "mission" projects to Mexico and Central America consisting of the donation of emergency vehicles, medical equipment and the screening and fitting of used eyeglasses on the needy. In 1994-95, the group served almost 7,000 people with eyeglasses in Mexico, as well as donating $200,000 of medical equipment, 5 ambulances, a school bus, a water wagon and a station wagon. Helmer has been recognized by the Government of Guatamala and received the Fire Departments Medal of Honor for his efforts in that country, and in 1994 was named by the International Associaton of Lions Clubs as one of the "Top Ten" in the world of International Relations.

Helmer was born in Arkdale, Wisconsin on June 27, 1931 attended a one-room elementary school, the Adams-Friendship High School and the South Central Vocational School at Pewaukee where he received an Associate Degree in Safety Engineering. He is a member of the Lutheran

Church, the American Legion, Quincy Masonic Lodge #71, a Thirty-Second Degree Mason, Quincy Eastern Star #177, Central Wisconsin Beef Producers, American Tree Farm Family and a Life Member of the following: Adams County Agricultural Society, Adams County Memorial Hospital Association and Adams County Historical Society. He is a Director and Vice-Chairman of the Board of the Adams County Housing Authority, served as Director and President of the Board of the Adams County Co-op Credit Union, a past Director and Past Executive Secretary/Treasurer and Manager of the Arkdale Mutual Fire Insurance Company. A member of the Arkdale Trinity Lutheran Church, he served as Secretary and President of the Church Council, as Youth Coordinator for nineteen years, as a delegate to the International Lutheran Convention and to the Wisconsin southern district conventions. A Korean War veteran, Helmer served for five years as a past counselor for the Boy Scouts of America, past Board Member and Treasurer of the Castle Rock-Petenwell Lakes Chamber of Commerce, Director of the Board for the Central Wisconsin Beef Producers Association, Past Director of the Central Wisconsin Jr. Livestock Show, 4-H Club General Leader for 18 years, owner/operator of Lecy Construction Company for thirteen years, a member of the Roche-A-Cri Elementary School PTO, and spent 17 years as Emergency Fire Warden for the State of Wisconsin Department of Natural Resources.

Helmer and his wife Myrt were married in 1954 and have four children: Loren, Janis, Jodi, and Lonny. Loren and Lonny are very active in the Lions and each has served as president of his home Lions Club.

Past International Director Harry T. Merriman

The Lions, Lionesses, Leos, and their family members from all around the world, were hosted by the great people of Brisbane Australia for the 74th International Convention, June 18-21, 1991.

There, the Lions of the world honored the Lions of Wisconsin again by electing Harry T. Merriman as the eleventh Wisconsin Lion to serve on the International Board.

Merriman became a Lion member when he joined the Green Bay Downtown Lions in 1958, and has maintained a perfect attendance record since. He served his club as Treasurer in 1965-67, Third Vice-President in 1967-68, and as President for the 1968-69 year. During these years, he has chaired or worked on numerous club projects, including four state conventions and three District Conventions.

On the District level, he served as Cabinet Secretary-Treasurer (1970-71), CARE Chairman (1971-72), Extension Co-chairman (1972-73), and Sight Conservation Chairman of Co-chairmen (1973-77). He was a delegate to many District Conventions, served as a 100 Per Cent District Governor 1977-78, and drafted district constitution and bylaws in 1983-84. During his term as Governor of District 27-B2, the first two Lioness clubs in the district were organized. In 1986 he drafted the first Multiple District 27 Policy manual for the Council of Governors.

On the state level, Harry served as Director, Wisconsin Lions Foundation (1973-77), President, Wisconsin Lions Foundation (1975-76). During this year, the Endowment Fund and Executive Committee were established and the size of the Board of Directors was reduced. He was chairman of the State Elections Committee (1975), served on the State Rules and Procedures Committee (1976-77), was Ex-Officio Member of State Council (1978-79), served on the State Bowling (1979-81), State Resolutions/Constitution and Bylaws (1982-91), and the International Activities (1984-86) Committees, and as a delegate or alternate to 27 state conventions.

On the International level, he served on the International Nominations Committee (1975 and 1984), as Presenter, International Convention (1978), as Unofficial or Official Parade Marshal for Wisconsin Delegation (1979-82 and 1984-85), as delegate or alternate to 24 international conventions, and as a Discussion Leader to the USA/Canada Lions Forum (1985).

He has received many club and district honors which include two special District Governors Awards, a 100 Per Cent District Governors Award, the International President's Certificate of Appreciation, the International Leadership Award, and three International President's Awards. He is also a Melvin Jones Fellow.

Director Merriman is a member of the American and Wisconsin Institutes of Certified Public Accountants, a Past Officer of the Interfaith Seamen's Ministry, active member of St. John the Evangelist Church of Green Bay, is a cantor and choir member, and on the church personnel committee. He is a senior partner of a Green Bay CPA Firm, and has 30 years in public accounting practice.

Lion Harry and Lioness Kathy Merriman have been married 32 years. They have three daughters: Anne, Paula and Ellen, and two granddaughters.

International Director Phillip J. Ingwell, Sr.

Phil Ingwell of Deerfield was elected to serve a two year term as Director of the International Association of Lions Clubs at the Association's 77th International Convention held in Pheonix, Arizona, July 12-15, 1994.

A life member of the Madison Central Lions Club with perfect attendance for 28 years, he has served as Lion Tamer, Treasurer, Secretary, Vice-President and President. He served as District Governor of District 27-D1 and Council Chairman in 198687. Director Phil has served in numerous capacities on the District and Multiple District levels.

Ingwell received the 100% District Governor Award, District Governor's Appreciation Award, the International President's Certificate of Appreciation, International Leadership Award, International President's Commendation and two International President's Awards. He is a Progressive Melvin Jones Fellow.

Ingwell retired after 25 years as Human Resource Administrator of the Madison Metropolitan Schools. He has been actively involved in the Scouting Program, American Legion and his church.

Director Ingwell has been married to Lioness Betty for 38 years. They have two children, Linda and Phil. Jr., and one granddaughter.

State Convention Cities

The Convention City Pins in my collection begin with the 1972 pin issued by Appleton, which we believe is the first pin issued by a Convention City.

The list of Convention Cities starts with the 1922 Convention which was held in Decatur, Illinois, when Wisconsin was divided between Districts Nine and Two.

1922, Decatur

1923, Madison

1924, Green Bay

1925, Fond du Lac

1926, La Crosse

1927, Wausau

1928, Appleton

1929, Milwaukee

1930, Sheboygan

1931, Oshkosh

1932, Madison

1933, Marinette

1934, Stevens Point

1935, J anesville

1936, Sturgeon Bay

1937, Racine

1938, Marshfield

1939, Menasha

1940, Lake Geneva

1941, Madison

1942, Stevens Point

1943, Marinette

1944, Lake Geneva

1945, * Janesville

27-A, Fort Atkinson

27-B, Weyauwega

27-C, Rhinelander

27-D, Janesville

1946, Rhinelander

1947, Sturgeon Bay

1948, Milwaukee

1949, Baraboo

1950, Wausau

1951, Manitowoc

1952, Milwaukee

1953, Superior

1954, Madison

1955, Stevens Point

1956, Fond du Lac

1957, Delavan

1958, Eau Claire

1959, La Crosse

1960, Rhinelander

1961, Green Bay

1962, Waukesha

1963, Superior

1964, Lake Delton

1965, Minocqua

1966, Green Bay

1967, West Allis

1968, Chippewa Falls

1969, Lake Delton	*1978, Green Bay*	*1987, Stevens Point*
1970, Stevens Point	*1979, Oshkosh*	*1988, Oshkosh*
1971, Green Bay	*1980, Wauwatosa*	*1989, Milwaukee*
1972, Appleton	*1981, Lake Geneva*	*1990, Eau Claire*
1973, Lake Geneva	*1982, Eau Claire*	*1991, La Crosse*
1974, Eau Claire	*1983, Superior*	*1992, Wausau*
1975, Madison	*1984, La Crosse*	*1993, Two Rivers*
1976, Rhinelander	*1985, Wisconsin Dells*	*1994, Lake Geneva*
1977, Wausau	*1986, Rhinelander*	*1995, Superior*

* In 1945, due to the curtailment in transportation facilities and wartime conditions in general, separate District business and election meetings were held instead of a state convention. These meeting sites are listed above and dates held on, are as follows: District A-June 24; District B-June 16; District C-June 23; District D-June 2.

Since 1923, there were a number of times when the convention was awarded to a city, but had to be changed. Sites where the convention was actually held are listed. In 1967, facilities for the convention were not ready by convention time, so it was decided to have the convention, curling and bowling cities bid two years in advance to give more time to make all necessary arrangements.

Wisconsin Lions Bowling Tournament Cities

The earliest known Bowling City Pin that I know of is the 1979 Greenville pin. The bowling city each year after that issued a pin.

With the help of Lion Edward Ehlert, long time Secretary for the Manitowoc Lions Club, we learned that Manitowoc lost the position and honor of being known as the first Club to host the Wisconsin State Lions Bowling Tournament. While searching through back issues of the Lions periodicals, Ehlert found an April, 1937 issue of the *The Badger Lion* announcing the winners of the 1937 bowling tournament. It stated that "The eighth annual bowling tournament for District 27 came to a close at Menasha..." Menasha also has a record from Lions Clubs International which states that the Club hosted the State Bowling in 1937.

Records of the Manitowoc Club included a copy of the December 1936, *The Badger Lion* which showed that the 1937 District Bowling Tournament City was Menasha. Later, Lion Ed found a record that the Appleton Lions held the Wisconsin State Lions Bowling Tournament in 1936 and a team from Clintonville won it with a score of 2924.

With the help of Debi Lutz, the following information was found in the state records: "At the eighth Wisconsin Lions Convention which was held in Sheboygan, May 26-27, 1930, District Governor Lion Frank Birch reported that, "Fond du Lac conducted the first annual 27th District Lions' Bowling Tournament."

At the 1936 Convention in Sturgeon Bay, Menasha asked if the Neenah Lions Club could co-host the 1937 bowling tournament with them. This was granted.

In 1937 at Racine, Manitowoc went on record as wanting to host the Lions of Wisconsin to bowl in Manitowoc, but would withdraw and support Madison for 1938.

Not much mention was made about bowling in the earliest days, and for the first number of years, it appears that the District Governors picked the bowling city. This may have been changed in 1937, when the convention delegates started to vote on the bowling city. It was not until 1939 at the Menasha convention that they voted to rotate the bowling tournaments by districts.

Bowling Cities 1930-95

1930, Fond du Lac
1931, New London
1932, Watertown
1933, Two Rivers
1934, Stevens Point
1935, Sheboygan
1936, Appleton
1937, Menasha
1938, Madison
1939, Manitowoc
1940, Stevens Point
1941, Fort Atkinson
1942, Green Bay
1943, Rhinelander
1944, Beloit
1945, Wauwatosa
1946, Appleton
1947, Merrill
1948, Janesville
1949, Lake Geneva
1950, Manitowoc
1951, Land O'Lakes
1952, Madison

1953, Eau Claire
1954, Menomonee Falls
1955, Two Rivers
1956, Rhinelander
1957, La Crosse
1958, Chippewa Falls
1959, Beaver Dam-Juneau
1960, Marinette
1961, Stevens Point
1962, Tomah
1963, Menomonie
1964, Wauwatosa
1965, Antigo
1966, Marshfield
1967, Madison
1968, Eau Claire
1969, Waukesha
1970, Appleton
1971, Marinette
1972, Wausau
1973, Merrill

1974, Tomah
1975, Menomonie
1976, New Berlin
1977, Brown Deer
1978, Green Lake
1979, Greenville
1980, Wisconsin Rapids
1981, Merrill
1982, Sun Prairie
1983, Chippewa Falls
1984, Menomonie
1985, Caledonia
1986, Watertown
1987, Appleton
1988, Antigo
1989, Marshfield
1990, Medford
1991, Monona Grove
1992, Genoa-Stoddard
1993, Chippewa Falls
1994, Altoona
1995, New Berlin

Greetings:

The Members of the Lions' Club of Manitowoc cordially welcome to this city and to this bowling tournament, all Wisconsin Lions. We are happy to have the opportunity to act as host to the Lions' State Bowling Tournament and hope your visit to our city will be one that will give you much enjoyment.

Enjoy the facilities of the Elks Club–the entire building is yours to enjoy–and make use of the hospitality which Manitowoc is honored to extend.

Please report your lineups for teams to the Secretary of our Bowling Committee, John Vierig, or the Lion who is representing him, at least one-half hour before you are scheduled to bowl.

We are indebted to the advertisers who have contributed to this schedule and to them we extend our thanks. Bowlers both visitors and residents are urged to patronize them whenever possible.

Lionistically yours,

The Bowling Committee
John Kasper, Chairman
R.W. Parish, John Vierig, Jr., Alois Fischl, Sr., Wm. Huchthausen, Earl Haugh.

This was the greeting extended to the bowlers who attended the Wisconsin Bowling Tournament in Manitowoc, March 18-April 30, 1939. Bowling took place at the Elks Club on South 8th Street and at other alleys when available.

The Official Schedule listed 105 teams, 168 doubles, plus an estimated 20 doubles from the Manitowoc Club, and 130 singles, plus an estimated 40 singles from Manitowoc.

A Hotel Manitowoc advertisement for the tournament shows 75 rooms, private toilet, running water, $1.75 to $2.25; 75 rooms, private bath, $2.50 to $3.00. Sunday Dinner, served from 11 a.m. to 9 p.m., cost $1.00

One ad identified Kingsbury Beer, "The Aristocrat of Them All," from Kingsbury Breweries Co. in Manitowoc-Sheboygan,

Wisconsin. Another ad said, "Try Gold Coast, The Beer without a Peer" from Bleser Brewing Co., Manitowoc, Wisconsin. A third ad said, "Help Wisconsin Labor by Buying Nash Cars."

A few jokes were included:

> Says a Lion: "There's nothing strange in the fact that the modern girl is a live wire, she carries practically no insulation."

> Daughter: "I can't marry that man, mother, he's an atheist and doesn't believe there is a hell."
> Mother: "Marry him, daughter and between the two of us, we'll convince him he's wrong."

The following information was received from PDG Lion John Esch of Madison, who served as secretary of the State Bowling Committee since its inception in 1951 and Treasurer since 1953 when this duty was added to the secretary's position.

In the years prior to 1952, Lion's bowling tournaments in the state of Wisconsin were run without benefit of any rules or regulations.

The state convention in Manitowoc in 1951 remedied this situation by enacting Article III, Section 3 and Article VI, Section 10, providing for the appointment of a State Bowling Committee consisting of a member from each District, with each District Governor recommending a Lion in good standing from his district.

The Lions appointed for a three-year term were: Marty Inkmann, Milwaukee, District A; Tony Kerscher, Manitowoc, District D; and T.S. Saari, Menomonie, District E. The committee met at the Loraine Hotel in Madison on January 19, 1952 with Ray Bate acting as chairman, since the tournament was to be in District 27-D that year. Ray Bate, who fathered the idea of having a state bowling committee and John H. Esch, who was elected the secretary of the committee, had prepared a set of rules and regulations which the committee, with some changes, approved. The committee also met in joint session with the State Council, secured its blessings and its recommendations for amendments to the constitution relating to working funds for the committee and qualifications of bids by clubs aspiring to act as host for the tournament. These amendments were enacted at the State convention in 1952 at Milwaukee.

In 1953, Marty Inkmann moved from Milwaukee and Harry Hart of District A, Menomonee Falls, replaced him for the balance of his three-year term.

One of the big changes inaugurated by the State Bowling Committee was changing from the so-called "Fellowship" tournament to a handicap tournament under ABC rules. Judging from increased interest in the tournament, this has proven to be a beneficial move.

The first State Bowling tournament played under these rules was held in Madison, March 29-April 27, 1952. Singles bowled at Schwoeglar's Lanes and the doubles at the new Bowl-A-Vard Lanes. Eighty-nine clubs were represented by two hundred teams, 338 doubles and 676 singles entries. These records are broken year after year.

Curling Bonspiel

On Saturday, May 25, 1957 at the Wisconsin State Lions Convention held at Delavan, Wisconsin, International Counsellor and Chairman Art Best made the following report:

Resolution No. 1 for State Curling Bonspiel
Whereas, curling is one of the oldest and purely amateur sports and is a game that lends itself well to our concept of Lionism. Whereas, now, there is a considerable amount of interest and enthusiasm in this wholesome sport among the Lions of Wisconsin.
Now, therefore be it resolved, that the State Council of Governors appoint a committee to consider the organization, promotion, and promulgation of a State Curling Bonspiel for the Lions of the State of Wisconsin."

Governor Farwell asked for a motion and a Lion from Wauwatosa moved that the resolution be accepted. Lion Wagner of North Lake seconded it, and the resolution was carried.

Curling Bonspiel Cities

1959, Medford
1960, Pardeeville
1961, Appleton
1962, Medford
1963, Galesville
1964, Stevens Point
1965, Monroe
1966, Waupaca
1967, Appleton
1968, Galesville
1969, Medford
1970, Two Rivers
1971, Stevens Point

1972, Galesville
1973, Waupaca
1974, Medford
1975, Waupaca
1976, Trempealeau
1977, Waupaca
1978, Stevens Point
1979, Ettrick
1980, Appleton
1981, Medford
1982, Holmen
1983, Pardeeville

1984, Whittlesey
1985, Marshfield
1986, Trempealeau
1987, Waupaca
1988, Medford
1989, Pardeeville
1990, Marshfield
1991, Galesvlle
1992, Genoa-Stoddard
1993, Chippewa Falls
1994, Waupaca
1995, New Berlin

State Lions Golf Tournament

For a number of years, District 27-A had been sponsoring a District Golf Tournament. On September 22, 1962, Lion Dave Herb presented to the State Council a list of the rules and regulations which District 27-A used in their golf tournaments–just in case they were thinking about sponsoring an All-State Lions Golf Tournament.

It was talked about in the years that followed, but nothing was done about an All-State Lions Golf Tournament until during a Council meeting held on September 19, 1965, when then District Governor Jerry Radlinger proposed holding an annual State Golf Tournament on the lines of the present State Bowling and Curling Tournaments. Governor Radlinger was requested to make a further study so that a resolution could be made.

On November 6, 1966, Governor Radlinger presented a proposed resolution for an All-State Lions Golf Tournament and that it be held in 27-C as it was the district instrumental in bringing it about. During the February 26-27, 1966 Council Meeting, it was decided to hold a State Golf Tournament starting in July 1966.

At the June 26, 1966 Council meeting, Lions Louis Rundquist and William Brendell, representing the Phillips Lions Club, presented a detailed report and final plans for a July 30-31 weekend start, and they were told to go ahead.

On July 30-31, 1966, at the Westward Country Club located on the shores of beautiful Long Lake at Phillips Lion President James Parent welcomed all present for the tee off of the first annual State Golf Tournament. Lion Roland Zerneke, Immediate Past President of the Wausau Lions Club, won the first place trophy.

At the October 30, 1966 Council Meeting it was proposed that the Council consider a resolution that the Golf Tournament be blanked for

1967 and set for 1968 so that the host club would have two years to prepare for it. A motion was passed during the February 19, 1967 Council Meeting that the State Golf Tournament would not be held in 1967 and would be delayed until 1968.

The Sun Prairie Lions Club, the successful bidder for the Second State Golf Tournament, advised the Council at their May 5th, 1968 Council Meeting that their Club was withdrawing from the 1968 State Golfing Tournament. The Council thought that the tournament held during the Convention was adequate and that the other one should be canceled.

At the 1968 State Lions Convention, the Lions of Wisconsin passed a resolution which ended the All-Wisconsin State Lions Golf Tournament.

State Directories

The first Wisconsin State Lions Directory was published in the years 1965-66. On Sunday, September 19, 1965, the Council of Governors meeting was held in Wisconsin Rapids and the following notation was made in the minutes for that meeting:

19. <u>Wisconsin Lions Clubs Directors:</u>
> State Council Chairman District Governor Sheahan, pointed to the excellent District Directory published by District 27-A, and proposed the publication of a similar one to all of our 5 Lions Districts in Wisconsin combined. Motion by Governor Foster, seconded by Governor Radlinger, and carried, of the advisability of such an action, and that the State Council Chairman Governor Sheahan be authorized to make the necessary study on this, to check with Governor Robert Spruce 27-A, conveying to him the compliments of the State Council on their District 27-A Directory, to secure the necessary quotations, and to go ahead with the printing of an all-Wisconsin Lions Clubs Directory.

Saturday, November 6, 1965. Meeting held at Past International President Lion Frank V. and Mrs. Rose Birch's home in Milwaukee.

5. <u>State Lions Club Directory:</u>
> As decided at the previous meeting of the State Council, Governor Spruce reported that 700 copies of the proposed combined directory of the Wisconsin Lions Clubs, as per sample presented, will cost $550. Motion by Governor Foster, seconded by Governor Anderson, and carried to authorize Governor Spruce

to go ahead in the coordination of the necessary material, and the printing of 700 copies of the combined Wisconsin Lions Clubs combined directory, or rather better, if the price is not much more, even have 1,000 copies of the combined directory printed. The District Governors will provide the necessary material about their respective Districts.

January 8, 1966, the 4th Council meeting was held at Hotel Northland, Green Bay.

5. State Directory:

The State Directory will be mailed out to all District Governors this coming week with the balance sent to State Secretary Shafeec as extra copies for those who may want them.

February 26-27, 1966 (Saturday and Sunday), the Council Meeting as held in the Twilite Motel in Marshfield.

4. State Directory:

Governor Spruce reported that the new Wisconsin Lions State Directory has been printed. Quantities of the new Directory were presented by Governor Spruce to all the District Governors for mailing to their respective District Cabinets, International, and State Officers in their Districts. Motion by Governor Anderson, seconded by Governor Foster and carried, to thank and commend Governor Spruce on a job well done, and for payment of $613 for the 826 copies printed.

While at the 1986 Wisconsin State Lions Convention at Rhinelander, I spoke with PDG Lion Robert Spruce, and asked him about both the State and District 27-A Directories, and if he had any copies of the District 27-A directory which the State Directory was based on. Since then, he has sent me a copy of District 27-A's 1960-1961 directory, as well as the 1965-66 directory. In my efforts to find out when the first directory for District 27-A was printed, PDG Bob Spruce suggested I contact PDG Dr. O.J. Turek. Turek informed me that District A printed their own Directory from year 1957-1958, during the governorship of Lion E.J. Mueller, thru 1965-66, during Lion Robert Spruce's term as

Governor. Doc Turek suggested that I contact PDG Lion E.J. Mueller. PDG Mueller checked through some of his old files, and sent me a copy of District 27-A's 1957-58 Directory. PDG Mueller suggested that I contact Lion Leonard Bartell who served as Cabinet Secretary-Treasurer for then District Governors Nord, Snyder, Rowoldt, Lucareli and Metcalfe for more history.

For the years, 1966-67, 1967-68, and 1968-69, I had the pleasure of putting the directories together. They were printed and bound in Withee, Wisconsin by John Isaacs Printing.

In 1966-67, we celebrated the Fiftieth Anniversary of Lions Clubs International, and the theme for that year was, *Peace Is Attainable* by our *Search For Peace* through our *Peace Essay Contest.* The back cover showed a picture of the first Totem Pole presented, as a gift from the Lac du Flambeau Lions Club, to the Wisconsin Lions Camp. Schutte Bros. of Wausau, Wisconsin, hauled this Totem Pole from Lac du Flambeau to our Lions Camp via Green Bay where it appeared in the Wisconsin State Lions Convention Parade in Green Bay.

The 1967-68 Directory showed a picture of Copper Falls, which is located near Mellen, Wisconsin. Our theme that year was to *Keep Wisconsin Beautiful.*

The back cover showed one of the first aerial photos of our Lions Camp. I believe it was taken the second year that photos of the camp were taken from the air.

The 1968-69 Directory showed the first color aerial photo of our camp in Wisconsin.

The back cover showed a composite of pictures of the Lions of Wisconsin–SERVING–and some of the many projects they accomplished. These pictures were secured from Past International Director Lion Ray Galipeau Sr., Managing Editor of the Wisconsin State Lions Magazine.

All future issues of the Wisconsin State Directory were handled by the State Secretary, and the front and back covers of the 1969-70 Directory showed the front gate to Our Camp In Wisconsin.

Improvements have been added to this directory over the years, and today it contains all the latest information of the Wisconsin State Lions, and each directory is an information file, and another chapter on Wisconsin Lionism.

Back Patch

The first back patch issued in Wisconsin was made in 1966-67, the Golden Anniversary Year of Lions Clubs International.

There were four themes incorporated in this Wisconsin Patch: Dairy Land, Vacation Land, Packer Land, Industrial Land. They were represented by a cow, with a milk bottle and cheese for Dairy Land and fishing, skiing, a deer, plus lakes and rivers for Vacation Land. The Brule River was added for then District Governor Bernard Klugow, Brule. A star was added for our state capital at Madison, but we forgot to add a symbol for our Wisconsin State Lions Camp at Rosholt.

In the years that followed, the design was altered - a pine taken out, a snowmobile added. Some patches were a bit rough or homely but they represented our willingess to try something new. In 1989, a new, professional-looking back patch was introduced.

Trading Pins

Whenever and wherever Lions, Lionesses or Leos meet, sooner or later you will hear, "Do you have a pin to trade?" or simply, "Trade?"

No matter who they are, or where they are from, whatever language they may speak, pin and banner trading has become a part of Lionism. Trading has broken all barriers and helped forge many great friendships world wide.

The first trading pin was issued by the Lions of Texas in 1952, followed by Nebraska in 1953. After that, other districts started to issue trading pins. In these early days, pins were called "tokens" and handed out in a friendly manner as an ice breaker at meetings. Today, most every club has a trading pin and many individuals have their own pins.

Each year, many Lions, Lionesses and Leos spend many hours in planning and designing new pins, hoping that their's will be a winner and will be wanted by everyone else.

The history of trading pins in Wisconsin begins at the third meeting of the Council of Governors held December 2, 1962 at Past International President Frank Birch's home in Milwaukee. Ellsworth "Zeke" Hart was commissioned to get some information on pins for the next meeting.

The fourth meeting of the Council was held January 6, 1962 at the Mead Hotel in Wisconsin Rapids. Zeke presented a sample of a Wisconsin Pin with a Lions emblem and a Bucky Badger with Wisconsin printed across it. The general opinion was that it was good. Zeke was to get prices of pins in quantities of 5,000 and 10,000.

The Edgewater Hotel in Madison was the site of the fifth meeting of the Council on February 3, 1961. Don Quistorff reported the prices of pins for the international convention as follows:

Silver or Gold:

5,000, 15 cents; color, 17 cents; pins attached, 19 cents. 7,500, 14 cents; color, 16 cents; pins attached, 18 cents. 10,000, one cent less.

Bronze:

Four cents more

Color: Blue on Gold - Red on Silver - White on Bronze.

A motion by Dean that we purchase 10,000 simulated silver medallions with red color and with matching pins attached; and with "Multiple District 27, Nice, France, 1962" on back, as quoted January 2, 1962 by West Shore Mfg. Co., Kewaunee, and as per drawing submitted with prices of 17 cents each. Seconded by Zeke and carried.

On February 16, 1962, the sixth Council meeting was held in the bank at Tomah, Wisconsin.

After the minutes of the Madison meeting were read, a motion by Zeke and seconded by Russ that the minutes be accepted after the following corrections are made.

Item 2 under report on Pins: Silver or Gold 10,000 at 13 cents color, 15 cents; pins separate, 17 cents.

Item 3 was a motion by Dean that we purchase 10,000 simulated silver medallions with red color, with matching pins attached with "Multiple District 27, Nice, France, 1962" on the back, as quoted Janunary 2, 1962 by West Shore Mfg. Co.

The Seventh Council meeting was held April 13-14, 1962 at the Avalon Hotel in Waukesha, Wisconsin and on April 14, 1962 in the White Room at 8:04 a.m. Don Quistorff reported that within the next 14 days the pins would be ready for shipment as recommended by Lions International. He was given the go ahead.

The 1961-62 Council of governors Included:

District A: David Herb, Council Chairman, Menominee

District B: Ellsworth "Zeke" Hart, Greenleaf

District C: Russ Nachreiner, Adams

District D: Verdine Johnson, Madison

District E: Gene King, Cadott

Donald Quistorff, Kewaunee, was a 1960-61 Governor.

PDG Lions Ellsworth "Zeke" Hart and William Johnson from Wisconsin Rapids advised that 500 pins were made with the blue spot on the Lions Logo for the Governors.

I also heard that this pin was not considered attractive compared with other pins and they were tossed to the kids in Nice, France like popcorn.

Zeke also advised me that there were two other samples made, one in bronze and another one in white and it had a red spot in the logo and a read sweater on Bucky Badger in the same color as the word Wisconsin.

I have also been told by a Lion at the 1984 La Crosse state convention that he has seen a number of the 1962 pins in a bronze color.

At the Wisconsin Lions Convention in Rhinelander in 1986, I met Lion Ken Wychen from DePere, who was walking around with all the Wisconsin State Trading pins, including the 1962 bronze pin. This was the first bronze 1962 pin that I had ever seen and he let me take it home so that I could have a picture taken of it.

The front of the pin has the same design that all the 1962 pins have, but the back does not show any printing. It was explained to me by Zeke Hart, who was at the plant when the pins were made, that the manufacturer tried out various metals and designs. They struck a few trial pieces in bronze and Ken Wychen acquired one of them. Zeke also explained that a silver pin was made with the Lions logo, the sweater of Bucky Badger, and a banner with "Wisconsin" on it, colored in red. All the 1962 pins have a red Wisconsin banner. He also advised me that he was in charge of getting these pins made and he must have lived at the plant until the pins were delivered.

Trading Pins for 1963, 1964 and 1965

The front cover of the October 1979 issue of the Wisconsin Lions Magazine and an article in the June 1983 issue, advised that there were pins issued in 1962, 1963, 1964, then none for 1965, 1966 and 1967 and each year thereafter. This is incorrect. According to the state secretary's records, pins were issued for 1962, 1965, 1966, 1967 and each year thereafter.

At the international convention in Los Angeles, California, July 7-10, 1965 we used the silver pin for trading. PID Jerry Radlinger gave us the pins for trading. My wife Irene went with Helene Galipeau when they traded pins and they always came back with nicer pins than any I received.

From the 1962-63 Council of Governors minutes, there was no mention of pins at any of the meetings in those years except one as listed as follows.

July 23, 1962: *Hotel Northern, Chippewa Falls:* no mention.

September 22, 1962*: Frank Birch's Home, Milwaukee:* no mention.

December 1, 1962*: State Office, Wausau:* no mention.

January 26, 1963: *A Sturms & Sons Office, Manawa:* no mention.

March 2, 1963: *Mead Inn, Wisconsin Rapids*: It was noted in Item 8: a letter was presented from the West Shore Company, Kewaunee, manufacturer of the Wisconsin pins for last year's international convention, offering their services for this year's international convention. Motion by Governor Johnson, Second by Governor Strye, that no action be taken on this matter.

May 5, 1963: *Wisconsin Rapids Lions Clubhouse, Wisconsin Rapids:* No mention.

May 23, 1963*: Androy Hotel, Superior:* no mention of pins. The information which I received from the governors of that year was that they believed that there were enough pins left over and that no more were needed. Also, that there was little interest and no budget for new pins.

July 27, 1963: *Mead Inn, Wisconsin Rapids*: no mention.

September 14, 1963: *State Office, Wausau:* no mention.

December 7, 1963: *Frank Birch's Home, Milwaukee:* no mention.

March 14, 1964*: Dell View Hotel, Lake Delton*: no mention.

April 10, 1964*: Dell View Hotel, Lake Delton:* no mention.

May 21, 1964*: Dell View Hotel, Lake Delton*: no mention.

August 1-2, 1964*: Long Lake, Clintonville.*
State pins. Governor Rosenfeldt was also appointed to investigate this matter with the company which made the 1962 pins and report as to the availability of the dies and costs at the next Council meeting.

September 20, 1964*: C. Sturms, Manawa*: no mention.

December 6, 1964*: Frank Birch's Home, Milwaukee.*
Item 8. State Pins. The State Secretary presented a large number of different state souvenir pins which he received from his colleagues on the field staff of Lions International. After some discussion and scrutinizing of the various sizes, price quotations and pins, it was decided that the State Secretary ask the manufacturer of the Missouri pins, for the prices of pins in the shape of our state in enamel, for which we will provide the dies, in quantities of 1,000, 3,000 and 5,000 with Wisconsin Lions in white metal and the background in cardinal red.

February 21, 1965*: Clubhouse, Wisconsin Rapids Lions.*
Item 16: State Pins. Quotations as requested by the Council were presented by the State Secretary from the Frigerio Diamond Tool Co., for 20 cents each, without enamel, as per their letter of January 14, 1965, with no die charge, to be supplied and paid for 2,500 this year and 2,500 next year. Inquire if the 2,500 pins for the next year could be enamelled, if so desired, by next year's State Council.

March 28, 1965*: Fischer's Supper Club, Lake Delton, Wisconsin.*
Item 8: International Convention: Wisconsin State Pins. The State Secretary reported that the 5,000 pins were duly ordered by him from the Frigerio Diamond and Tool Co., of Jersey City, New Jersey, to be delivered in two shipments of 2,500 each, one for this year and the other for 1966 and to be paid for as delivered, half this year and

half next year, as decided by the State Council. The first 2,500 will be delivered on April 15.

Motion was made by Governor Petrykowski, second by Governor Wedeward and carried, to put in escrow from the Wisconsin Promotion Fund $500 toward the payment of the other pins which will be delivered for the 1966 International Convention. It was further decided that the pins be distributed among the District Governors, for their transportation to Los Angeles.

March 28, 1965*: Bosacki's Minocqua, Wisconsin*
Item 10: International Convention. Council Chairman Governor Shaurette reported that a float is being ordered costing $900. Some minor changes were made on the design proposed. The State pins have been received and paid for. Each District Governor will be supplied with 500 for distribution at the international convention in Los Angeles. International Director Eddie Eick and Past International Director Ray A. Galipeau, will be given a supply by their respective District Governors for their use. The State Secretary will also be given a supply for his use. This was the silver pin which was traded in Los Angeles, California in 1965.

Trading Pins, 1965-1966

August 8, 1965*: Rainbow Supper Club, New London.*
5. Treasurer's report: State Council Treasurer Counselor Claud pointed also to the amount of $500 held in escrow in the $5,991.42 balance of the Wisconsin Promotion Fund, for the payment of the 2,500 remaining state pins ordered and withheld for completing as per the 1965/1966 State Council's wishes from the Frigerio Diamond Tool Company of New Jersey. The issuance of these 2,500 pins will have to be requested by the present State Council, if they so desire in their present design or they may be enamelled at a small extra cost if the Council so wishes

September 19, 1965*: Wisconsin Rapids Lions Club House.*
Item 7. State Pins: The 2,500 state pins still pending with the manufacturers of the 1965 state pins distributed at the 1966

International Convention in Los Angeles were discussed. $500 was withheld in escrow in the Wisconsin Promotion Fund for paying for these pins which are meant for distribution at the 1966 International Convention if the present State Council decides to do so. The State Secretary was requested to bring the details and samples of enamelled and non-enamelled other state pins, for consideration at the next Council meeting.

November 6, 1965: PIP Frank V. Birch's Home, Milwaukee.
Item 7. State Pins: After further consideration, it was decided that the State Secretary secure further details from the manufacturers on: (a) the possibility of a different color, either gold or bronze; (b) if enamelled, the cost and the sample. Also it is hoped that there will be no extra charge for having the remaining 2,500 pins in a different color as in (a).

January 8, 1966: Hotel Northland, Green Bay.
Item 11. Wisconsin State Pins: No report at present. Lion Shafeec has made repeated attempts by mail and telegraph to get an answer from the company, but no results yet. He finally was able to secure their present new address and is in communication with them. Lion Jerry moved we begin other inquiries from other sources in order to assure procurement of pins, from one place or another, by January 15th, if company not heard from. Second by Jim, carried unanimously. Lion Shaurette will secure figures through his connections.

February 26-27, 1966: Twilite Motel, Marshfield.
Item 5. State Pins: The State Secretary presented a letter received from Frigerio Diamond & Tool Company of Union, New Jersey with an enamelled Wisconsin sample pin. Ex-official Shaurette presented other quotations. Motion by Governor Spruce, seconded by Governor Foster and carried unanimously, that we order the remaining 2,500 state pins, enamelled from the Frigerio Diamond & Tool Co. of Union, New Jersey, which manufactured last year's pins for us at 33 cents each, as per their letter, this depending on the final decision by the Council on the color. The Frigerio Co. is to be requested to provide us with other samples in red and purple with golden insignia, it being understood that the finished products will have a "clutch back."

March 26-27, 1966: *Wisconsin Lions Lake, Rosholt.*
State Pins: State Secretary Shafeec reported on his communications with the Frigerio Diamond & Tool Co. of Union, New Jersey. The Council reviewed various samples. Motion was made by Governor Foster, seconded by Governor Spruce and carried unanimously, that the State Secretary order the 2,500 State Pins from the said manufacturers Frigerio Diamond & Tool Co., in accordance per the sample pin, enamelled, which they had sent for the consideration of the Council and that the enamelled State pins, with a clutch back, be delivered to the State Secretary within four or five weeks, or by May 1, as he was assured by the manufacturers.

May 1, 1966: *Northland Hotel, Green Bay.*
State Pins: State Secretary Shafeec reported that he contacted the manufacturers and was assured that the 2,500 pins are made already and are now in the process of being enamelled as per the State Council's decision and that they will be delivered to him in Wausau between May 10 and May 15 at the latest.

May 19-20, 1966: *Northland Hotel, Green Bay.*
Item 7. State Pins: The State Secretary reported the receipt of the 2,500 enamelled state pins manufactured by Frigerio Diamond & Tool Company, Mountainside, New Jersey and passed around samples thereof. Motion by Governor Radlinger, seconded by Governor Spruce and carried to distribute them five ways and that each Governor will share his with his successor, and that a quantity as will be requested (60 pins) be presented to Past International President Sturm (for the International Family) and 60 pins to Past International Directors Galipeau and Eick (for the Past International Directors); and 60 pins to the State Secretary 40 pins to Ex-official Shaurette (for his distribution). This distribution was effected right there.

This was the blue Enamelled Pin that was used for trading in New York City in 1966.

Wisconsin Lions Foundation

On July 31, 1956, Mrs. Glenn M. Wise, Secretary of State, signed the Articles of Incorporation of the Wisconsin Lions Foundation. The Lions had filed for incorporation shortly after we acquired what was then known as Kiolbassa Lake.

The first meeting of the Wisconsin Lions Foundation was held in 1956 and the following officers were elected: V.J. Lucareli, President; Fred Lewis, Vice President; Harold Johnson, Secretary; Charles Hoffmann, Treasurer; Walter Netterblad; Art Best; Edgar Mueller; Frank Birch; and Clarence Sturm.

Over the years, the number of board-members has varied, increasing and decreasing as the needs arose. Today, there are two members from each District.

The Foundation is in charge of our Wisconsin Lions Camp, Wisconsin Lions Eye Bank, Hearing Evaluation Clinics and Public Awareness Education, Temporal Bone Bank, Collection of Used Hearing Aids, Used Eye Glass Program, Glaucoma Screening Programs, Drug Awareness Program through QUEST and local school systems, diabetes research and education. The Foundation works with the Michigan Lions to promote the Leader Dog Program to place dogs with those who need them.

Wisconsin Lions Foundation Officers and Staff

V.J. Lucareli, 1956-59 *Harold Johnson, 1964-66*

Fred Lewis, 1959-62 *Hugh Scott, 1966-68*

Clarence Sturm, 1962-63 *Vern Volz, 1968-70*

Vern Metcalf, 1963-64 *Clifford Thrall, 1970-71*

William Johnson, 1971-73

J. Eugene Roshell, 1973-74

Howard Heimke, 1974-75

Harry Merriman, 1975-76

Dr. Alton Rosenkranz, 1976-77

John Schoonenberg, 1977-78

George Hoffmann, 1978-79

Daniel Stevens, 1979-80

Gene Ender, 1980-81

Willis Vallet, 1981-82

Peter J. Meyer, 1982-83

Helmer N. Lecy, 1983-84

Robert G. Peterson, 1984-85

Hal Helwig, 1985-86

DuWayne Carl, 1986-87

Gerald H. Rabbach, 1987-88

Ivan Ryan, 1988-89

Wayne Tyree, 1989-90

Ronald Husby, 1990-91

Robert Welch, 1991-92

Herb Schneider, 1992-93

Ron Duffe, 1993-94

Alfred Kohlway, 1994-95

Wisconsin Lions Foundation Office: *Joe Desch, Executive Administrator.*
Wisconsin Lions Camp: *Tony Omernik, Camp Director.*
Those who served as Camp Directors since 1965 are: *Ray Hempel, Frank Hanna, Wayne McKay, Richard Carroll, and Tony Omernik.*

The Wisconsin Lions Camp

For many years, geologists have been studying the geology of Wisconsin. Their records show that rock formations from the Pre-Cambrian Era, the earliest known period of time, have been located in various parts of the state. The Pre-Cambrian dates back to 1,200 to 1,700 million years ago. Sometime during the latter part of this era records of the first plant and animal life are found. This era was followed by the Paleozoic Era (old life), the Mesozic Era (intermediate life) and the Cenozoic Era (recent life). It was during the Cenozoic Era that the glacial period or the Ice Age occurred.

Sometime during the earliest era, Wisconsin was covered by a large mountain range. The peaks and ridges of this range were similar to the Alps. Fossil finds show that these mountains were among the oldest in the world. Periods of erosion were followed by periods of uplift. At times the mountains were submerged beneath a great ocean. (If you go to the top of Rib Mountain near Wausau, you will be able to see rocks which have ripple marks which were caused by wave action. Al Foster, a rock hound from Germany who lived in Wausau for a number of years, found crystals in local rotten granite sites that are similar to the same kind of crystals found high up in the Alps, thousands of feet above the rotten granite sites near Wausau. Lava intrusions are also found in various parts of the state, one can be found in a cut on Highway 52 year Brokow and other spots are located in the Interstate Park on the St. Croix River.)

The Pleistocene Period with its Ice Age and Glaciers, is estimated to have started more than 722,000 years ago. During this period it is believed that there were at least four separate and distinct times that this area was subjected to glaciation: first, the Nebraskan; 200,000 years later, the Kansan; 300,000 years later, the Illinoisian; 200,000 years later, the Wisconsinian, the last of the glacial periods.

The Wisconsin Glacier gave the state many thousands of lakes and it was the Green Bay Lobe of this Glacier that left the one special lake which we now call Lions Lake.

As the Wisconsin Glacier melted, its retreat was followed by trees, plants, animals and people. In time, the area which we now call Lions Lake became the home of the Pottawattamie Indians and they called the lake Big Fish Lake. As late as 1865, stagecoach travelers reported as many as 75 lodges in the Indian encampment on the southwest corner of the lake. The Indians raised corn on several acres that they had cleared over the years.

They also had a burial ground and there is a legend that an Indian Chief is buried there. The legend tells that the Chief rode into the village from the west on a beautiful pony with an even more beautiful saddle studded with gold and diamonds. He became known as the "Chief of the Land of the Setting Sun," or "Chief of Setting Sun." When he became old and died, he was buried in the burial ground along with his pony and saddle. There are no dates as to when this Chief arrived or when he died, but the result was that the Indian burial ground was continuously looted in the hope of finding this valuable saddle.

By the late 1880's, with white settlers occupying the land, only a few Indians remained near Big Fish Lake. The settlers gave the lake many names. Prior to 1870, it was known as "Kvella Laken," which might be translated as the "Lake of the Evening," although "Kvella" was also the name of a nearby homesteader.

In the late 1870's, Gunder Lia, a Norwegian emigrant, settled on two forties on the south side and erected a root cellar, some other buildings and planted apple trees on a spot a little west of the peninsula just east of the Indian clearing. While working alone constructing a log shelter to store wild hay near the south shore of the lake, Gunder was injured in an accident. Two logs rolled down and pinned one leg above the knee and crushed it. It was well in the evening before his wife and daughter went to look for him and found him. She realized that he needed medical attention and, there being no doctor in the area, she asked the Indian medicine man to help her. Legend has it that he decided that the leg had to be removed, and with the aid of the injured man's wife and daughter, and possibly some neighbors, the Indian amputated the leg with his Bowie knife. After recovering from this surgery, Mr. Lia fashioned a peg leg for himself and used it for the rest of his life. He died in 1891 and the farm was sold to a family named Freimart. In time the roof of Lia's root cellar fell in, but the hole remained and, along with the apple trees, could be seen long after he was gone.

At the turn of the century, the property was purchased by Peter Kiolbassa, a prominent Polish-American political leader from Chicago. The Kiolbassa family built a summer home on the southeast shore of the lake in the vicinity of the present administration building and gave the lake a new name, Kiolbassa Lake.

The lake continued to be owned by the Kiolbassas until the Lions acquired it. Then, by legislative action it was renamed Lions Lake.

Lions Lake is spring fed and has a substantial year-round flow. Its outlet is located on the west end and forms Bailey Creek, (a famous trout stream). It flows northwest, makes a hairpin turn, swings south for some distance then turns northeast for several miles through a heavily wooded area before joining the Little Wolf River. The lake has approximately 1.5 miles of shoreline, mostly all a beautiful sand and gravel beach. The shoreline is ringed with white birch, white pine, maple, hemlock, basswood and elm trees. The original virgin forest around the lake had trees so thick that it required three men to stretch their arms around them. The Lions property, including the lake, contains 240 acres in Section Sixteen and 155.39 acres in Section Nine.

Lime jugging was practiced by the locals on this lake. This consisted of putting some slack lime and water into a glass jug, sealing the lid on tight, weighing this with a brick or rock which was wired to the jar and thrown into the water. When the jug exploded, the fish would rise to the surface and they would then take the large fish and the rest which were left would revive.

Every spring before they left the area, Indians would assemble just west of the Indian burial ground and go to Stevens Point to pick up the annual payment for the sale of their land to the federal government. It reportedly consisted of $10 in cash and one blanket per year.

The Indian payment day usually fell near St. Patrick's Day. Irish immigrants to Portage County had a grand celebration and the Indians, who camped where the University of Wisconsin–Stevens Point was later built, joined in the fun.

"When You're Blind, You Can't Go To Outdoor Camps And Stuff Like That."

Those were the words Lion Ray Hemple of Poysippi heard from two blind 12-year-old boys he visited in a hospital, after he asked them if they had ever attended any type of camps. The year was 1953 and this casual remark set Lion Hemple to thinking. He was an avid camper, Boy Scout leader, and a Lion, so it didn't take him long to decide that what was needed, and what the Lions could do, was start a camp for the blind. He soon brought the idea to his club and they accepted it. In 1954, they rented a Boy Scout camp in the area and introduced five visually-impaired local youths to outdoor life. Lion Hemple accepted the camp director's job.

In 1955, their club again ran this camp, but because the grounds could only be rented for a short period of time at the end of the summer, it did not allow them enough time to give all the deserving blind children a treat at camp.

During the 1955 Wisconsin State Lions Convention at Stevens Point, the Poysippi Lions, headed by Lion Ray Hemple, petitioned the District Governors for assistance. The conventioneers appointed a committee of three: Governor Fred Lewis of Stevens Point; Deputy District Governor Harold Johnson from Adams, both of District 27-C; and Governor Charles Hoffman from Manawa of District 27-C to search for a permanent campsite in the coming year and report their findings at the next State Lions Convention scheduled for Fond du Lac in May 1956.

During that year they looked everywhere and could not locate anything that would be suitable. Lion John C. Wozniak, a member of the Stevens Point Noon Club, told me that shortly before the Fond du Lac convention, Lion Lewis reported to his club that they had looked everywhere in east-central Wisconsin and the only thing they could find was some land that abutted on part of a lake in the Baraboo-Lake Delton area, and that they had made a $50 deposit on it which was to hold it until they reported to the convention. (Past District Governor Harold Johnson, was not able to verify this report.)

At about the same time, it happened that Lion Wozniak, who was a loan officer for the First National Bank of Stevens Point, examined the Kiolbassa Lake property. A couple wanted to get a loan to buy it as a place to set up a photography studio. After visiting the property, Lion John just did not believe that it was the logical place for a business of this nature and did not grant the loan.

During this transaction Lion John also had contact with Charles Anderson of Rosholt. He was the agent handling the sale of the lake property. (Charles Anderson later became president and chairman of the board of the Peoples Bank in Wausau and an active member of the Wausau Lions Club.)

Lion Wozniak told Lion Lewis about the property, that it had a lake on it not far from Rosholt and that he thought it was just what the Lions were looking for. He also told him to contact Charles Anderson. As soon as he finished talking with John, Lion Lewis phoned Charles Anderson and found out the property consisted of 240 acres of land, several buildings and the lake. The asking price was $18,000.

Lion John told me that Charles Anderson told him that he was to get $18,000 and anything over that would be his commission, but for the Lions, he would sell it for $18,000 and not take any commission. He also agreed to hold the property until the Lions approved the purchase at their convention. When it became known that this property was for sale, he received many higher bids, one even for $30,000. Anderson kept his word to the Lions and two weeks later at the Wisconsin Lions Convention, the delegates voted overwhelmingly to accept the property.

Over the years our camp has grown from 240 acres to 395.39 acres. A visitor would say that there are sure a lot of buildings there and he would be correct. Many buildings are necessary for the proper operation of the camp in order that all campers' needs and desires are properly taken care of.

The camp site includes separate areas for boys and girls, seven cabins for the girls and eight cabins (one cabin is divided into three sections) for the boys. There are also separate bath houses for the girls and boys. Pinewood Lodge was built in 1989 and has eight apartments which couples can use.

The other buildings and facilities include the caretakers home, camp garage, shop buildings, and a modern water and sewer system.

For the campers, there is a dining hall and kitchen, gift and refreshment shop, health lodge, handicraft shop, a swimming beach and boats, canoes and paddle boats. They can take a canoe trip down the river, go on overnight camping trips or enjoy a trip around the lake on a tractor-drawn wagon. Their days are well planned, and the time goes by very quickly.

For a number of years, young men and women from Denmark have been coming over to work at the camp as counselors at no cost to the camp.

In 1990, the camp handled 264 visually-impaired children, 422 hearing-impaired children, 704 mentally-impaired children, and 382 visually- and hearing-impaired adults for a total of 1,772 individuals.

There are campers who cry when they are left at the camp by their parents. By the end of their one-week or two-week stay, they cry when their parents come to pick them up.

This Wisconsin Lions Camp is known around the world as one of the finest of its kind.

Louie The Lion

Louie the Lion, who proudly stands guard over all activities at our Wisconsin State Lions Camp has led a very interesting and colorful life, and has the scars to prove it.

Louie came into existence way out west in Salem, Oregon during 1935 and 1936. And now for the rest of the story, as it was given to me by Past District Governor Louis J. Gardipee of Black River Falls:

"Back in the 1930s, this lion was given to "Hod" McManners, Black River Falls, as a gift. And, of course, there are many rumors concerning the origin and arrival of this concrete creature. One rumor has it that because "Hod" was a good Republican, a fellow GOP supporter shipped this lion to him by flat car, all the way from California. "From one good Republican to another," goes the legend. Although why two loyal Republicans would be so concerned over one old concrete lion, I don't know. This legend, however, is just that – legend."

The following account is the true history of the Lion. Back in 1935, "Hod" McManners was visiting some relatives in Salem, Oregon. While there, he admired the lion statues produced by a local industry. Not long after, to "Hod's" surprise, Mr. Ed McLean stopped at Black River Falls with a bus he was delivering to Detroit. His only passenger was a lion, a fearless fellow, constructed of concrete and old gun barrels.

For many years this lion served as a landmark at 803 Main Street in Black River Falls. Every Halloween the young fry of our town found it a great challenge to try to tip Mr. Lion over. Finally this challenge seemed to present itself all through the year and Mrs. Lila Gilbertson Greenlee, daughter of "Hod" McManners, with the patience of Job, would have to call an auto wrecker to once again right the lion. After his many skirmishes with the younger set, the lion lost part of his tail and two legs.

In 1957, Mrs. Greenlee donated the lion to the local Lions Club. Because of his weight and many battle scars, the Lion was difficult to display. The Lions kept him in storage.

In 1960, Don "Coogan" Woodford was doing some work at the Louis Gardipee residence and asked Lion Louis about the disappearance of the lion. "Coogan" suggested that the Lion's Camp at Rosholt, Wisconsin, was the ideal residence for the lion.

The same day, Lion Gardipee and some willing helpers, including Frank Kubina and his auto wrecker, brought the damaged lion to the site of the new Jackson County jail. There, in the evenings, Frank Stein and Ed Zillmer repaired friend lion. Both artisans in concrete, Ed and Frank remade the legs and tail and embedded the feet in a reinforced green-colored concrete platform. Thanks to this platform, our lion would no longer lose his dignity by being tipped over. For the Lion's platform, Mr. Gardipee had a brass plate engraved by Mr. Don Berg. The plate was to bear our lion's name, *Leo*, and that of his donors. But, a sense of humor intervened and the plaque was changed to read "Louie the Lion," from the Black River Falls Lion's Club.

After further refurbishing by Dick and George Gardipee, (that is, a washing down with muriatic acid and then a gilding with gold) Mr. Lion was transported to Rosholt where he looks over the peaceful Lion's Lake and still bears the name "Louie." Our lion stands as a proud and majestic guardian over the youth of the Lion's Camp.

Hear Those Bells

As you tour the camping area at Lions Lake, you may first spot the old bell that is located near the kitchen. Then later, as you get in line to get a chicken dinner, you will spot the other bell that is located on the mantle of the fireplace in the shelter building. Both of these bells have an old history and an interesting story connected with them.

With all the reported storms in the area, and other possible dangers, it was considered that there was a need for an alarm system to warn the campers.

During 1962-63, when William Johnson was District Governor, Zone Chairman Lion Edward Parker of Stevens Point served as a Zone Chairman along with me. It was during this time that Lion Ed Parker told me about the bell, and just recently, Past District Governor Harold Johnson filled in other details and further confirmed that the bell near the kitchen came from a fire engine. This bell has the following information on it: C.S. Bell Co. 2 Hillsboro, O.

Lion Parker, a member of the Stevens Point Noon Lions Club, was working as a Fireman at the Stevens Point Fire Department south side fire station. Lion Carl Maslowski was the Stevens Point Fire Chief, also a member of the Stevens Point Noon Club, and he worked at the North Water Street Station. He and Ed secured the bell, fixed it up, and presented it to the Camp.

After the bell had been installed, it was found that it was not loud enough to be heard throughout the camp, so it was decided by a few, which included Lion John C. Wozniak, to find something that would be louder, and could be heard over the entire camp area. He told his good friend John Gannon, a civil engineer who worked on the Soo Line Railroad. Gannon told John of a number of old bells that were lying around the Soo Line roundhouse at Fond du Lac, and that he would see what he could do about getting one of those bells for the camp.

Shortly, he had to go to Minneapolis where he contacted the President of the Soo Line Railroad, and received permission to have one of the bells cleaned up and presented to the Lions Camp. When John informed some of those connected with the camp about the new bell, it stirred up some opposition and was never set up. It is engine bell number 12819, was used on steam locomotives and it remains on the mantle.

Wisconsin Lions Eye Bank

A list of Eye Banks for November 1965, contains 76 eye banks in 38 states. At that time, only one eye bank was listed for Wisconsin, and that was the Wisconsin Lions Eye Bank located at the Milwaukee Blood Center, Inc., 763 North 18th Street, Milwaukee 3, Wisconsin.

The Lions Eye Bank divided Wisconsin into nine regions. Today, there are 99 Regional and Branch Eye Banks located in these nine regions in Wisconsin, and there are two Eye Bank Centers which accept delivery of eyes. One is located at the Medical College of Wisconsin, Eye Institute, 8700 West Wisconsin Avenue, Milwaukee 53226. The other is located at University of Wisconsin Clinic and Hospital, 600 Highland Avenue, Madison, 53706.

Research laboratories have been added to the Madison facility. The Lions of Wisconsin have donated $500,000 to this project and these two research laboratories are named the Wisconsin Lions Eye Research Laboratories.

Each laboratory has 480 assignable square feet of space with researchers sharing heavy equipment, coldroom and darkroom facilities. Laboratories are of standard Clinical Sciences Center construction with four 10-foot lab benches, one 3-foot stainless steel, corrosion-resistant sink, one 2-foot sink, and a 5-foot vented fume hood. Each laboratory is further equipped with 110V and 220V electrical service, resilient floors with mounting track on side walls and suspended ceilings with fluorescent lighting. Laboratory benches are equipped with 110V and 120V electrical, natural gas, vacuum, cold and hot water, distilled water, and below counter, vented, flammable chemical storage. Shelves and cabinets are mounted above benches.

The eyes suitable for transplanting are used in Wisconsin and other states as needed. Eyes not suitable for transplanting are used for research.

For 1991, the Wisconsin Eye Banks collected the following number of eyes.

1991 Eye Disposition List				
Hospital	**Transplant**	**Research & Training**	**1991**	**1990**
Adams-Friendship	6	16	22	14
Arcadia	0	0	0	0
Ashland	4	34	38	26
Baldwin	3	5	8	6
Baraboo	6	6	12	8
Barron	2	12	14	12
Beaver Dam	6	26	32	20
Beloit	8	12	20	24
BlackRiver Falls	12	12	24	10
Bloomer	2	6	8	14
Boscobel	0	0	0	0
Chippewa Falls	10	34	44	42
Clintonville	0	0	0	0
Columbus	0	0	0	0
Cuba City	0	0	0	2
Cumberland	0	0	0	0
Dallman FH	0	6	6	0
Darlington	8	10	18	0
Dodgeville	7	23	30	16
Durand	0	0	0	4
Duluth	0	0	0	0
Eagle River	2	6	8	4
Eau Claire:				
Luther	4	22	26	36
Nursing Home	2	0	2	0
Sacred Heart	17	47	64	82
Edgerton	0	0	0	2
Fort Atkinson	5	15	20	44
Frederic	0	0	0	0
Hayward	10	24	34	48
Hillsboro	0	0	0	0
Hurley	0	0	0	14
Iola	0	0	2	0
Janesville	8	32	40	56
Keehr FH	0	2	0	-
La Crosse:				
Lutheran	34	119	153	134
St. Francis	8	58	66	58
St. Francis Home	0	2	2	-
Ladysmith	7	27	34	49
Lancaster -				
Fenimore	0	0	0	6
Lodi FH	0	0	0	2
Madison:				
Anatomy Dept.	0	2	2	-
Central Wi Ctr.	0	2	2	-
Dane Co. Morgue	0	0	0	2
Funeral Home	0	2	2	4
Hospice Care	0	0	0	3
Madison-Meriter	30	66	96	96
Nursing Homes	0	2	2	2

Hospital	Transplant	Research/ Training	1991	1990
St. Mary's	26	44	70	72
University	55	73	128	72
Veterans	6	32	38	26
Marshfield	31	86	117	72
Mauston	4	6	10	8
Menomonie	0	18	18	14
Merrill	2	8	10	10
Monroe	7	13	20	34
Neillsville	2	4	6	0
Oshkosh	16	32	48	60
Osseo	2	10	12	8
Park Falls	1	15	16	18
Phelps	2	0	2	0
Platteville	2	8	10	4
Portage	2	2	4	6
Prairie du Chien	8	34	42	42
Reedsburg	1	3	4	10
Rhinelander				
Peterson	0	20	20	48
St. Mary's	26	59	85	112
Rice lake	5	25	30	50
Richland Center	0	0	0	2
River falls	0	2	2	2
Shell Lake	0	0	0	2
Sparta	2	8	10	8
Nursing Home	0	2	2	-
Spooner	2	0	2	2
St. Croix Falls	0	0	0	2
Stevens Point	4	30	34	28
Stoughton	0	20	20	8
Funeral Home	2	0	2	-
Superior	4	20	24	40
Taylor County	2	8	10	26
Tomah	7	3	10	2
Care Center	0	2	2	0
Tomahawk	4	14	18	16
Viroqua	0	4	4	0
Waupaca	6	8	14	12
Waupun	2	4	6	10
Wausau	53	65	118	119
Whitehall	0	0	0	2
Wild Rose	0	0	0	2
Wisconsin Rapids	8	28	36	30
Woodruff	24	53	77	92
TOTALS	523	1405	1928	1925

In the earlier days, various means were used to get these eyes to either Milwaukee or Madison. Some made arrangements with the airlines, others with the sheriff's department where one sheriff's squad would meet another squad and transfer the eyes from one squad to the next until they got to Madison or Milwaukee. Nowadays, each club has volunteers who can be called on at any time of the day or night to carry eyes directly to the lab. Not only are eyes collected, but nearly all the organs can be used. Currently, a big drive is being made to make people aware of how important these organs can be to someone else. As the Lions say, **"Give the gift of sight**."

Wisconsin Used Eye Glass Program

The earliest records available of when the Wisconsin Lions started the collection of used eyeglasses is from a letter I have from Shafeec Mansour, dated June 28, 1987. In it, he tells that he started this program with the Janesville Lions Club in the early 1950s. It was after his return from India, after starting his first club there in 1956. With the help of both the Janesville and Wausau Lions Clubs, Wisconsin was able to ship 20,000 pair of used glasses to the Bombay Lions Club in India.

The late Jawaharial Nehru told Shafeec that the Lions and Lionism which he brought into India are accomplishing miracles in the social welfare of his country.

During October 1957, Noshir Pundole, the first President of the Bombay Lions Club, and then a Past District Governor, along with his wife Roshan, came to Wausau to visit with Shafeec and Eleanor.

Shafeec and Eleanor took the Pundoles to visit the Jonas Mink Ranch which LeRoy Jonas owned in Rib Mountain. There they got acquainted with LeRoy, who was the District Care Chairman. Noshir told LeRoy of the great need for used eyeglasses in India, and he would greatly appreciate what LeRoy could do to help them out with used eyeglasses. LeRoy got busy and asked all the local clubs to help in collecting used eyeglasses.

Later, in a letter dated February 18, 1964, he asked all the clubs in Wisconsin to start collecting used eyeglasses, and send them to him for shipment to India. Shafeec, in his travels around the state and Upper Michigan, also promoted the collection of used eyeglasses.

The sorting, wrapping and packing of the used glasses into cartons took place in the Jonas Warehouse, where many of the local Lion Clubs members would get together and help. These cartons were then put into a large crate and were shipped to CARE in Philadelphia, Pennsylvania, via Spector and Midstate Truck Lines - free of charge. Then CARE would take over and see that they were loaded onto a ship for Bombay, India.

In all, LeRoy and the Rib Mountain Lions Club, with the help of other Lion Clubs, ended up shipping 40,000 pairs of used eyeglasses to India, 20,000 to Chile, 10,000 to Equador, and 45,000 pair to the Philippines.

After March 2, 1970, the Stettin Lions Club took over the project for about two years, when the Wausau Noon Lions Club took it over.

If Wisconsin was not the first state, it was one of the first, to collect and ship used eyeglasses. I do know that the Rib Mountain and the Wausau Noon Lions Clubs have received glasses from many of the states, including Alaska. So, it would seem that Wisconsin could be the first state to have the used eyeglasses program.

Richard Eiseman, a member of the Wausau Noon Lions Club, now in charge of the Wisconsin State Lions used eyeglasses program, took over the sorting, packing and shipping of the used eyeglasses many years ago. He told me that Wisconsin will soon obtain its 6,000,000 pair of used eyeglasses shipped to the poor and needy of the world.

He tells that these shipments by mail must not exceed 28 pounds in weight. All glasses are shipped out via the U.S. postal service with the exception of those that go to Mexico. These are picked up by the medical mission groups like VOSH (Volunteer Optometric Service for Humanity). These groups travel to Africa, Central and South America, India, Philippines, as well as Mexico and work very closely with the local Lions Clubs in that country there. This has also resulted in large savings in postage.

These doctors give freely of their time and money to perform this humanitarian service free to the needy, and they cannot be thanked sufficiently. The Lions of the world are most grateful to them.

Further, he tells that we have many wonderful clubs and individual Lions who make this project work, and that the Janesville Noon Lions Club fly their used eyeglasses to Wausau.

On the humorous side, he had to tell me about some of the things that they found while unpacking and sorting through the cartons. On various occasions, mice would jump out of the cartons. During the past eighteen years, they've found such things as dentures, a ladies stocking, bubble gum, bras, boxes of cookies, half-chewed candy, coins, children's mittens, a single shoe, a 1910 rusted toaster, a single pair of glasses in a special container with a note insisting it be given only to a U.S. citizen, a magnifying glass, several false eyes, a toupee, half used pencils, old neckties, an old mouth organ, several old shaving kits, combs, body lotion and hair spray.

He went on, "...but of course, mostly good used eyeglasses and yes, hearing aids, all of which were a godsend for the needy."

Leader Dogs
"For Whither Thou Goest."

It is a chance for a new life for a visually-impaired person and to gain a new lifetime friend who will furnish mobility.

If they could talk, they would say "Fear not, I am your Eyes, I will help you, I will lead you wherever you wish to be taken, for I am your eyes for as long as I live, I am a **Leader Dog.**"

This pledge has been given over and over again many hundreds of times as each visually-impaired person receives his Leader Dog. Leader Dogs have given the visually impaired a new life – a new life of confidence, mobility, freedom and a chance to become a productive individual in today's society.

Leader Dogs for the Blind, a great success story, came into being as a result of many events over a period of time.

The following was taken from the book, "Leader Dogs for The Blind," which was written by Margaret Gibbs and published by the Deninger's Publishers, Ltd. Box 76, Fairfax, VA 22030.

It was early in the summer of 1938 when, Club President Lion Donald Schuur, (the founder of Leader Dogs for the Blind), and the other members of the Uptown Detroit Lions Club met in order to see what they could do to help Dr. Glenn Wheeler, who was blind. Most of the members knew him personally, and they wanted to secure a dog guide for him.

Donald Schuur had phoned The Seeing Eye in Morristown, New Jersey, and informed them that his club would like to pay all expenses for the training of both dog and Dr. Wheeler. He was informed that the applicants could not be sponsored by any organization or individual and that any and all contributions were used where needed. The turn down of the Club's offer was a shocking, disappointing set back, but they could understand The Seeing Eye's policy.

During the discussion that followed, many thoughts and questions were brought up. Should Dr. Wheeler be encouraged to apply for entrance to the school and the club make a contribution to The Seeing Eye School of an amount that would cover the supposed costs of training this man and dog team?. Or, should they try some place else? Is The Seeing Eye the only place that trains dogs?

President Donald Schuur sadly explained that in 1938, The Seeing Eye was the only organized, nonprofit school in North America devoted to the training and placement of dog guides.

Following World War I, there was an effort made in Germany to use specially trained dogs to help people who were visually handicapped. In France during the same period, they introduced the white cane. And all during this time, other means were tried, such as having someone else lead around a blind person or with the limited use of dogs.

In 1916, the Germans started a program at Oldenburg to see if the German Shepherd could be trained to take the place of human guides. After the war, they expanded this training to Potsdam and Munich. The dogs were trained to avoid traffic, stop at obstructions, curbs and stairs, plus a few other instructions.

The dogs learned fast and the Germans were very pleased with the results. More and more people were able to experience a freedom of movement that they had never dreamed possible before.

In 1923, Dorothy Harrison Eustis (an American by birth), along with her husband George, founded the Fortunate Fields research, breeding and training center for German Shepherd dogs on Mount Pelerin, near Vevey, Switzerland.

In 1927, *The Saturday Evening Post* asked Dorothy to write an article about her successful programs at Fortunate Fields. The article that she wrote, printed during November, 1927, did not tell about her work but about the dogs being trained to lead the blind and she entitled it "The Seeing Eye."

In the huge pile of mail that resulted from this article, was a letter from Morris Frank, a blind teenager from Nashville, Tennessee who had asked for one of these dogs in order to get the freedom that he knew that a dog would give him. He was sure that there were other visually-impaired people who felt the same, and he pledged that if she could help him get a dog, he would foster a dog guide movement within the United States.

The American Foundation for the Blind refused to sponsor a dog within the United States.

The Potsdam School refused to sell Dorothy a dog, so she decided to bring Morris over to Switzerland and train a dog for Morris herself. The female German Shepherd Dog, Buddy, became the first Seeing Eye Dog.

After Morris returned to the United States in June, 1928, he spent the rest of his life giving as much time possible to The Seeing Eye. Morris was 72 when he died on November, 1980.

Shortly after Dorothy Eustis incorporated her Seeing Eye School at Fortunate Fields, the first class of two graduated. In 1938, Mrs. Eustis closed The Seeing Eye School in Switzerland and returned to the U.S. Also in 1938, Donald Schuur learned of qualified dog trainers emigrating to the United States, and one such breeder and trainer was Glen Staines, who Donald contacted. The four dogs he agreed to provide and train, at $800 each, were provided to Dr. Wheeler; Earl Morrey from Detroit; William Joyce, a law student; and Paul Brown, a brother of Joe E. Brown, from Toledo, Ohio. The Park Avenue Hotel in downtown Detroit offered free accommodations for as long as it took to train these students.

The Lions Clubs throughout the United States were asked to furnish a name for the school. On December 14, 1938, it was announced that The Lions Club of Coulterville, Illinois submitted "Lions Leader." Later, this was changed to Lions Leader Dog Foundation and later changed to the Leader Dogs Foundation.

During this time, The Seeing Eye did not resent the formation of this school, but was concerned about the quality of training. This concern resulted in the Leader Dogs Foundations decision to use trainers and instructors who had served an apprenticeship in dog guide work.

In June 1939, the Leader Dogs Foundation found a small farm on the corner of Rochester and Avon Roads, just outside of Rochester, Michigan, which the owner agreed to rent for fifty dollars per month. In 1940, the Lions purchased this fifteen-acre site, and today, the major buildings include general offices, garages, kennels, student dormitory and many parking areas. Today, with their large dormitory, they can take care of thirty-two students and their kennels can hold 300 dogs.

The dogs receive a five-month training and the students go through a four-week training course with the dog that is picked as most suitable for them.

Helen Keller often told that the thing that troubled her the most as the result of her handicaps was the fact that she had to always rely on others in order to get around. The Leader Dogs free visually-impaired people of that dependence.

Wisconsin State Lions Magazine

Past International President Lion Frank V. Birch graduated from the University of Wisconsin in 1918. While in school, he edited *The Badger* yearbook, so it was little wonder that when he became Deputy District Governor, he decided to make up and mail out the first ever Wisconsin Lions Newsletter which he called the *Badger Lion*. It was September, 1928.

One year later, the staff was enlarged to include William C. Hyde and John C. Viets as editors. They published a two-page newsletter.

District Governor Olson was appointed editor of the *Badger Lion* in 1935, and he changed the format.

After the division of District 27 into three subdistricts, the Board of District Governors authorized the 1937-38 issue of the *Badger Lion* to become a four-page publication. This allowed the editor to give more prominence to the activities of the Wisconsin Lions. And, as in the past, these copies were distributed to the clubs through the club secretaries.

At the 1939-40 convention, Lion Oliver Wordell was appointed to serve as Editor of the *Badger Lion*. In 1941, A.A. Storsheim of Weyauwega was made editor of the state magazine with Lion Pete Walch, also from Weyauwega, as associate editor. The last known issue that they put out was dated June, 1953.

During his term as International Director in 1952-54, Ray Galipeau saw the need of a state publication and mailed out a 6 x 9 magazine in November 1954 to all State and Club Officers.

In March 1955, the first 8-1/2 x 11 issue of the *Wisconsin Lions Magazine* was mailed out in a limited number. The next issue appeared in April 1955, and it was sent out through the new state office in Merrill. Ray Galipeau became the editor, and Shafeec Mansour the associate editor.

In October 1955, Lion Art Jones of Glidden, the editor of an industrial publication, took up the editorship of *The Wisconsin Lions Magazine* until February 1956, when he passed away.

In 1956, the State Council of five District Governors appointed a State Editorial Board to pick someone for the position of editor for the state magazine. This Board appointed Ray Galipeau.

After the death of Ray Galipeau on November 21, 1981, bids were asked for the editing and publication of the *Wisconsin Lions Magazine*. Managing Editor Lion Erik Madisen, Jr., of the Madisen Publishing Division, Appleton, Wisconsin won the bid. He has done a fine job with this magazine ever since.

A few years ago, the Lions of Wisconsin voted to have the number of issues of this magazine increased to ten each year.

Following are copies of the various headings under which the Lions news has been published.

Vol. XVII, No. 6   Lions International, Districts 27 A-B-C-D, Wisconsin   May 1944

February 1994

International Counsellors and Past District Governors Organization

The Past District Governors Organization of Lions Clubs International District 27-Wisconsin is made up of the Past District Governors who have served as District Governors of the many Sub-Districts in Wisconsin and membership is also open to any Past District Governor who has served as a District Governor in some other District outside of Wisconsin but now resides in Wisconsin.

During the First Convention in Dallas, Texas, in 1917, Committees arranged for the districting of the United States and for the appointment of Governors to be in charge of these Districts. At the 2nd International Convention, this plan was adopted and nine Lions, recommended by the Clubs in their District or State, were appointed to serve as District Governors of their District or State. They were:

Arkansas: T.J. Parker, Little Rock

California: Jesse Robinson, Oakland

Colorado and Wyoming: Louis K. Cameron, Denver

Illinois: George W. Milligan, Chicago

Iowa: E.J. Wenner, Waterloo

Louisiana: F.C. Brinkman, Jr. Shreveport

Minnesota: William. P. Repke, St. Paul

Oklahoma: A.V. Davenport, Tulsa

Texas: G.M. Cunningham, Houston

Tennessee: John E. Lippitt, Memphis

Some of their duties included supervising club activities and organizing clubs in their respective states. The bylaws relating to the duties of these District Governors empowers each one to call an annual state convention which should prove a valuable stimulus to both present and prospective clubs in each District.

The 3rd International Convention was held in Chicago, Illinois during July 9-11, 1919 and Judge John F. Garner of Quincy, Illinois was appointed to serve as District Governor for the year 1919-1920. The first District Convention of then District Nine was held in Quincy in 1920 and the delegates elected him to serve for a second term.

So, Lions George Milligan of Chicago, and William Repke of Saint Paul became the first Past District Governors of the two Districts that had jurisdiction over Wisconsin in 1918.

At an International Board of Directors meeting which was held April 22, 1940, the Directors established the honorary title of International Counsellors for those District Governors who ably served. "The action of the International Board elevated the past District Governors and gave them an enduring, up-to-date and permanent position. Through this medium, men who ably serve as District Governors are not shelved as past District Governors and remembered only as those who once served but they are elevated and given permanent recognition. They are men of honor and respect, men of experience, men of Lion service, men capable of helping and counselling–Lions International Counsellors.

"The Counsellor holds an honorary office in the association. He is not limited to a Zone, District, State or Nation. He may move from one part of the country to another, but he remains an International Counsellor as long as his membership is active."

Later, they established one week in November as International Counsellors' Week.

At the meeting of The International Board of Directors held in Washington, D.C., September 23-25, 1965, the "Advisory Committee," of the board recommended: "In the interest of clarity and to be understandable to Lions everywhere, your Advisory Committee recommends the following titles for Lions who have served our Association: International President – *Past International President;* International Director – *Past International Director;* District Governors – *Past District Governors.*

"The recommendation was unanimously adopted but only following consideration of the questions raised at two previous Board meetings. Basically, the reasons given for "rescinding" the title concerned clarity (the title meant different things in different countries, status wise–in some countries an International Counsellor was higher in status than an International Director) and "equality" of treatment in recognition of those who served as officers of The Association. The words of the late Past International President Briggs were succinct on the latter point when he said "we propose to call those who served in this office by the exact same terminology as we did the Past President and the Past Director and the rest of them, all on exactly the same basis...what is good for a Past President, or a Past Director, ought to be good for a Past District Governor...Since the Board gave the title in 1940, the Board had power to take it away in 1965."

This information was included in order that every one will understand why the title of the International Counsellor was originally created and why it had to be rescinded.

During the 1952-1953 year, an invitation was sent out by International Director Ray Galipeau along with Counsellors R.J. Cronin and J.H. Hamilin, all from Merrill, to all the International Counsellors of Wisconsin, including Counsellors G.W. Milligan, J.J. Garner and J.W. Scott of Illinois, to meet at Merrill, Wisconsin on January 25-25, 1953 in order to organize the International Counsellors Association of the State of Wisconsin.

The weekend conference started out with a 7:30 p.m. banquet held in the Badger Hotel in Merrill on January 24, 1953. Due to the inclement weather, many who had planned to attend were not able to make it, but records show that the following were in attendance: International Counsellors Victor Miller, St. Nazianz; Dr. Robert Haggerty, Park Falls; Hugo Baumann, Marinette; Clyde Jewett, Janesville; Edward Heller, Marshfield; G.I. Wallace, Madison; Clarence L. Sturm, Manawa; C.J. Blaska, Oconomowoc; Frank V. Birch, Milwaukee; R.J. Cronin, Merrill; J.H. Hamlin, Merrill; Harold Frank, Kaukauna; Chester R. Bell, Milwaukee; Ray Galipeau, Merrill; Emil C. Gehrke, New London, Norman A. Krueger, Wausau and their wives, a group of Merrill Lions and their wives, four of the five District Governors of the state and their wives, and special guests, Lions International Secretary William R. Bird and Mrs. Bird of Chicago, Special Representative of Lions International, S.A. Mansour and Mrs. Mansour. The records I used did not list International Counsellor Louis Gardipee and his wife Inez as being in attendance, but a letter dated September 15, 1990 from PDG Gardipee advised that "I remember being to the meeting there, but I'm hazy about it. I remember a night meeting and a morning breakfast get-together." So let the record show that they were there.

After attending church services of their choice on Sunday, January 25th, the International Counsellors called their organization meeting at 11:00 a.m. They elected: President, Chester R. Bell; Vice President, Dr. Robert Haggerty; Secretary-Treasurer, Emil C. Gehrke.

They set the dues at $5 per year and decided to hold the meetings as early as possible after the State convention of 1953 and invite the new State Council of District Governors. They also planned to hold their next meeting in Superior on the evening before the opening day of the State convention.

The purposes, objectives and bylaws of the new Association were thoroughly discussed and with a few revisions were accepted as follows:

> (1) To advance and further assist the Cause of Lionism throughout the great State of Wisconsin. (2) To help in the promotion of a close and friendly inter-district relationship among the Lions Clubs of Wisconsin. (3) To lend our assistance and cooperation, whenever and wherever possible, with the duly elected officers of this association in Wisconsin, so that this encouragement and cooperation will be a constructive aid in the furtherance of the "On Wisconsin Program."

This group became an official part of Wisconsin Lionism through adoption of a resolution by the delegates of the State Lions Convention in Stevens Point in 1955.

International Counsellors, Past District Governors, Past Presidents

1953, Chester R. Bell, Milwaukee

1953-54, Chester R. Bell, Milwaukee

1954-55, Chester R. Bell, Milwaukee

1955-56, Ray A. Galipeau, Merrill

113

1956-57, Eugene J. Nord, Milwaukee

1957-58, Eugene J. Nord, Milwaukee

1958-59, Dr. Robert Haggerty, Park Falls

1959-60, Dr. L.E. Nelson, Marinette

1960-61, Arnie S. Sader, Fremont

1961-62, Edward S. Eick, Chilton

1962-63, Leo T. Kehl, Madison

1963-64, Thomas W. McLean, Nekoosa

1964-65, Dr. O.J. Turek, Milwaukee

1965-66, Hugo R. Bauman, Marinette

1966-67, Russell Nachreiner, Adams-Friendship

1967-68, Walter E. Ender, West Salem

1968-69, Louis J. Gardipee, Black River Falls

1969-70, Claud Petrykowski, Hales Corners

1970-71, Frank Zahorik, Crivitz

1971-72, Fred R. Louis, Stevens Point

1972-73, James W. Wedeward, Stoughton

1973-74, Marvin J. Roshell, Chippewa Falls

1974-75, Frank A. Polski, Milwaukee

1975-76, Warren Zander, Milwaukee

1976-77, Donald Leverentz, Endeavor

1977-78, Louis Becker, DePere

1978-79, Donald Shaurette, Amherst

1979-80, Ray A. Galipeau, Sr., Merrill

1980-81, William Mellin, Tomah

1981-82, Len Amberg, Memomonie

1982-83, George W. Hoffman New Berlin

1983-84, Alfred Kohlwey, Grafton

1984-85, Max Harrington, Plainfield

1985-86, Melvin Pethke, Manawa

1986-87, Arnold Driscoll, Port Edwards

1987-88, Daniel Stevens, Rhinelander

1988-89, Hal Helwig, Stone Lake

1989-90, Henry Q. Turville, Madison

1990-91, Gene W. Ender, West Salem

1991-92, Ronald L. Duffe, New Richmond

1992-93, Raymond Seidel, Waterford

1993-94, Wayne Tyree, Sussex.

1994-95, Herb Schneider

Wisconsin Lions Past District Governors Organization - 1989-90

Officers: President, Henry Q. Turville, Madison, D1;

First Vice-President: Gene W. Ender, West Salem, D2;

Second Vice-President: Ronald L. Duffe, New Richmond, E2;

Third Vice-President: Raymond Seidel, Waterford, A1;

Secretary-Historian: Wayne Tyree, Sussex, A2;

Treasurer: Herbert Schneider, Sheboygan, B1;

Sergeant-At-Arms: Lloyd Eggleston, Clintonville, B2;

Director: Gary M. Lutz, Stevens Point, C1;

Director: Edward J. Sirek, Rhinelander, C2;

Immediate Past President: Harold Helwig, Stone Lake, E1.

Since their organization on January 24, 1953, the International Counsellors Organization (changed in 1965 to the Past District Governors Organization) has been active in improving Lionism in the State of Wisconsin by: establishing teams of past district governors to conduct new member orientation sessions, conducting seminars at the Wisconsin state conventions, studying the feasibility of a statewide project, developing a state Lions Slide Library where loans of slides are made by Past District Governors for presenting programs in their district.

District Governors Who Served Wisconsin

1918 -19
George Milligan

1919-20
Judge John Gardener

1920-21
Judge John Gardener

1921-22
Dr. John Scott

1922-23
Rev. J. A. Holmes

1923-24
Rev. J. A. Holmes

1924-25
John Baker

1925-26
Robert Hine

1926-27
Walter Wittich

1927-28
Giles Putman

1928-29
Rev. M. S. Weber

1929-30
Frank Birch

1930-31
George Dobbins

1931-32
Lawson Lurvey

1932-33
Roman Heilman

1933-34
Sid Kaye

1934-35
Rev. J. Olson

1935-36
Judge A.M. Scheller

1936-37
Dr. W.L. Boyden

1937-38
A. Dr. H.J. Watson
B. E.W. Mackey
C. Ralph Kennedy*

1938-39
A. Dr. J. J. Watson*
B. A.U. Stearns
C. Alfred Gerhard

1939-40
A. Dr. J.M. Jeffers
B. August Fanslau*
C. Dr. Van Patter
D. Leo Kehl

1940-41
A. Glen Dalrymple
B. Harold Frank
C. J.H. Hamlin
D. Leo Kehl
E. C.J. Blaska*

1941-42
A. Arnold Klentz
B. Clarence Sturm
C. C.J. Blaska*
D. Alvin Loverud

1942-43
A. Arnold Klentz
B. Francis Flanagan
C. Dr. Robert Haggerty
D. Louis Means*

1943-44
A. Alvin Seegers*
B. Robert Connelly
C. Louis Gardipee
D. Louis Means

1944-45
A. John Winterburn
B. Arnold Sader
C. Dr. S. T. Donovan
D. Clyde Jewett*

1945-46
A. Chester Bell
B. Edward Eick
C. Ray Galipeau, Sr. *
D. John Esch

1946-47
A. Chester Bell
B. Hugo Bauman*
C. Howard
   Dankemeyer
D. Dr. B. I. Pippin

1947-48
A. Dr. Emmet Cook*
B. Norman Taylor
C. Dr. N. Reppen
D. Harland Hill

1948-49
A. Paul Junghans
B. Austin Smith
C. Robert Cronin
D. Solon Pierce*

1949-1950
A. A.W. Bearder
B. Robert Grimmer
C. Norman Hoel*
D. Walter Curtright

1950-51
A. Edward Daley
B. Emil Gehrke*
C. Edward Heller
D. G.I. Wallace
E. J. Earl Vesser

1951-52
A. Eugene Nord*
B. Victor Miller
C. Norman Krueger
D. Henry Schmid
E. John Kraft

1952-53
A. Eugene Nord
B. Dr. L.E. Nelson
C. Roman Jungers
D. Leonard Porter
E. Rufus Dimmick*

1953-54
A. K.I. Snyder
B. Dr. L.E. Nelson
C. Fred Lewis
D. Ed Hofmeister*
E. Herbert Schultz

1954-55
A. Art Rowoldt
B. Charles Hoffman
C. Fred Lewis*
D. Ed Steul
E. Thomas Tobola

1955-56
A. V.J. Lucareli
B. Edgar Mueller*
C. Harold Johnson
D. Walter Netterbald
E. Arthur Best

1956-57
A. E.V. Metcalfe*
B. Dr. H.G. Fehl
C. Larry C. Jensen
D. Art Farwell
E. Lorn Johnson

1957-58
A. E. J. Mueller
B. William Farnum
C. W.W. Quinlan
D. Lester Johnson
E. V. L. Droog*

1958-59
A. Clarence Black
B. Frank Zahorik
C. Thomas McLean
D. Walter Ender*
E. Fred Friedrich

1959-60
A. Leo McGlade
B. George Kalcik
C. A.P. Haemmerle*
D. Freeman Fox
E. Bennie Erickson

* Council Chairman

1960-61
A. Dr. O.J. Turek
B. Donald Quistorff*
C. Clifford Thrall
D. Dan Goeden
E. Arthur Swenson

1961-62
A. David Herb*
B. Ellsworth Hart
C. Russell Nachreiner
D. V.J. Johnson
E. Eugene King

1962-63
A. James Wenzel
B. LeRoy Styre
C. William Johnson
D. William Brewer
E. Marvin Roshell*

1963-64
A. Ray Kraft
B. Carl Schuster
C. Clair Baehman
D. George Crandall*
E. Aurthur Ripplinger

1964-65
A. Claud Petrykowski
B. Edward Rosenfeldt
C. Don Shaurette*
D. James Wedeward
E. Donald Dedrickson

1965-66
A. Robert Spruce
B. Louis Sheahan*
C. Jerry Radlinger
D. Earl Johnson
E. James Foster

1966-67
A. Harold Patzer*
B. Leslie Rose
C. Donald
   Rasmussen
D. F.R. Grieneisen
E. Bernard Klugow

1967-68
A. Frank Polski
B1. Howard Heimke
B2. Frank Feivor
C. Edward Ludwig
D. Harvey Brandau
E. J. Eugene
    Roshell*

1968-69
A. Warren Zander
B1. Vern Ruhl
B2. M.W. Millard
C. Douglas Gould
D. K. Schellpfeffer*
E. Robert Muza

1969-70
A. Herbert Velser
B1. Herbert Schneider
B2. Mel Pethke
C1. Howard Whaples*
C2. Lester Schlink
D. Dale Doering
E. Paul Sylla

1970-71
A. Thomas Sheehan
B1. Donald Leverentz
B2. Louis Becker*
C1. Joseph Boettcher
C2. Dr Harvey Hougan
D. William Mellin
E. Fred Geske

1971-72
A. Dr Alton Rosenkranz
B1. Everett Lee*
B2. Marlow Strehlow
C1. John Tetzlaff
C2. John Gehring
D. Justin Williams
E. Len Amberg

1972-73
A1. Joseph Wimmer*
A2. Carl Klug
B1. Ray Kauffung
B2. Vern Volz
C1. Arnold Driscoll
C2. W.Dan Zimmerman
D. Leroy Herbeck
E. L. Rhodes Lewis

1973-74
A1. George Hoffmann
A2. Dick Kapp
B1. Max Harrington
B2. Lloyd Eggleston
C1. John Plumb Jr.
C2. Charles Francis
D. Gene Ender
E. Robert Crase*

1974-75
A1. John Coleman
A2. Roy Schwalbach
B1. Donald Kringel
B2. William Allen
C1. Ray Ohlsen
C2. Roy Buckland
D. Henry Q. Turville*
E. Norman
    Panzenhagen

1975-76
A1. Arthur Gulrud
A2. Alfred Kohlwey
B1. Donald Mattison
B2. Robert Peterson
C1. Donald Carl
C2. Daniel Stevens*
D. Peter Meyer
E. Dr. Willis Valett

1976-77
A1. Raymond Noonan
A2. Rueben Sader
B1. John Schneider
B2. William Meyer
C1. John Tabakos*
C2. Carl Torkelson
D. Arnold Schlicht
E. Harold Helwig

1977-78
A1. Raymond Seidel
A2. John Nezworzski
B1. Clem
    Schoenborn Jr.
B2. Harry Merriman*
C1. Gary Lutz
C2. Cecil Dixon
D. Lloyd Lewis
E. Gordon Berg

1978-79
A1. John Fleischer
A2. John Rickert
B1. Clarence Weller*
B2. Norbert Klatt
C1. Adolph Gorke
C2. Harold Knauf
D. Richard Ledford
E. Howard Ackley

1979-80
A1. Lester Jacobs
A2. Gerald Bogart*
B1. Orvin Doede
B2. Lloyd Keeney
C1. Helmer Lecy
C2. Frank McKay
D. Lee Winch
E. Edward Kolar

1980-81
A1. Lloyd Addie
A2. Harold Doege
B1. Glenn Murty
B2. David Bahr
C1. Dale Splinder
C2. Bob Maletzke
D. Ivan Ryan
E1. Lyle Fechtelkotter
E2. Lynn Steglich
    Helmer Lecy*

1981-82
A1. Harlan Unger
A2. Ralph Mehlos
B1. Fred Holtz
B2. Ken Linzmeyer
C1. Charles Iverson
C2. Charles Franz
D1. Gregory Johll
D2. Harold Alston
E1. James Bailey
E2. Dr. Bill Sperling
    Dale Splinder*

1982-83
A1. Dave Sugden
A2. Wayne Tyree
B1. Vernon Pautz
B2. Ken Capelle
C1. Gary Frahm
C2. Leroy Jensen

117

1982-83 cont.
D1. Jerry Whitford
D2. Ed Carpenter
E1. Edward Ludwig
E2. Marvin Lansing
    James Bailey*

1983-84
A1. Robert Welch
A2. Michael Travis
B1. Milton Wood
B2. Eugene Fischer
C1. Wallace Meuret
C2. Edward Sirek
D1. James Hopkins*
D2. Dr. C.J. Laridaen
E1. Edwin Williams
E2. Ronald Duffe

1984-85
A1. Robert Ahler
A2. Gerald Bloedel
B1. Eugene Norberg*
B2. Herbert Johnson
C1. Leslie Heath
C2. Harvery Conley
D1. James Guy
D2. William Smillie
E1. Mel Samplawski
E2. Ronald Husby

1985-86
A1.Thomas Ellenson
A2. Robert Mantei
B1. Thomas Koch
B2. George Madon
C1. E. William Laudert
C2. Oscar
    Kretzschmar*
D1. Glen Spring
D2. Dave Ruetten
E1. William Sigafoos
E2. Thomas Le Cleir

1986-87
A1. Robert Kolosowsky
A2. Donald Roskopf
B1. Dennis Kitchen
B2. Robert Entringer
C1. Fran O'Brien
C2. Ron Alexander
D1. Phillip Ingwell*
D2. Dennis Koranda
E1.Robert Zimmerman
E2. Larry Butler

1987-88
A1. Gary Thompson*
A2. Carl Schuett
B1. Dwaine Habrat
B2. Donald Sykes
C1. Bernard Dahlke
C2. Mike Condella
D1. Peter Cerniglia
D2. Ron Lauden
E1. James Snyder
E2. Henry Kurth

1988-89
A1. Thomas Pizzo
A2. Arnold Holming
B1. Paul Tadych
B2. Don Pavlat
C1. Herbert Carlson
C2. J. Bellefeuille
D1. Roger Babcock*
D2. Ray Horstman
E1. Ed Bonn
E2. Jim Skorlinski

1989-90
A1. Warren Ackerman
A2. Gerald Rabbach
B1. Thomas Thorson*
B2. Ted Hendrick
C1. Harry "Mike"
    McMeeken
C2. Clarence Helwig
D1. Marvin Staskal
D2. Darrel Talcott
E1. Peter Hubin
E2. Peter Hendrikson

1990-91
A1. Lee Ketterhagan
A2. Robert Sielaff
B1. Victor Voigt
B2. DuWayne Carl*
C1. William Jajewski
C2. Francis Hyland
D1. Donald Johnson
D2. Dick Nestingen
E1. A. Pat Mrotek
E2. William Setterlund

1991-92
A1. Jerome Willms
A2. Dr. Steven
    Johnson
B2. Robert Showers
B2. William Ratzburg
C1. Roger Poteat
C2. Dale Schroeder*
D1. George
    Ringelstetter
D2. Elwyn Beane
E1. Larry Blahauvietz
E2. Albert Johnson

1992-93
A1.Gene Zawikowski*
A2. David West
B1. Gordon Hoffman
B2. Rudolph Messar
C1. Louis "Mike"
    Carter
C2. Donald Jante
D1. Roland Buchholz
D2. David Mocco
E1. Bonar Carlson
E2. David Kaiser

1993-94
A1. Sherman Allen
A2. Del Hintzmann*
B1. Kenneth Rohde
B2. Ronald Grosskopf
C1. John Rung
C2. Edward Sirek
D1. Michael Tiber
D2. Les "Mike"
    Levendoski

1993-94 continued
E1. William Sigafoos
E2. Delmar Plank

1994-95
A1. Robert Blunck
A2. Harold Nagler
B1. Clayton Sengbusch
B2. Curt Kjendalen*
C1. Sharon Cherek
C2. Ted Bonkowski
D1. Gordy Brandt
D2. Joe Persons
E1. Bertram Ancel
E2. Ronald Myhers

Wisconsin's International District 27 Listing

Club Name	Original Date

District 27-A1

Big Bend Vernon	06/03/55
Burlington	03/09/50
Caledonia	04/21/67
Cambridge Area	09/22/80
Cudahy	03/29/50
Darien	02/14/84
Delavan	05/16/38
Dousman–Ottowa	02/10/65
Eagle	03/16/64
East Troy	12/10/37
Elkhorn	10/15/52
Fontana-Big Foot	11/18/81
Fort Atkinson	02/28/30
Franklin Noon	04/30/87
Franklin	10/01/57
Genoa City	10/18/60
Greendale	11/10/55
Greenfield	09/10/57
Hales Corners	10/16/56
Jefferson	05/15/78
Johnson Creek	06/24/85
Kenosha Noon	12/28/48
Kenosha Greater	10/12/67
Lake Geneva	03/30/37
Lake Mills	02/17/70
Lyons	03/19/86
Milwaukee Bay View	02/10/86
Milwaukee South Shore Noon	03/25/87
Milwaukee Lake	01/06/50
Mukwanago	12/04/60
Muskego	02/16/50
New Berlin Industrial	12/10/74
New Berlin	04/19/50
North Prairie	05/26/50
Oak Creek	06/10/58
Paddock Lake	04/10/95
Palmyra	02/22/82
Prospect	02/10/50
Racine	11/25/29
Sharon	03/18/81
South Milwaukee	09/13/37
St. Francis	04/14/70
Sturtevant	02/04/71
Tichigan Lake	02/20/69
Union Grove	02/22/49
Wales Genesee	03/06/73
Waterford	11/06/60
Waukesha Noon	09/28/37
Waukesha Evening	03/05/70
West Allis West	03/11/74
West Milwaukee	10/28/37
West Allis	01/14/38
West Allis Central	12/08/75
Whitewater	02/17/39
Williams Bay	08/08/46
Wind Lake	03/22/66

District 27-A2

Allenton	01/08/82
Ashippun	12/21/78
Beaver Dam	06/24/53
Belgium	03/16/53
Brookfield	11/29/62
Brown Deer	05/13/60
Brownsville	04/13/65
Butler	02/01/50
Cedarburg	07/29/46
Clyman	03/18/85
Columbus	01/31/87
Delafield Summit	07/28/54
Elm Grove	04/06/81
Fox Point Bayside	01/13/50
Fox Lake	01/23/86
Fredonia	09/12/73
Germantown	10/26/60
Glendale	04/16/69
Grafton	06/24/46
Hartford Kettle Moraine	06/28/93

Hartford	01/27/39	Appleton Evening	12/03/63
Hartland	11/18/31	Appleton Noon	03/01/22
Horicon	03/05/84	Berlin	06/13/40
Hustisford	07/12/51	Black River -	
Iron Ridge	03/08/73	Town of Wilson	08/26/94
Ixonia	03/15/76	Brillion	06/10/29
Jackson	04/23/80	Butte Des Morts	02/27/76
Juneau	05/18/39	Campbellsport	07/23/31
Kewaskum	05/20/70	Cascade	05/12/76
Lannon	05/24/65	Chilton	02/12/73
Lebanon	01/31/83	Cleveland	06/04/63
Lomira	09/26/44	Collins	11/30/79
Mayville	01/26/54	Coloma	05/30/72
Menomonie Falls	07/01/46	Dundee Long Lake	06/01/92
Milwaukee–Greater		Eden	02/24/76
Milwaukee	10/21/74	Eldorado	08/26/85
Milwaukee–Honey Creek	02/13/95	Elkhart Lake	06/14/71
Milwaukee–North		Endeavor	10/26/55
Milwaukee	05/31/50	Fairwater	01/06/64
Milwaukee–North Central	01/31/83	Fond du Lac Noon	02/15/22
Milwaukee Central	06/10/21	Fond du Lac Evening	06/05/73
Newburg	01/31/86	Francis Creek	08/15/62
North Lake Merton	10/14/52	Green Lake	11/04/61
Oconomowoc	10/26/38	Greenbush–Glenbeulah–	
Okauchee	04/14/50	Green Glen	05/16/83
Pewaukee	10/31/66	Hancock	10/26/70
Port Washington	01/20/71	Harrisville	04/30/75
Reeseville–Lowell	04/19/82	Hilbert	01/04/74
Richfield	01/16/50	Hingham	12/13/94
Saukville	06/14/77	Howards Grove	06/27/73
Slinger	05/27/93	Kiel	05/11/66
Stone Bank	02/19/51	Kingston	02/07/63
Sussex	02/02/39	Larsen-Winchester	04/30/74
Theinsville–Mequon	04/13/50	Manitowoc	01/10/22
Theresa	04/12/76	Maribel	01/21/65
Waterloo	12/09/30	Markesan	08/23/65
Watertown	03/28/30	Menasha,Town Of	11/04/76
Waupun	11/28/62	Menasha	03/31/36
Wauwatosa	04/05/38	Mishicot	01/09/46
Wauwatosa Mayfair	12/27/73	Montello	12/03/64
West Bend	07/19/60	Neenah	03/23/36
		Neshkoro	04/17/74

District 27–B1

Adell	04/07/75	New Holstein	04/09/70
Amsterdam	10/03/78	Newton	10/23/75

Oakfield	12/06/66	Black Creek	12/13/67
Omro	02/17/75	Bonduel	11/16/50
Oshkosh Lakeshore	03/15/66	Brussels	03/31/60
Oshkosh	11/23/23	Caroline	03/02/87
Oxford	06/13/55	Casco	04/10/75
Packwaukee	08/17/76	Cecil	05/18/73
Pickett	05/13/81	Clintonville	07/23/24
Plainfield	02/25/57	Coleman–Pound	09/12/51
Plymouth	04/02/64	Crandon	02/18/46
Poy Sippi	11/05/51	Crivitz	02/27/51
Princeton	11/22/49	De Pere	03/25/69
Random Lake	12/12/51	Denmark	11/17/55
Red Granite	07/12/55	Dyckesville	05/27/70
Reedsville	09/02/38	Egg Harbor	10/25/56
Ripon	12/07/55	Florence	12/11/69
Rosendale	01/15/68	Forestville–Maplewood	03/26/63
Sheboygan Evening	01/30/22	Freedom	10/14/76
Sheboygan Falls	09/16/52	Gillett	02/09/51
Sheboygan Noon	11/12/68	Goodman–Armstrong	
Sherwood	04/17/68	Creek	04/01/87
St. Peter	11/04/76	Grand Chute	06/20/77
St. Nazianz	06/11/52	Green Bay N.E.	05/27/59
Stockbridge	04/03/74	Green Bay Downtown	11/28/21
Two Rivers	03/21/23	Green Bay West	10/31/62
Valders	09/14/38	Greenleaf	10/17/55
Van Dyne	05/06/77	Greenville	09/17/73
Waldo	03/24/86	Gresham	03/11/53
Wautoma	10/30/29	Hortonville	11/01/63
Wayside Morrison	03/09/51	Howard-Suamico	02/18/77
Westfield	03/06/69	Hyland Lakes	11/19/64
Whitelaw	04/12/65	Iola	11/30/48
Wild Rose	11/24/52	Kaukauna	05/12/36
Winnebago East Shore	01/11/61	Kewaunee	04/28/53
		Laona	03/02/51

District 27–B2

		Lena	03/24/71
		Luxemburg	04/05/85
		Manawa	06/28/29
Algoma	10/27/52	Marinette	01/20/30
Antigo	11/13/48	Marion	04/10/62
Ashwaubenon	02/17/75	McCaslin	01/09/73
Baileys Harbor	06/17/52	Medina–Dale–Readfield	08/16/66
Bear Creek	03/06/73	New London	01/22/24
Bellevue	02/03/95	Niagara	11/15/66
Big Falls	05/01/85	Oconto Falls	05/18/84
Birnamwood	01/28/31	Oconto	06/07/54
		Pearson-Pickerel	01/27/87
		Peshtigo	10/28/37
		Pulaski	09/26/67

Seymour	03/19/63
Shawano	02/03/59
Shawano Lake	04/14/64
Shiocton	05/16/66
Sister Bay	05/14/52
Sturgeon Bay	05/17/29
Suring	03/28/74
Tigerton	08/17/48
Wabeno	12/07/28
Washington Island	01/29/35
Waupaca	03/30/25
Wausaukee	09/04/58
Weyauwega Fremont	04/02/28
Wild River	01/12/71
Wittenberg	01/24/51
Wrightstown	06/29/39

District 27–C1

Abbotsford	05/01/68
Adams-Friendship	06/21/50
Almond	01/30/51
Arnott	11/17/75
Arpin	03/06/73
Athens	09/12/67
Auburndale	05/15/67
Bancroft	05/04/82
Berlin-Hamburg Area	09/23/85
Bevent	10/26/83
Castle Rock L.C.	02/03/77
Colby	01/22/63
Curtiss	10/31/80
Dorchester	06/14/56
Easton White Creek	08/08/85
Easton Hewitt Wausau	06/22/84
Edgar	12/12/50
Fenwood	04/26/82
Grand Rapids	04/09/73
Grand Marsh	03/06/73
Greenwood	11/09/71
Halder	09/03/77
Junction City	10/19/66
Kronenwetter	09/19/91
Lake Dubay	11/17/80

Lake Mason	02/09/73
Loyal	10/15/68
Maine	06/30/58
Marathon	10/06/65
Marshfield Sunrise	06/30/88
Marshfield	02/26/31
Milladore	09/16/69
Mosinee	09/26/39
Neillsville	09/22/64
Nekoosa	03/06/51
Pittsville	06/08/55
Plover–Whiting	11/04/65
Port Edwards	05/19/65
Rib Falls	01/19/84
Rib Mountain	10/08/70
Roche-A-Cri	04/11/72
Rome	02/18/80
Rosholt	03/20/46
Rothschild-Weston	12/28/57
Rozellville	06/08/73
Rudolph	04/27/70
Schofield	10/13/50
Spencer	02/06/41
Stettin	02/12/57
Stevens Point Morning	05/15/87
Stevens Point Noon	03/05/26
Stevens Point Evening	09/19/69
Stevens Point-Wisconsin River	12/19/77
Stratford	09/20/39
Thorp	07/09/31
Tomorrow River	10/28/48
Town of Texas	02/10/59
Vesper	01/23/64
Wausau	04/19/22
Wausau Monarch	02/16/87
Wausau Noon	01/29/69
Wausau–Big Bull Falls	01/31/85
Wisconsin Rapids	03/25/46
Withee	08/04/54

District 27-C2

Arbor Vitae Woodruff	09/21/49

Ashland	12/26/84	Sugar Camp	02/21/67
Barnes	03/21/75	Three Lakes	03/18/52
Boulder Junction	03/06/72	Tomahawk Royal	06/11/90
Butternut	08/26/58	Tomahawk	01/29/46
Cable & Area	10/05/65	Tripoli–Brantwood	06/13/67
Catawba–Kennan	04/13/66	Washburn	10/23/39
Conover	10/06/49	Whittlesey	06/03/77
Eagle River	04/13/49	Winchester	10/20/70
Elcho–Pelican Lake	10/17/51		
Fifield	11/02/65		

District 27-D1

Gilman	05/29/51	Albany	02/08/68
Gleason & Area	04/05/85	Argyle	08/26/57
Glidden	01/28/54	Arlington	06/08/73
Hazelhurst	11/09/66	Belmont	02/09/55
Hodag	08/21/81	Beloit Evening	06/30/75
Hurley	09/24/52	Beloit Noon	11/23/23
Irma Birch Rock Falls	06/30/87	Boscobel & Area	01/26/93
Irma	01/23/86	Brodhead	08/27/57
Iron River	01/15/63	Cassville	04/09/74
Jump River	10/27/77	Cobb	09/26/51
Lac du Flambeau	01/11/50	Cottage Grove	04/10/74
Lake Tomahawk	10/18/67	Cross Plains	10/25/78
Land O' Lakes	10/25/49	Cuba City	05/24/62
Manitowish Waters	02/25/71	Darlington	11/02/83
Medford	01/31/51	De Forest	05/31/56
Mellen	08/22/50	Deerfield	06/02/42
Mercer	09/07/50	Dickeyville	02/12/76
Merrill Noon	10/29/76	Dodgeville	01/14/72
Merrill	02/25/27	Edgerton	11/12/40
Minoqua	02/14/46	Evansville	12/21/25
Ogema	10/10/50	Fennimore	03/28/62
Park Falls	10/19/37	Fitchburg	01/20/84
Phelps	10/19/81	Hazel Green	02/20/68
Phillips	04/11/62	Highland	10/01/46
Prentice	02/25/59	Janesville Evening	01/21/85
Presque Island	06/08/73	Janesville Noon	05/26/22
Rhinelander	08/19/40	Lancaster	06/04/71
Rhinelander–Harmony	04/20/93	Lodi–Dekorra–	
Rib Lake	04/14/66	Lake Wisconsin Area	01/22/85
Saxon–Gurney	06/07/84	Madison Evening	06/30/91
Sayner–Star Lake	09/19/60	Madison Central	05/04/22
South Shore	09/11/50	Madison West	01/29/64
St. Germain	03/17/52	Marshall	01/03/79
Stetsonville	06/29/87		

Mazomanie	03/20/50	La Farge	02/13/73
McFarland	12/12/62	Lake Delton	05/21/51
Middleton	05/05/86	Mauston	03/12/68
Mineral Point	11/12/82	Mindoro	05/28/68
Monona Grove	11/13/57	Mormon Coulee	05/04/79
Monroe	06/11/51	Necedah	10/26/72
Monticello	10/30/78	New Lisbon	11/16/59
Mt. Horeb	08/28/57	North Bend	04/23/80
Muscoda	04/27/66	Norwalk	01/08/52
New Glarus	08/18/41	Onalaska	05/29/52
Oregon	06/11/80	Plain	06/20/50
Pardeeville	02/18/77	Prairie du Chein	04/14/83
Platteville	04/19/82	Reedsburg	04/23/51
Portage	10/10/68	Richland Center	09/14/42
Potosi–Tennyson	12/17/86	Sauk Priairie	03/25/47
Shullsburg	01/06/47	Seneca	04/30/87
Stoughton	12/21/23	Soldiers Grove	11/20/51
Sun Prairie	09/26/33	Sparta	10/19/61
Verona	01/05/87	Spring Green	11/28/49
Waunakee–Westport	06/29/80	St. Joseph's Ridge	04/30/77
West Grant	10/10/63	Stoddard	02/24/70
Wisconsin Dells	04/20/78	Tomah	02/17/30
		Viroqua	10/30/47

District 27-D2

		Warrens	04/29/85
		Wauzeka	05/18/84
Bangor	12/28/77	West Castle Rock Lake	04/28/88
Baraboo	08/03/42	West Salem	10/13/48
Barre Co-Ed	01/04/91	Westby	09/01/59
Boaz	01/23/78	Wilton	07/01/70
Brice Prairie	05/07/92		
Camp Douglas	05/26/72		
Cashton	01/05/49		

District 27-E1

Chaseburg	12/10/74	
Coon Valley	03/14/60	Amery	09/03/80
De Soto Area	06/19/91	Barron	06/09/86
Elroy	03/14/52	Birchwood	02/11/61
French Island	06/25/74	Bloomer	05/31/84
Gays Mills	06/16/59	Boyd	05/08/51
Genoa	05/09/78	Brule River	07/30/58
Hillsboro	01/31/86	Cadott	10/02/47
Holmen	02/29/60	Chequamegon	11/17/94
Ithaca	01/08/86	Chetek	12/05/67
Kendall	10/14/48	Chippewa Falls	05/03/56
La Crosse North	11/02/81	Clayton	12/08/65
La Crosse	11/20/52	Clear Lake	09/26/66
		Cornell	06/25/31

124

Danbury	03/26/74	Black River Falls	10/08/37
Eagleton	04/19/89	Blair	03/24/58
Frederic	01/10/74	Boyceville	06/15/92
Grantsburg	05/13/75	Cochrane–Buffalo City	04/18/67
Hawkins	12/06/50	Deer Park	12/22/75
Hawthorne	06/05/80	Durand	03/08/65
Hayward	03/07/63	Eau Claire Evening	12/06/79
Jim Falls	01/05/60	Eau Claire Seymour	11/22/83
Ladysmith	12/12/68	Eau Claire	05/11/46
Lake Holcombe	11/09/72	Eleva Strum Area	05/19/81
Lake Nebagamon	02/12/68	Elk Mound	11/18/76
Lake Wissota	07/11/73	Ellsworth	10/20/30
Luck	11/14/60	Ettrick	07/18/51
Minong-Wascott	11/18/63	Fairchild	11/14/68
New Auburn	04/07/75	Fall Creek	03/22/54
Osceola Area	10/28/80	Foster Area	04/03/95
Pattison Park Area	09/29/80	Fountain City	09/07/51
Poplar–Wentworth	11/12/63	Galesville	08/12/46
Prairie Farm	12/04/67	Glen Hills	03/03/81
Rice Lake	10/30/67	Hammond	10/22/82
Sheldon	01/19/53	Hudson	01/23/87
Shell Lake	01/21/60	Independance	08/08/51
Siren	05/26/69	Knapp	05/18/53
Solon Springs	05/10/56	Menomonie	10/16/46
Spooner-Trego	09/21/72	Merrillan	02/14/74
Springbrook	05/19/82	Mondovi	04/29/59
St. Croix Falls	03/25/52	Nelson	09/30/85
Stanley	04/09/46	New Richmond	10/22/86
Stone Lake	01/12/70	Osseo	02/15/74
Superior Evening	04/30/87	Pepin	08/24/72
Superior	11/05/45	Pigeon Falls	05/31/60
Tilden	12/04/73	Pleasantville	10/31/68
Turtle Lake	05/01/52	Plum City	03/13/67
Unity Area	06/10/57	Prescott	10/20/80
Wanderoos	01/16/84	River Falls	11/22/37
Webster	12/13/66	Roberts	01/10/59
Winter & Area	03/13/75	Spring Valley	10/21/47
		Star Prairie	10/01/68
District 27-E2		Taylor	01/26/70
		Trempealeau	06/19/72
Alma	03/21/68	Waumandee Area	12/01/93
Alma Center	01/30/67	Whitehall	07/01/46
Altoona	02/21/61	Woodville	01/03/52
Arcadia	07/17/51		
Augusta	11/20/39		

The
Wisconsin
Lions
Today

Lions lead the parade in community service throughout Wisconsin, raising millions of dollars for local, state and international projects. In Sussex, the Lions Daze celebration has been held every year since 1967. Riding the first float in 1994 were third-generation Lions President Tom Halquist and Lioness President Diane Ehnert.

127

The Lions committment to programs related to vision is basic to the club and takes many forms, as in Sun Prairie, where Lions President Tom Tucker presented a check for $1104 to Assistant Library Director Sharon Zindars to purchase and rent books for the visually-impaired.

Age is no obstacle for Lions or Lions programs. The Leo organization is made up of teenagers who also serve. (above) Eight Madison West Leo Club members took part in the "Walk For The Cure" sponsored by the Madison Chapter of the Juvenile Diabetes Foundation, with Molly Bosold, Diane Hoyt and Mark Daluge stopping for a photo. (below) In Dodgeville, the Lioness Club went trick-or-treating to collect food for the county food pantry.

In Cecil, (above) eight and nine-year-old Little Leaguers were equipped with bright orange tee shirts, courtesy of the Lions, while in Janesville, (below) Leos and Lions turned out on a rainy October day to spruce up the Lions Beach swimming hole/ice skating pond.

Volunteer fire and emergency medical services (above) are among the leading benefi-
ciaries of Lions fund raisers. First Responders in the Barre Mills area received one of
many checks from the Barre Co-ed Club (l-r), Andrea Page, Steven Kreibach, Bob Moch,
Elaine Stelloh, Richard Stelloh and Ray Neimeier. The Old Car Show (below) sponsored
by Krause Publications brings hundreds of thousands of Studebaker-lovers and other
car buffs to Iola. It all began in 1972, when Iola Lion Chet Krause invited a few of his
friends to show off their vintage cars at the Lions Chicken BBQ. Today, 14 area Lions
Clubs work at the Show to raise funds for their programs.

Helping neighbors near and far is part of the Lions creed. (above) Cable Lions President Dale Schone and Russell Mroz presented a check to Kathy and Kevin Schone, Clam Lake, after Kathy lost her sight during the birth of her baby. (below) Taking senior citizens Inez Brunner, Gene Mommsen and Art Schafargel fishing was the happy chore of Spooner-Trego Lions Jim Leonard, Buck Ferger and Stan Stone.

(above) Ripon Lions Earl Schrader, Rollie Polakoski, Kevin Kaiser and Hubert Rohde turned out to present $500 to transplant patient Rebecca Haberkorn. The Newburg Lions (below) purchased a Telesensory Color CCTV Monitor to assist vision-impaired, but avid reader, Nicole Norgel.

McFarland Lion and author Robert Mecum (above), who is blind, received a little help from his club towards the purchase of a computer system that enables him to write his own stories. A little less high-tech, but equally important help to a neighbor, came from the Caledonia Lions who built a handicapped ramp on the house of a young woman diagnosed with multiple sclerosis.

The number of students educated over the years with the aid of Lions Club
contributions would fill every college in Wisconsin many times over. (above)
Luxemburg President Marv Bini distributed checks to college-bound students
Tracey Baierl and Jessica Alsteen. (below) In Crivitz, Lions President Herald
Polfilio presented checks to young scholars Shawn Nelezen, Travis Dahlke, Sara
Hansen, Jennifer DeGroff, Kim Ducaine and Mike Glish.

The Lions/Quest program helps prepare students for adult life while the Service Project
Award encourages young people to acquire the skills of service. (above) District
Governors John Rung and Del Hintzmann joined Wisconsin Lions Foundation
President Ron Duffe to hold up the banner awarded to Thorp Elementary School.
(below) Campaign SightFirst reflects the Lions' decades-old commitment to vision
programs. Raising funds for SightFirst are Charlie Graiugel and Hiram Valliere of the
Lac du Flambeau Lions.

The Peace Poster Contest is one in a long line of Lions programs promoting world peace. Pete Fannin of the Greenville Club presented prizes to Jesse Gitter, Elizabeth Neumann and Jenny Huss. Elizabeth's poster won the district award and went on to international competition.

The Wisconsin Lions Eye Institute, Eye Banks and Hearing Center are supported by every Lion in the state. In 1993, Wisconsin Lions contributed over $500,000 for new research laboratories in the Department of Ophthalmology at the University of Wisconsin, Madison. (above) Wisconsin Eye Institute technical specialist Carol Keuler demonstrates a corneal excision for District Governor Ted Bonkowski and Foundation Director Dave Kaiser.

"United to give light to your eyes," is the sentiment expressed on the sign announcing the Wisconsin Lions Mission to Mexico. With the most recent trips coordinated by Past International Director Helmer Lecy, Wisconsin Lions have made five trips south since 1991. In 1993, '94 and '95 the Lions conducted basic eye exams and distributed eyeglasses in the city of Rio Bravo just across the border from Texas in northeastern Mexico.

(above)Lions from all over Wisconsin have made the long drive south of the border. In addition to distributing eyeglasses, the Lions have donated 17 ambulances and other vehicles for community service in Guatemala and Mexico. (below) The auto-refraction device enables non-professional Lions volunteers to determine which set of eyeglasses will correct a vision problem. The Lions take two auto-refractors with them, with each exam requiring about one minute to complete. Working together, they have been able to distribute 5,000 pairs of eyeglasses a year. Here Lion Orv Kittel does the reading, Darrel Kittelson records, and Ana Kittel, who is bilingual, interprets.

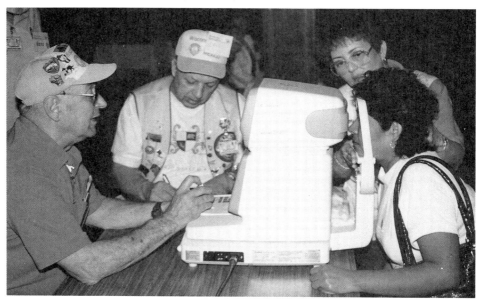

(above) To fit properly, eyeglass frames must be shaped. In Rio Bravo, the fitting crew uses hot water, hot sand and hot salt to bend the frames into the correct shape. (below) The volunteers from Wisconsin, Texas and Mexico in 1994: (front, l-r) Dwaine Hebert, Orv Kittel, Jim Shiferl, Ana Kittel, Pauline Shiferl, Avis Ping, Mario Blanco and "Elloy." (middle l-r) Tom Melberg, Ethel Batz, Mary Melberg, Marge Gorke, Michelle Guegero, Dorothy Wood, Lois Brown, Arnoldine Guleynski, Pat Carlson, Bev Schultz, Duane Sackett. (rear, l-r) Bob Showers, Jerry Ping, Bob Guleynski, Doug Bresina, Helmer Lecy, Herb Schneider, Milt Wood, Bernie Dahlke, Bill Brown, Harlan Schultz, Bonar Carlson, Adolph Gorke.

Just because you are visually, hearing or mentally impaired doesn't mean you can't try archery or stand up on a tube and fall into the lake—that's the spirit behind the Wisconsin Lions Camp.

Since its opening in 1956, tens of thousands of children and adults have attended the Wisconsin Lions Camp near Rosholt. They learn new skills, have new experiences and have fun in ways most of them have not been able to try. Of all Lions projects, perhaps none more expresses the ideal of "doing something for someone else" than the camp. As one Lion said, "Everybody should see what they get those kids to do out there. It really makes you feel good about being a Lion."

Having fun and helping neighbors is part of being a Lion (above), whether it means cooking up burgers, fries and homemade pies–and sampling them too–as these Mondovi Lions do every year, or muscling ice out of Pioneer Lake at Prairie Farm (below). The ice is stored and used to cool beverages during the Prairie Farm Fair. Working on the ice are Glenn Thompson, Bud Lindemer, Cheryl Thompson and Dave Olson.

As they approach the 75th Anniversary of Lionism in Wisconsin in 1996, Lions look to the future. Thanks to the efforts of computer science teacher Pat Phillips and the Janesville Noon Lions, Janesville Leos will be able to communicate with other Leos around the world via the Internet telecommunication system. As Phillips pointed out, Leo Clubs are found around the world and linking her students to them by computer is an ideal way for them to learn about the world beyond Janesville. Acting locally, thinking globally, Lions ideals are demonstrated once again.

The
Lions
International

William Perry Woods M.D.

Founder, owner, twice President of
the International Association of Lions Clubs

Dr. William Perry Woods, an Evansville, Indiana physician and surgeon, founded and served as the president of the Royal Order of Lions, from the day he incorporated it on August 18, 1911, until it was terminated on December 31, 1950.

On October 25, 1916, he incorporated the International Association of Lions Clubs. Thus he became the originator and first owner of the International Association of Lions Clubs. At the first International Convention, held in Dallas, Texas on October 8-10, 1917, he was elected as first president of the Lions Clubs.

The records of the Dallas convention show that Mr. M.E. Throwbridge of Shreveport, Louisiana, nominated Mr. L.H. Lewis of Dallas to be president of the Association.

Mr. Lewis immediately declined, saying that he sought no favor at the hands of the convention. He moved that Dr. Woods be elected to the office of president, saying that the doctor deserved this consideration. Mr. J. Landry from Beaumont, Texas seconded the nomination. Dr. Woods was unanimously elected, and he voiced his appreciation, saying that he would not have been disappointed had he failed in the election, and invited the cooperation of all the clubs and their members.

William Perry Woods, born on May 20, 1877, in Page County, Iowa, was the son of Renwick and Nellie Tracy Woods. He married Anna Emily Augusta Rietz in 1904. Dr. Woods died January 28, 1966. Anna Emily Augusta Rietz was born in Manitowoc, Wisconsin on November 4, 1877, and died March 1, 1969. Both are buried in the Lutheran Cemetery, in Evansville, Indiana.

Renwick Woods, a son of James, was born near Hopkinton, Iowa, was a farmer, and died in 1932. His wife, Nellie Woods, died in 1931.

James "Pappy" Woods, son of Hance Woods, was born in County Tyrone, Ireland, died in 1892 and is buried in Blanchard, Iowa. He married Nancy Smith who was born in Pennsylvania.Nancy died November 10, 1895 and is buried in Iowa.

Hance Woods was born in N. Bracken, Tyrone County, Ireland c. 1775-1795, died August 1825, and is buried in Allegheny County Pennsylvania. He married Jane McCracken who was born c.1775-1795, place unknown, and died before 1828, place unknown.

The Woods children had a five-mile walk to a one-room school called Lynn Point, Iowa. Then went on to "College," (which was like our high school), at College Springs College.

Dr. William Perry Woods' father wanted Perry to become a farmer, but Perry wanted to become a doctor. (He was called Perry by his family.) A farming accident which nearly cost Perry his leg because of no available local medical care, was the reason that Perry wanted to be a doctor.

Because he did not follow his fathers wishes, Perry had to put himself through school by doing odd jobs and taking time off to teach school.

He finished high school in three years and then attended Amity College in College Springs, Iowa, where he completed eight years of study in six years. He then went to the University of Missouri Medical School.

He tells that he picked Missouri because they had just opened their medical school, and offered free tuition to anyone outside the state who wanted to study medicine.

He finished his medical career at the Chicago College of Physicians and Surgeons fourth in his class, and interned at St. Mary's Hospital in Chicago.

Anna Rietz was in Chicago teaching at the Chicago Business School. Anna and Perry became acquainted at a boarding house where she was boarding and where Perry was waiting on tables.

Perry was encouraged to come to Evansville to take over the practice of, and fill in for his brother-in-law, Dr. P.C. Rietz, who was going to take a post graduate course in Pennsylvania. He took a great liking to Evansville, and decided to stay and start up his own practice.

He set up his first office in the old Boehne building, at Eighth and Main streets. Later on he joined his brothers-in-law, Dr. P.C. Rietz, along with Dr. A.R. Rietz, a dentist who had offices in the old American Trust and Saving Bank building at Sixth and Main streets.

Evansville was a large German speaking area, and Anna taught Perry how to speak some German, and she translated for him from the patients.

For the first few years, Dr. Woods made his rounds on a bicycle. He recalled the distances between house calls saying, "I did more work pumping the bike than I did among my patients."

After a while Dr. Woods went "modern" and bought a horse and buggy for transportation from patient to patient. After driving a horse for four years, he bought an automobile. His was the 24th car in Evansville.

During some of his trips to Clarinda, Iowa to visit, he was called on to do several operations which, over the years, included removing his brother Earl's appendix, a large tumor from his brother Earl's wife Mary, even repair of a neighbor's hernia, all done on a kitchen table with the local doctor giving the anesthesia.

During a banquet held in Indianapolis on October 7, 1954, Dr. Woods was honored by the Indiana Medical Society for having administered to the sick and injured for fifty years. During all of his practice, he never refused help to the sick and made calls at all hours. His services as a physician were sought long after he retired.

The Woods had three daughters–Evelyn Eckstein, Lorraine Able, Florence Foster–and five grandchildren.

Royal Order of Lions

The Royal Order of Lions, a fraternal benefit society, was organized on August 18, 1911, by Dr. William Perry Woods and four other men in Evansville, Indiana.

Sometime before this date, a minister whose name is unknown, stopped in Evansville and became acquainted with Dr. Woods. Dr. Woods had been active in organizations during his college days and, with the help of this minister, put together a fraternal benefit society called the Royal Order of Lions.

The order had a ritual with six degrees. Three of the degrees were given in the *Subordinate Den*. The fourth degree was conferred on the state level, the *Supreme Den*, and the fifth was worked on by past officers of the Supreme Den. The sixth, and final degree, was given to select members of the fifth degree.

Reading the Book of Daniel in the Bible influenced the organizers to adopt the Lion as their namesake. They admired its loyalty, courage, strength, regal bearing, and the ferocious way it protected its family. They also adopted the colors of royalty–purple and gold–as the colors of their order.

As a fraternal benefit society, the Royal Order of Lions would help members during sickness and distress, and help defray funeral expenses of any member of a den in good standing.

The constitution and bylaws of the Royal Order of Lions contains a list of their officers, and it shows that the organization had expanded throughout Indiana and into Illinois, Pennsylvania, Ohio, Nebraska, and Oklahoma. Each Den issued a Classified Business Directory, divided by professions or services such as Attorneys, Accountants, Awnings and Tents and Auto Bus Service.

In front of some names there appeared a <u>T</u> for Trade Contract Members who would "sign your coupons," i.e. give a discount for services. Another note says that every business or professional man listed should be patronized by members of the Order.

The Royal Order of Lions had people who traveled and organized new dens. Mr. B.A. Hicks and Mr. G.M. Cunningham, who were working in the Ohio and Pennsylvania areas, asked to be transferred to the southeast.

In the south, they started dens by going to the main hotel in a city and telling the manager of the hotel that they were going to organize a luncheon club. They asked him for the names of some of his friends who he would like to see as members of a club and invited them to lunch. As soon as they found out that they were being asked to join a secret society, and not a simple luncheon club, many men objected directly to Dr. Woods.

He said, "if that is what they want, then we will give it to them." At this point, he started to organize the International Association of Lions Clubs.

On October 24, 1916, Dr. Woods filed another Article of Incorporation with the State of Indiana which incorporated the *International Association of Lions Clubs* as a service and social luncheon club and not as a fraternal benefit association.

In the early 1920s, the Ku Klux Klan was experiencing a resurgence, not just in the South, but throughout the United States. Many members of the Royal Order of Lions joined the KKK and wanted the Lions organization to follow. As soon as they found out who these people were, the officers of the Royal Order of Lions dropped them from membership. This loss was a severe blow to the Royal Order of Lions. The membership and number of dens decreased until it seemed that the only den left was the original one in Evansville.

Although the KKK lost much of its popularity after a few years, the Royal Order of Lions did not recover. When the Great Depression of the 1930s began, the few organizations left also went under.

The last available record of the Royal Order of Lions was dated December 31, 1950. It appears that this was the last year it was active.

The Directory of the Royal Order of Lions contained a statement whose meaning has far outlived the organization. It reads:

The Definition of a True Lion

The man who is clean inside and outside, who neither looks up to the rich or down on the poor, who can lose without squealing, and can win without bragging, who is considerate of his brother and assists him in his struggle for success, who is too brave to lie, too generous to cheat, and too sensible to loaf.

It is a poor species of humanity that does not desire to do some good that will live beyond the limit of his own life.

He who helps others, helps himself.

Articles Of Incorporation Of The Royal Order Of Lions

Known All Men By These Present, That,

W. P. Woods, A.B. M.D.
Stanford E. Pomroy,
Theodore J. de Sabla
George J. an Allstyne
William E. Loos

All of Evansville, Vanderburgh County Indiana, being desirous of associating themselves together for the purpose of forming a body corporate under the laws of the State of Indiana for the Incorporation of Voluntary Associations, approved March 9th, 1901 and all acts and laws amendatory and supplementary thereto; do make and adopt and mutually agree to, and abide by the following articles to-wit:

Article 1. Name
The name of the society or association shall be known as the Royal Order of Lions.

Article 2. Capital
There shall be no capital stock, the Association not being organized for pecuniary profit or reward.

Article 3. Object - Plan
The object and purpose of this Society or lodge is social intercourse and entertainment; to do deeds of charity within its membership and to mutually aid and assist a member when in need or distress.

Plan:

First – The proposed plan for carrying out the object and purposes of this Society is to organize into what is known as a lodge with a ritual, and to adopt such secret work as may be necessary to accomplish this purpose.

Second – To adopt suitable bylaws, rules and regulations to govern the society.

Third – To provide in the bylaws, rules and regulations of the society for the payment of monthly membership dues by each member for the support and maintenance of the society, and to provide for the relief of its members when in sickness or distress.

Article 4. Names and Places Of Each Incorporated Party

The names and residences of each of the incorporating parties are as follows:

> W. P. Woods, A.B. M.D., Evansville, Ind.
> Stanford K. Pomroy, Evansville, Ind.
> Theodore J. de Sabla, Evansville, Ind.
> Geo. J. Van Allstyne, Evansville, Ind.
> William E. Loos, Evansville, Ind.

Article 5. Domicile

The Domicile of the society shall be at the City of Evansville, County of Vanderburgh, State of Indiana, but the society reserves the right to establish subordinate organizations elsewhere.

Article 6. Term

The society not being organized for profit, its term of existence shall be perpetual.

Article 7. Seal

The seal of the Society shall be a round metal disk, on the upper margin of which shall appear the words "ROYAL ORDER OF LIONS" on the lower margin thereof the name and number of the lodge; in the center shall appear a facsimile of a Lion's head with the word "SEAL," said seal to be so constructed, that by its use a raised impression of same will be made on paper.

Article 8. Officers Of The Supreme Royal Den

The officers of the Supreme Royal Den shall be as follows:

> A Supreme Royal President.
> A Supreme Royal Vice President.
> A Supreme Royal Secretary and Treasurer.
> A Supreme Royal Overseer.
> A Supreme Royal Guard.

Article 9. Supreme Royal Governing Board Of Trustees

There shall be a Supreme Royal Governing Board of Trustees consisting of five members who shall manage the business and prudential affairs of the Order.

The election of the Supreme Royal Governing Board of Trustees and their term of office to be, as provided for in the constitution and bylaws

The Supreme Royal Governing Board of Trustees for the first year and until their successors are duly elected and qualified shall be as follows:

> *W.P. Woods, A.B. M.D.*
> *Stanford K. Pomroy*
> *Theodore J. de Sabla*
> *Geo. J. Van Allstyne*
> *William E. Loos*

The International Association of Lions Clubs

The organization of the International Association of Lions Clubs grew out of the confusion and discontent in the early days of the Royal Order of Lions.

Many men who had entered the Royal Order of Lions thinking that they were joining a luncheon club were surprised and unhappy to learn that they had signed onto a fraternal organization.

Dr. Perry Woods and other officers of the Royal Order decided that if some club-members wanted a luncheon club, they should have one.

A luncheon club and a fraternal order could not operate under the same charter so Dr. Woods started to put together a new one. On October 25, 1916, he incorporated under the laws of Indiana, an association known as the **International Association of Lions Clubs.** The articles of incorporation were signed by Dr. William Perry Woods as President. His secretary, Miss C.R. Conen, became an officer; Carmi Hicks, a friend with an insurance office across the hall, became the Secretary-Treasurer; but Miss Conen kept the secretary's records.

They planned to organize 100 clubs and then call a convention, but Dr. Woods soon found out that the members could not wait. He agreed to an offer from the new Dallas club to serve as host. Dr. Woods then sent out a letter to each one of the thirty-three clubs organized in the southwestern states, and invited them to send a Delegate to meet in a convention in Dallas, Texas at the Adolphus Hotel on the 8th, 9th, and 10th of October, 1917.

The 33 Clubs represented here are now known as the Founder Clubs of the International Association of Lions Clubs.

Oct. 25, 1916
Holmer L. Cook
Secretary of State

Articles of Incorporation of the "International Association of Lions Clubs."

We, the undersigned, being citizens of the United States and twenty-one (21) years of age, and desiring to become incorporated under the acts of 1889 of the laws of the State of Indiana, with reference to the organization of societies, associations and clubs, not for pecuniary profit, do hereby make, execute and adopt the following articles of Incorporation, to wit:

Article I

The name or title by which said corporation is to be known in law is, "The International Association of Lions Clubs."

Article II

The purposes for which it is formed are as follows:

First – To take an active part in movements for the commercial and civic betterment of cities, states, and nations in which this association may be established or represented.
Second – To encourage high ethical standards in business and professions by the exchange of business methods and ideas.
Third – To foster the business of its individual members and emphasize the value of each business as a means of earning a livelihood and serving humanity.
Fourth – To study the work of organized clubs; how they best serve the individual members and communities and circulate such information for the benefit of all clubs and mankind in general.

Article III

The principal office or place of business shall be in the City of Evansville, County of Vanderburg, State of Indiana.

Article IV

This corporation not being organized for pecuniary profit its Charter shall be perpetual. There shall be no capital stock.

Article V

The seal of this corporation shall be as herein described, which is as follows:
A circle rope indenture. A smaller circle point indenture. Between the circles or the top indenture the words "LIONS CLUBS" and at the bottom "INTERNATIONAL." Within the smaller circle two parallel point indentures with the word "SEAL" indented between them.

Article VI

The number of directors of this corporation who shall manage its business and prudential concerns shall be three, with the privilege of increasing the number to seven.

Article VII

The names of the three directors selected for the management of Article VI. for the first year of the corporation's existence are as follows:

W.P. Woods
C.R. Conen
Carmi Hicks

157

Article VIII.

The qualifications required of officers and members and the election of directors and officers are as specified in the Constitution & bylaws of the Corporation.

IN WITNESS WHEREOF, We, the parties hereby incorporating, have hereunto subscribed our names, this *24th* day of *October.* A.D. 1916.

signed	*W.P. Wood*	signed	*Carmi Hicks*
signed	*C.R. Conen*		

The Dallas Meeting

Dallas, Texas was one of the fastest-growing cities in Texas. It was a hub for railroads, cattle-raising, farming, oil, and the gateway to the southwest.

During the early 1900s, many fine hotels were constructed in Dallas, and none finer than the Adolphus. It was named after St. Louis beer baron Adolphus Busch who, when he decided to expand his Anheuser-Busch beer empire beyond the confines of St. Louis, chose Dallas as the site of his new brewery. Traveling by private railroad car, he made many visits to Dallas, and considered it his second home.

In time, a delegation from Dallas met with Busch and asked him to underwrite a palatial hotel for the city. He enthusiastically agreed and so threw himself into the project that he added some of the design touches himself.

On the Commerce Street facade of the Adolphus sculptured fixtures depict Night and Morning. The top portion of the building is decorated with terra-cotta representations of Mercury, Ceres, Terpsichore and Apollo. The gargoyles, cherubs and heraldic devices are reminiscent of the Louis XIV style, with touches of Louis XV and Louis XVI as well. Circular decorations near the top of the facade resemble the ends of beer barrels, and the beautiful turret on the southwest corner of the building looks like a beer stein.

Inside the lobby, there still hangs one of two huge chandeliers that hung in the French Pavilion of the St. Louis World Fair in 1903. In 1904, Busch purchased them both, put one in the hotel, and the other in the stables of his Clydesdale horses.

The French Room, the most impressive dining room in the hotel, is decorated with clouds, cherubs, and gilt flowers of the hops plant, an ingredient of beer.

159

Adolphus Busch gave his hotel to the city of Dallas. It opened for business on October 5, 1912, promoted as the most beautiful building west of Venice, Italy.

Over the years, many great and famous people visited the Adolphus. Three-time presidential candidate William Jennings Bryan spoke there. Generals John J. Pershing and Douglas MacArthur reviewed parades from one of its balconies. President Franklin D. Roosevelt dined there during the Texan Centennial celebration in 1936. Guests who stayed there included Charles Lindberg, Harry Truman, Jack Dempsey, Max Schmeling, Primo Carnera and Joan Crawford. Its Century Room became the hottest nightspot in town, featuring Rudy Vallee, Bing Crosby, Phil Harris, Sophie Tucker, Artie Shaw, Hildegarde, Glenn Miller, Joe E. Lewis, and many Ice Shows.

In the 1950s, as the automobile replaced the railroad and the motel replaced the hotel, the Adolphus started to decline. It was almost razed to the ground several times until, in 1981, a group of investors financed a $60 million restoration. The new Adolphus has earned virtually every architectural, interior design, and hospitality award in the industry and has been named one of the most outstanding meeting facilities in the United States.

The Adolphus was in its early heyday as one of the finest hotels in the United States when it became a worthy site for the first meeting of the International Association of Lions Clubs.

In the summer prior to the October convention, Melvin Jones came to Evansville, Indiana and met with Dr. Woods. This was the first time that these two had ever met. Melvin Jones told Dr. Woods that he had heard about the Lions Organization, and they had several private conferences on that day and the following day. Melvin Jones informed Dr. Woods that he was the Secretary of a club in Chicago called the Business Circle which had about thirty-five members and that they would like to affiliate with some national organization.

Dr. Woods told him that he had just incorporated the International Association of Lions Clubs under the State Laws of Indiana, and that a convention had been called to meet in Dallas, Texas, that notices had already been mailed to each club in the southwest requesting them to send delegates to this convention. Jones asked how many clubs Woods had and was informed that there were 33. Jones then asked if his club could get a charter, and Dr. Woods agreed to it and also to having some one as a delegate from the Chicago club attend the Dallas convention.

Melvin Jones and a Mr. Trienens came to Evansville in time to join Dr. Woods on the train trip to Dallas. Sometime after they left St. Louis, Jones came to Dr. Woods' Pullman apartment and asked Woods if he thought that Jones had a chance of being elected secretary of the Lions. Jones said that he would like to be secretary and Woods said that he thought that he had as good a chance as anybody else. Woods suggested that Jones mix with the boys, be a good fellow and try to boost his own stock, and that he would be behind him. Dr. Woods did support him and Melvin Jones was elected secretary.

The Dallas Morning News for October 8th was filled with reports on World War I, which the United States had entered the previous spring, but it also carried the following article on the first Lions Convention.

Lions' International Meeting Opens Today
Delegates began arriving here last night for first annual convention.

Mayor Joe E. Lawther will officially welcome about forty delegates to the first annual meeting of the International Lions' Club in the palm garden of the Adolphus at 10 o"clock this morning.

Delegates to the meeting began arriving last night. Dr. W.P. Woods, president of the club, has been in Dallas for several days, preparing for the convention. Last night he and a number of other delegates were dinner guests of L.H. Lewis of Dallas at the Adolphus.

Although this will be the first international convention, delegates said the gathering will be more in the nature of a meeting than a convention. The meetings today, tomorrow and Wednesday will be to perfect the organization and to make plans for its expansion.

They were in Dallas and would convene that morning on the 15th floor of the Hotel Adolphus to try to erase their differences and unite into one common group. Present were 37 delegates and 8 alternates from 23 cities in 8 states, together with a number of interested observers who were not in a position to participate

The Dallas Lions Club's President, L. H. Lewis, opened the meeting and presented the Mayor of Dallas, Joe E. Lawther. He gave the welcoming address after which Dr. W. P. Woods presided.

The wrangling began when the former Vortex Club, now represented as the St. Louis Lions Club, demanded that the name of the club be reconsidered. Their object hardly needed explanation. The St. Louis boys wanted the Association to forget the Old Monarch and adopt the stirring name of *Vortex*. This was easily understood by at least three other delegates who had come to Dallas with similar plans. It was also understood—and resented—by the bulk of the delegates who were already pretty good Lions, at least to the extent that they didn't want to be called anything else.

The outcome was that some of the groups changed their minds about joining an International Organization and went home. Those who remained found new subjects for bickering. What sort of an outfit was this going to be? Who was going to pay for it? Who was going to collect? Who was going to be in it, who was it going to profit? And, what did it stand for?

Out of this melee and in this explosive atmosphere, there came a real basis for permanent unity. Whatever else the loud-voiced delegates said to elevate each other's blood pressure, they were at least in vague agreement on the fundamental reason for their existence as an Association.

They agreed that one reason for their existence could be reconstructed from the one idea they made part of the Constitution that the Convention finally adopted. It says:

> **No member would be permitted to make a racket of his club by using it as a means of financial gain—an echo of the old theory: "You don't get anywhere until you do something for somebody else."**

Once they agreed on this point, others followed. The people who wanted the Lions to go by the name of *Vortex* or *Phalanx* or *Sigmoid* or *Elmer* had already left. The delegates approved a Constitution and voted for Gold and Purple as the Lion's Colors, formally approved the granting of Charters, then adjourned in almost breathless harmony.

Many matters of great importance in the development of Lionism had to be left for subsequent conventions, but committees were formed to take of care these matters.

Now read about the happenings as reported by *The Dallas News* dated October 9, 1917.

From The Dallas Morning News - October 9, 1919

LIONS' ORGANIZATION IS BEING PERFECTED
Club of Business Men Convenes Here For First Annual Meeting

The Lions' Club may be the first mutual business organization in the world to recognize woman constitutionally as a business entity and provide for women members.

Whether or not women will be made constitutional members of the club will be decided today at the second day's session of the first national convention of the Lions at the Adolphus. Bylaws and a constitution are being drafted by the convention. Most of the work was completed yesterday. Shortly before adjournment Charles J. Kirk delegate from Houston, suggested that women be made constitutional members. Several prominent business women of Houston are active workers in the Lions' Club of that city, Mr. Kirk said.

L.H. Lewis, president of the Dallas club, made the suggestion that the members of the club be limited to white persons.

Change of Name Suggested

Delegates from the St. Louis club want the name changed from the Lions' Club to the Vortex Club. E.N. Kaercher presented the St. Louis Club's request. Mr. Kaercher's home club succeeded the Vortex Club of St. Louis, which was one of the two clubs bearing the name. The other was located at Detroit. The name, "Vortex," it was contended, emphasizes the idea of "bringing together," F.N. Calvin of Waco will take the floor against changing the name. The delegates are divided as to whether the organization shall be called "national," "international," or "general."

Yesterday morning was spent in preliminary ceremonies. Mayor Joe E. Lawther welcomed the Lions to Dallas. "We feel that you have honored our city by coming here to hold your first con-

vention," Mayor Lawther said. "Your organization is made up of men who accomplish things; men who recognize no obstacles. No enterprise looking to the betterment of the city has been undertaken since the local club was organized in which its members did not have an active part."

Melvin Jones of Chicago responded to the address. Applause and laughter greeted Mr. Jones' statement that he wished "Chicago might change Mayors with Dallas." Some of the local delegates answered saying "there's not a chance." Mr. Jones complimented Dallas on it excellent drinking water, declaring that "with such fine water I am not surprised that Dallas has gone dry."

W.P. Woods, president of the organization, appointed Tom Finty Jr., of the Dallas club to be secretary pro tempore of the convention in the absence of the secretary, who was unable to attend the convention.

Committees Are Appointed

The following committees were named by Dr. Woods: Credentials, W.A. Lebrand, H.A. McDonald and F.H. Matthes; Election Committee W.J. Power. Melvin Jones and W.L. Dickey; Resolutions and Constitution Committee. Joseph Trienons, L.H. Lewis and E.N. Kaercher; Business Methods and Conventions Committee. A.W. Dreus, J.W. Conner and W.A. Grimes; Public Affairs Committee G. Richardson, Tom Finty Jr. and Charles J. Kirk; Education Committee, H.P. Henderson, Hunter Martin and M.E. Trowbridge; Publicity Committee, C.L. White and Charles W.A. MacCormack.

L.H. Lewis entertained all of the delegates and officers of the club at the luncheon at the Adolphus at noon. Speeches were made by Mr. Lewis, A.C. Eble of Dallas and others. A number of dialect sketches portraying Italian and German life were given by James P. Landry of Beaumont.

At the afternoon session the report of the committee on credentials was adopted. Charles W.A. MacCormack of Austin and H.F. Endsley of Texarkana told of the things being done by their local clubs.

The remaining portion of the afternoon was spent in considering the report of the committee on constitution and bylaws. Most of the provisions were adopted without difficulty, but there was extended debate on the section which declares the purposes of the association and the clubs composing it. An amend-ment was offered to this section by W.A. Lybrand and J.C. Leonard of Oklahoma City, who led a fight for its adoption. The amendment declared that 'no club shall by its bylaws, constitution or otherwise hold out the financial betterment of its members as its object." Mr. Kirk of Houston led the debate against the adoption of this amendment, saying that the members were benefited in their business by membership in the Lions' Club and that there should be no concealment of the fact. The Oklahoma members conceded that such might be the facts, but they did not want it stated as an object of the organization. Although the amendment was defeated, 12-10, it is probable that it will be offered today in another form.

—————

The chair appointed the following committees:

Credentials Committee
W.A. Lybrand, Oklahoma City, Oklahoma

H.A. McDonald , Beaumont, Texas

F.H. Matthes, Abilene, Texas

Election Committee
W.J. Powers, St. Louis, Missouri

Melvin Jones, Chicago, Illinois

W.L. Dickey, Tulsa, Oklahoma

Resolution and Constitution
L.H. Lewis, Dallas Texas

Joseph Trienens, Chicago, Illinois

E.N. Kaercher, St. Louis, Missouri

Business Methods and Conventions
A.W. Dyeux, Port Arthur, Texas

J.W. Comer, Chickasha, Oklahoma

William Grimes, Fort Worth, Texas

Publicity Committee
Grant Richardson, Shreveport, Louisiana
Tom Finty, Jr., Dallas, Texas
Charles J. Kirk, Houston, Texas

Education Committee
H.D. Henderson, Texarkana, Texas
Hunter Martin, Tulsa, Oklahoma
M.E. Trowbridge, Shreveport, Louisiana

Public Affairs
W.J. MacCormack, Austin, Texas
R.A. Kleinschmidt, Oklahoma City, Oklahoma
E.A. Corbett, Fort Worth, Texas

Club Ethics
Jason L. McRae, Memphis, Tenn.
J.W. McNeese, Paris, Texas
Russell D. Law, Colorado Springs, Colorado

Mr. Lewis spoke briefly, saying that it was his contention that the International Association had not yet been perfected and that the way was open for making a constitution anew.

In response to questions, the President, Dr. Woods, said the Association had been duly chartered under the laws of Indiana, but no convention had been held previously to the present gathering.

The convention reconvened at 1:30 p.m.

The Committee on Credentials, W.A. Lybrand, Chairman, reported that there were no contests, and that the following named representatives and alternates were present and entitled to be seated in the convention.

Representatives

Abilene: F.H. Matthes
Ardmore: O.C. Lasher
Austin: W.A. MacCormack, Harry Reasonover

Beaumont: H.A. McDonald, J.F. Landry
Chicago: Joseph Trienens, Melvin Jones
Chickasha: J.W. Corner
Colorado Springs: Herbert Somer, Russell Law
Dallas: L.H. Lewis, Tom Finty, Jr.; Alternates: George L. Boedeker and S. Koenigsberg
Denver: M. Harry Mayers
Fort Worth: W.W. Wren, Wm. A. Grimes; Alternate: A.E. Corebett
Houston: Charles J. Kirk
Little Rock: H.T. Esterle
Memphis: James L. McRae, L.W. Hughes
Muskogee: F.E. Coss
Oklahoma City: B.A. Kleinschmidt, W.A. Lybrind. Alternates: R.E. Duval. J.C. Leonard, C.L. White
Paris: O.L. Gregory, J.W. DeWeese; Alternate: R.E. Duval
Port Arthur: A.W. Lycus, C.V. Palmer
St. Louis: W.J. Powers, E.N. Kaercher; Alternate: R.J. Dawson
Shreveport: R.E. Wheeless, Grant Richardson; Alternate: R.E. Trowbridge
Texarkana: H.D. Henderson, H.F. Endsley
Tulsa: W.L. Dickey
Waco: E.N. Calvin
Wichita Falls: B.F. Johnson

The report was unanimously adopted.

Under the head of Good of the Association, interesting addresses were made by Messrs. MacCormack of Austin, and H.F. Endsley of Texarkana, concerning the methods and achievements of their respective clubs.

The report of the Committee on Resolution and Constitution was presented by the Chairman of the committee.

The report was considered at length. Pending action, the convention adjourned until 10:30 a.m. Tuesday, October 9.

Morning Session, October 9, 1917

The convention was called to order at 11:30 a.m.

The report of the Committee on Constitution and bylaws was further considered.

Mr. Power of St. Louis moved to substitute the name "Vortex" for "Lions."

Mr. Kirk moved to table the motion. Carried.

Mr. Henderson moved that the name of the Association should be "The International Association of Lions Clubs." Carried.

Mr. Calvin of Waco moved that the motto of the Association and the clubs composing the same should be "Do it now."

Mr. Finty moved as a substitute that the subject of selection a motto or slogan should be referred to a committee of three, which shall report to the Board of Directors, which shall, in turn, report its recommendation to the next convention. Carried. The chair appointed as this committee Messrs. Richardson of Shreveport, McRae of Memphis and Kaercher of St. Louis.

Mr. Landry moved that the Board of Directors be instructed to copyright the name of the Association. Carried.

Mr. Kirk moved that a committee of three be appointed to report an endorsement of President Woodrow Wilson and the Liberty Bond sale. The Chair appointed as this committee Messrs. M. Harry Mayers, Denver, James L. McRae of Memphis, and Grant Richardson of Shreveport. Motion of Mr. L.H. Lewis of Dallas was seconded by Mr. A.W. Locus of Port Arthur and carried, that the constitution and bylaws, which had been considered seriatus, should be adopted as a whole.

The Convention recessed until 2 p.m.

The next order of business was the election of officers.

Mr. Trowbridge nominated Mr. L.H. Lewis of Dallas to be President of the Association.

Mr. Lewis immediately declined, saying that he sought no favor at the hands of the convention. He moved as a substitute that Dr. W.P. Woods should be elected to the office of President, saying that Dr. Woods deserved this consideration. Mr. J.P Landry seconded the nomination. Dr. Woods was unanimously elected and he voiced his appreciation, saying that he would not have been disappointed he failed of election and invited the cooperation of all the clubs and their members.

Mr. Richardson nominated Mr. L.H. Lewis of Dallas to be First Vice-President. Mr. Lewis was unanimously elected.

Mr. E.N. Kaercher of St. Louis was uninimously elected Second Vice-President.

Mr. Kirk nominated Mr. M. Harry Mayers of Denver to be the Third Vice-President. Mr. Mayers was elected by acclamation. When the election of the Secretary-Treasurer was reached, the chair laid before the Convention the following letter:

Headquarters
3rd Battalion
159th Depot Brigade
Camp Taylor, Kentucky
October 2nd, 1917

Delegates. Int. Ass'n of Lions,
Assembled in Convention
Dallas, Texas.

Gentlemen:
"Duty before pleasure" is an old saying, but a good one. It behooves us at all times to do our duty as our conscience dictates. I am trying to do mine in the service of my country, believing that I am rendering a better service here than I would possibly do by remaining home and serving as Secretary of the International Association of Lions Clubs.

Although I have not been stationed here long enough to get accustomed to the regular routine, suffice it to say that we are extremely busy in preparation for what we believe to be the greatest war in history - a war for democracy - and while we are in the service, whether in training or on the battle fields of France or Russia, we have confidence in those who remain behind, and we know they will do their duty. This has been proven by the subscription of the first issue of the "Liberty Bond" and the appeal of the "Red Cross." It is encouraging to me to know that in many cities the members of the Lions Clubs were the leaders in the campaign for Red Cross funds, and while we are fighting for victory may the Lions Clubs be victorious in any undertaking they may assume.

· Realizing that it is impossible to serve two masters, I am herewith tendering to the Board of Directors of the International Association of Lions Clubs my resignation as Secretary-Treasurer with an earnest desire that the work I have been instrumental in promoting will be carried forward conscientiously and with success.

Regretting that I am not able to be with you in person, but assuring you of my best wishes. I am,

Sincerely yours,
SAMUEL HICKS
Captain Infantry, O.R.C. Commanding

The Secretary was instructed to write to Captain Hicks advising him that the Association had accepted his resignation with regret and promising him that the Lions would back up the Army in every way possible.

Mr. Kaercher nominated Mr. Melvin Jones of Chicago to be Secretary-Treasurer. Mr. Jones was elected.

The Dallas Morning News, October 9, 1917

OFFICERS ELECTED BY CONVENTION OF LIONS
New organization to be "International Association of Lions' Clubs"

Dr. W.P. Woods of Evansville, Ind., was elected president of the International Association of Lions' Clubs at the election of officers yesterday. The first annual convention, which will close its sessions today, decided to retain the name of "Lions' Club" and rejected the proposal of St. Louis clubmen that the name be changed to "Vortex." The convention voted to open the rosters of the association's clubs to business women as well as business men and limited its membership to white persons.

Dr. Woods has been at the head of the movement to form an international organization of Lions' Clubs. L.H. Lewis, president of the Dallas club, who was nominated for the presidency, declined to permit his name to go before the convention, and nominated Dr. Woods. The latter was elected by acclamation. Mr. Lewis was elected first vice-president.

E.N. Kaercher of St. Louis was elected second vice-president; Mr. Harry Mayers of Denver, third vice-president Melvin Jones of Chicago, secretary treasurer. The following were elected directors for the three-year term: R.A. Kleinschmidt of Oklahoma City and J.L. McRee of Memphis; two-year term, H.F. Endsley, Texarkana, and Roger E. Wheeles, Shreveport; one-year term, A.V. Davenport, Tulsa, Okla., and Charles J. Kirk of Houston.

Dr. Woods read a letter from Samuel Hicks, secretary-treasurer of the association now a Captain of infantry in the United States Army, who resigned the office.

Delegates Are Entertained

The visiting Lions were the guests of the Dallas Lions at a luncheon at the Adolphus yesterday at noon. No speeches were made. Readings were given by James P. Landry of Beaumont and J.C. Leonard of Oklahoma City. Last night the Lions and their wives attended a banquet at the Adolphus.

The convention will choose the 1918 meeting place today. St. Louis and Austin have asked for the next meeting.

The convention adopted amendments to the constitution, which will permit clubs to accept non-resident members, providing that the cities in which the non-resident applicants have no local organization of Lions. The organization retained the name, "International Association of Lions' Clubs," and perpetuated the emblem now used. It is a lion's head, holding a club, marked "International." The motto for the association was referred to a special committee composed of Grant Richardson of Shreveport, and Messrs. McRee of Memphis and Kaercher of St. Louis.

Liberty Loan Endorsed

W.J. Power of St. Louis spoke in behalf of changing the name from "Lions" to "Vortex." E.N. Calvin of Waco, Messrs. Richardson and McRee and others contended that the name of Lions should be retained. Mr. Power's motion that the name be changed was tabled, 25 to 7. The motion to retain the present name was adopted, 24 to 6.

A motion that the home office of the club shall be at the home of the president was adopted. The name of the association will be copyrighted. Upon motion of Mr. Kirk a committee composed of Messrs. Mayers, McRee and Richardson was named to draft resolutions endorsing the Liberty Loan and President Wilson.

W.A. Lybrand of Oklahoma, in behalf of the visiting Lions, thanked the city of Dallas and the Dallas Lions Club for the entertainment provided and other courtesies shown during the meeting.

The delegates were given an automobile ride to the points of interest in the city yesterday morning.

The following officers were elected: Dr. W.P. Woods, President, Evansville, Indiana; L.H. Lewis, 1st VP, Dallas, Texas; E.N. Kaercher, 2nd VP, St. Louis, Missouri; M. Harry Meyers, 3rd VP, Denver, Colorado. Directors elected to serve three years were: R.A. Kleinschmidt, Oklahoma City, Oklahoma; J.L. McRee, Memphis, Tennessee. Directors elected to serve two years were: H.F. Endsley, Texarkana, Arkansas; R.E. Wheeles, Shreveport, Louisiana. Directors elected to serve one year were: Charles J. Kirk, Houston, Texas, A.V. Davenport, Tulsa, Oklahoma. Secretary-Treasurer: Melvin Jones, Chicago, Illinois.

No doubt-these debates generated the necessary heat to cause the fusion of the many Individuals, Clubs and Ideas into one great International Association–**THE LIONS–**.

Founders Clubs

This list was furnished by Lions Clubs International, and it did not include Pueblo, Colorado. The Shreveport, Louisiana club claims that it has a certificate that reads Organized on June 20, 1914 and Chartered Oct. 15, 1917. No doubt there can be other clubs that may have different dates. (Temple -then being formed- and San Antonio, Texas did not send any delegates to this convention, but sent word that they would go along with whatever was done. Some other names that were mentioned were, Fort Collins, Colorado, El Paso, Orange, Galveston, and San Angelo, Texas and Wichita, Kansas.)

Founder Club	Date Organized	Delegates
Little Rock, Arkansas	March 19, 1916	H.T. Esterle
Texarkana, Arkansas	February 19, 1917	H.D. Henderson, H.F. Endsley
Colorado Springs, Colorado	September 18, 1917	Russell D. Law, Herbert Somers
Denver, Colorado	June 26, 1917	Harry Mayers
Pueblo, Colorado	June 26, 1917	Harry Mayers
Chicago, Illinois	August 2, 1917	Melvin Jones, Joseph Trienens
Shreveport, Louisiana	November 6, 1916	Grant Richardson , R.E. Wheeles
St. Louis, Missouri	June 15, 1917	W.J. Powers, E.N. Kaercher
Ardmore, Oklahoma	February 12, 1917	O.C. Lasher
Chickasha, Oklahoma	July 28, 1917	J.W. Comer
Muskogee, Oklahoma	October 26, 1916	F.E. Coss
Oklahoma City,Oklahoma	September 1916	Walter Lybrand, R.A. Kleinschmidt
Tulsa, Oklahoma	September 1916	W.L. Kickey,Hunter Martin
Memphis, Tennessee	December 18, 1916	James L. McRee, L.W. Hushes
Abilene, Texas	May 23, 1917	F.H. Matthes
Austin, Texas	January 18, 1916	Harry Reasnover, W.A. MacCormack
Beaumont, Texas	September 16, 1916	H.A. McDonald, J.P. Landry
Dallas, Texas	September 1916	L.H. Lewis, Tom Finty Jr.
Fort Worth, Texas	September 26, 1916	W.A. Grimes,W.W. Wren
Houston, Texas	April 2, 1917	Charles J. Kirk
Paris, Texas	February 18, 1917	J. W. DeWerese, O.L. Gregory
Port Arthur, Texas	April 23, 1917	C.V. Palmer , A.W. Dycus
Waco, Texas	September 19, 1916	E.M. Calvin
Wichita Falls, Texas	July 16, 1917	B.F. Johnson
Temple, Texas	June 21, 1917	No Delegate Record
San Antonio, Texas	October, 1915	No Delegate Record

Melvin E. Jones

In 1872, the United States established the San Carlos Indian Reservation in what became Arizona and New Mexico. Military forts were built to pacify the Indians and to provide a place where they could receive annual payments for the land they had ceded to the U.S. Fort Thomas, in what is now southeastern Arizona, was one such post.

Melvin E. Jones was born at Fort Thomas on January 13, 1879. Rutherford B. Hayes was President and only three years had passed since the Sioux and other Plains Indians had defeated General George Custer at the Little Big Horn. While visiting Fort Thomas in the 1950s, Jones was asked exactly where he was born. He could never be sure but thought it was at his grandparents' home, located near the fort. His father wrote a letter stating that some of the money he earned as a scout and packer for the army was paid to the doctor at the fort for care given to Mrs. Jones.

Records of the Jones family go back to Martin Jones who left North Carolina for Georgia prior to 1850. Martin Jones had two sons, John Calvin Jones, born about 1850 at Blairsville, Georgia, and Melvin W. Jones, born near Atlanta, Georgia April 16, 1859.

After the Civil War the Martin Jones family decided to move farther west. Martin Jones and his son, Melvin W., arrived in Springerville, Arizona on April 2, 1875 and commenced ranching, later moving their cattle to the Gila Valley where they purchased the Clanton ranch.

John Calvin Jones stopped over in Kansas and married Lydia M. Gibler on February 22, 1874, and they moved to Fort Thomas, Arizona later on that year.

In 1879, Martin and his two sons John Calvin, and Melvin W., hired out to work for the U.S. Cavalry, including Company F of the 6th Cavalry, stationed at Fort Thomas. They worked as guides, packers and dispatch riders until their contract with the army expired in 1882. While working with the Apache Scouts, John Calvin was given the title of "Nig."

In 1890, the John Calvin Jones family moved to Colorado. Later on, they separated, with John Calvin staying in Colorado on business and Mrs. Jones taking the children to Missouri so they could get an education. Young Melvin E. Jones was a teenager in these years. The Jones family moved first to St. Louis, and later to Quincy, Illinois. Melvin took a course in the Union Business College, and studied law at Chaddock College in Quincy.

From there he got a job with the Johnson & Higgins Insurance Agency in Chicago, and later he went on to establish his own insurance business, located at 175 West Jackson Blvd, Room 1625. After the Lions International was formed, he ran the Lions business from Room 231 of the same building.

In 1909, he married Rose Amanda Freeman, who climaxed a spectacular golfing career by winning the National Women's Open Golf Title at Pinehurst, North Carolina in 1925. In 1954, Rose passed away and in 1956, Jones married Lillian M. Radigan. He passed away on June 1, 1961.

In March of 1913, Melvin Jones was invited as a guest of William Towne, to attend a luncheon meeting of The Business Circle in the Old Oyster House in Chicago's Loop. The Business Circle, like hundreds of similar clubs throughout the country, was composed of business and professional men from many fields of trade and commerce. Their slogan was, "You scratch my back and I will scratch yours." Their purpose in meeting together was to make business contacts, what a later generation would call "networking."

Organized in 1909, the Business Circle had attained a membership of 200 members before its decline and by 1913 was down to 39 members. Those successful manufacturers, merchants and professional men who remained, were bound together only because of a long acquaintance and a mutual respect for each other.

Jones, who had never belonged to any group before, was not to be considered a "Joiner," but he did enjoy meeting and making new friends. He took a great liking to the many new friends he made at that first meeting and became the newest member of the Business Circle.

Doing a great job on the various assignments he was given, and with the great interest he took in the club, he was elected to the position of secretary. On January 10, 1914 during his acceptance speech, he told the 18 or 19 members who were there that the club was turning around and it was now slated to go places. This enthusiasm stayed with him, and continued to build throughout the week as he talked to everybody he could, either in person or by phone and encouraged them to attend the next meeting on January 17.

His one-man campaign of rebuilding the club paid off. For the first time in many years there were 75 men in attendance at the next meeting and those that followed. Thanks to his efforts membership continued to grow and so did the correspondence, phone calls, personal contacts and other club work of Melvin Jones.

Jones continued to energize and increase the membership. He introduced new ideas and called on inactive members to become active again. Soon the membership increased to almost 200 successful, influential businessmen. Not one to rest on his laurels, Jones received permission from his club to contact similar organizations with the idea of forming a national association. After making initial contacts, he called a meeting at Chicago's LaSalle Hotel on June 7, 1917.

Some of the groups represented at the LaSalle meeting were the Optimists from Chicago and other cities, the Reciprocity Clubs, the Sheels, the Concord Club of Omaha, the Business and Professional Men's Association of Saint Paul, the Cirgonians of Los Angeles and the Vortex of Saint Louis and Detroit.

Dr. Perry Woods had incorporated the International Association of Lions Clubs in October 1916, but there is no record of Jones having invited the Evansville doctor to Chicago. However, it was not long after the June meeting at the LaSalle Hotel that Melvin Jones visited Dr. Woods in Evansville. In August, 1917 the Business Circle Club of Chicago joined the International Association of Lions Clubs.

Districting and Redistricting

During the first International Convention in Dallas in 1917, the Board of Directors parceled out the country into districts, and the districts were numbered from the West Coast. R. Roy Keaton told me that he thought the first system of districts was set up along time zones and it may have been so.

It could explain how California became part of District One, and Minnesota, North Dakota and South Dakota became District Two.

Plate One   (Page 18)

International records tell that under the first arrangement, the districts were numbered with more or less regularity, eastward from the Pacific Coast.

The districts were:

- **District One:** California, Oregon, Washington, Nevada, and Hawaii.
- **District Two**: Minnesota, North Dakota, South Dakota, and the western portion of Wisconsin.
- **District Three:** Colorado, Wyoming and Montana
- **District Four:** The western portion of Texas, New Mexico and Arizona
- **District Five:** The eastern portion of Texas, Louisiana, Mississippi, Alabama, Georgia and Florida
- **District Six:** Oklahoma and Kansas

- **District Seven:** Arkansas and Missouri
- **District Eight:** Kentucky and Tennessee
- **District Nine:** Illinois, Iowa, Nebraska, Ohio, Michigan and the eastern portion of Wisconsin.

At that time, because there were no clubs in the other states and no method for organizing or administering Lions Clubs, those states not mentioned and shown darkened in, were not included in any of those Districts. At times, Mississippi was attached to District Eight with Kentucky and Tennessee. If you check these districts against the time zones, you will find that, except for District Two, these lines do follow quite closely.

Plate Two (Page 19)

Lionism grew and spread much more rapidly than most persons had expected. Soon there were so many clubs in some districts, that the District Governor could not afford the time, and International could not afford the money to have them visited and cared for properly.

Also, Lions Clubs sprang up in states which were outside any district, and it was necessary to direct and control them. Therefore redistricting became an imperative matter.

During the fifth International Convention in Oakland, California in 1921 the Lions redistricted the country. Illinois became District One as an honor because it was then considered the birthplace of Lionism and where the International headquarters was located.

This redistricting caused some confusion. For example, District Five was calling itself District Six for a while.

- **District One:** Illinois, Indiana, Missouri, and the eastern portion of Wisconsin
- **District Two:** Texas, New Mexico and Arizona
- **District Three:** Oklahoma and Kansas
- **District Four:** California, Oregon, Washington and Nevada
- **District Five:** Minnesota, North Dakota, South Dakota and the western portion of Wisconsin.

177

Later on, this district was changed to become:

- **District Five C:** Saskatchewan
- **District Five M:** Minnesota, Manitoba, and Ontario
- **District Five N:** North Dakota
- **District Five S:** South Dakota
- **District Six:** Colorado, Wyoming and Montana
- **District Seven:** Arkansas
- **District Eight:** Louisiana and sometimes Mississippi
- **District Nine:** Iowa and Nebraska
- **District Ten:** Upper Michigan
- **District Eleven:** Lower Michigan
- **District Twelve:** Kentucky, Tennessee and Mississippi
- **District Thirteen:** Ohio
- **District Fourteen:** Pennsylvania

Following this redistricting, as soon as any of the states which were either attached or unattached to other districts had enough clubs of their own, they asked for District status, and when district status was granted, it was given the lowest number remaining open.

- **District Fifteen:** Wyoming and Montana
- **District Sixteen:** New Jersey, New York, Maryland, Delaware and the District of Columbia
- **District Seventeen:** Kansas
- **District Eighteen:** Georgia, Florida and Alabama
- **District Nineteen:** Washington, Idaho and British Columbia
- **District Twenty:** New York
- **District Twenty-One:** Arizona and part of California
- **District Twenty-Two:** Maryland, District of Columbia, and Delaware
- **District Twenty-Three:** Connecticut

- **District Twenty-Four:** Virginia
- **District Twenty-Five:** Indiana
- **District Twenty-Six:** Missouri
- **District Twenty-Seven:** Wisconsin
- **District Twenty-Eight:** Utah
- **District Twenty-Nine:** West Virginia
- **District Thirty:** Mississippi
- **District Thirty-One:** North Carolina
- **District Thirty-Two:** South Carolina
- **District Thirty-Three:** Massachusetts
- **District Thirty-Four:** Alabama
- **District Thirty-Five:** Florida
- **District Thirty-Six:** Oregon and part of California
- **District Thirty-Seven:** Montana, Alberta and the Northwest Territories
- **District Thirty-Eight:** Nebraska
- **District Thirty-Nine:** Idaho and Oregon
- **District Forty:** New Mexico and part of Arizona
- **District Forty-One:** Maine, New Brunswick, Nova Scotia, Newfoundland, Prince Edward Island
- **District Forty-Two:** Rhode Island
- **District Forty-Three:** Kentucky
- **District Forty-Four:** New Hampshire
- **District Forty-Five:** Vermont
- **District Forty-Nine:** Alaska and the Yukon Territory
- **District Fifty:** Hawaii.

When they achieved District status, the rest of the countries of the world used a different series of numbers and letters.

The Old Monarch

Some of our earliest records indicate that man always held a deep respect for the lion family. This admiration has become woven into the history of mankind as seen in the paintings, statues and use of lion symbolism by the ancient Egyptians, Assyrians, Ethiopians, Greeks, Romans, Chinese and others.

The Old Testament speaks of the heroic Lion of Judah and, of course, the fierce lions that the Prophet Daniel, through his faith, tamed into pussycats. As a symbol of wisdom, the lion is pictured with St. Mark the Evangelist and with St. Jerome, who translated the Bible from Hebrew to Latin in the Fourth Century AD. Although many kings and military leaders in Africa, Asia and Europe used the lion on their flags and shields, the most well-known is the 12th Century King of England, Richard the Lion-Hearted, who reputedly acquired a lion's courage by eating a lion's heart.

A long-time director of Chicago's Lincoln Park Zoo, Cy de Vary, told one Lions Club that he had known lions for forty years, and that he knew of a no truer friend with cleaner habits, or a more staunch defender of his rights. De Vary said he did not know who named the Lions organization, but whoever had selected the best name of all.

Melvin Jones, in recapping the virtues of a Lion, remarked that a Lion possessed courage, strength, activity, (always ready for action) and fidelity.

The January 1931 issue of the *Lions Magazine* had the following interpretation of the Association's name.

"Our name was not selected at random, neither was it a coined name. From time immemorial, the lion has been the symbol of all that was good and because of the symbolism the name was chosen. Four outstanding qualities–courage, strength, activity and fidelity–had largely to do with the adoption of the name. The last mentioned of these qualities, fidelity, has a deep and peculiar significance for all Lions. The lion has been a symbol of fidelity through the ages and among all the nations, ancient, and modern. It stands for loyalty to a friend, loyalty to a principle, loyalty to a duty, loyalty to a trust."

Lions Colors and Emblem

The Colors
After it was agreed to accept the Lions name, the selection of the Club Colors was simple–the tawny gold of the lion's coat, and the purple of his royal heritage.

To Lions:
Purple stands for loyalty to country, loyalty to friends, loyalty to one's self, and one's own integrity of mind and heart.

Gold signifies purity in life, sincerity of purpose, liberality in judgments, and generosity in mind, heart and purse toward one's fellow men.

The combination of purple and gold symbolizes cooperation, education, enlightenment, entertainment and recreation.

Our Emblem
In 1920, after many meetings with jewelers and draughtsmen, and long wrangling among the members involved, the Lions adopted the design of the emblem, as it now appears on lapel badges and letter-heads.

The history of the emblem's development records that most every man who had anything to do with it, made his own design and could not accept what anyone else submitted. So, as each committee failed, a new committee was formed.

The Lions Board of Directors who met in Oklahoma City on January 13, 1920, turned down the suggestion of the latest committee, and then appointed a new committee. They gave to the new group all the suggestions furnished by past committees, and challenged them to see what they could come up with.

When Jones returned to Chicago, he pulled out more than two hundred designs and suggestions that had accumulated in his files. With scissors and a glue pot, he started to make his own design. In time, he had a crude design put together, and presented it to Lion Maurice Blink, a commercial artist, and requested that he fix it up. It was noted that Blink was probably the only Lion who had never submitted a design of his own.

Within a few days, Blink returned with three sketches, one of which is virtually identical to today's emblem. A gold letter is mounted L on a circular purple field bordered by two lions, one lion facing the proud past, another confidently facing the future, both looking in all directions to do a service. The word *Lion* appears at the top and the word *International* at the bottom.

At their next meeting in Chicago April 12, 1920, the directors approved it and instructed Jones to order a supply in the form of lapel buttons.

Dog Face And Pug Nose Logos

After all the time and effort that was put into the development of the Lions emblem, we continue to see Logos used that are not the true Lions emblem.

One is called the "Dog Face," and the other could be known as "Pug Nose."

The Lions emblem is protected by a trademark in countries around the world and cannot be used freely by everyone.

Sometime in the past, a logo was made up to resemble or represent the Lions emblem which we now know as the "Dog Face." This was included with other altered types of logos representing other organizational emblems and sheets of these logos were sold or furnished to printing offices, banks, store, and wherever else there was a need. Through ignorance, these fake logos were used, much to the dismay of those who used it or knew the difference.

Later, "Pug Nose" came along. I do not know its history, but it appears that it was the result of a copy machine error, and its use is now becoming more wide spread as this defect is not that easy to notice.

Today with modern printing methods, it is now possible to clip a Lions Emblem or buy these emblems from Lions Clubs International for printing use. This way, you can be sure that your printing will have the official lions emblem.

Following are the Official Lions Emblems:

The following emblems are Official variations:

The following logos below the official Lions emblem are copies of the "Dog face" and Pug Nose." Please do not use them or allow them to be used with your printing.

Following are the rules from Lions Clubs International

Use of Lion Name and Emblem and the Marks *Lions, Lions Club, Lions International or Lions Clubs International:*

As a matter of legal protection to Lions Clubs International and its member clubs, the Association's name and emblem (and variations thereof) are registered under trademarks in countries around the world. As the owner so protected, the Association has a corresponding legal obligation to be alert to infringements thereon and to make all necessary steps to prevent and to provide against legal risks which may flow from unauthorized use thereof.

In fulfillment of this legal obligation, the International Board, through its General Counsel, seeks prompt cessation of any unauthorized use of the Association name and marks "Lions," "Lions Club," "Lions International" or "Lion Clubs International." Further, it has established the following rules of policy:

(a) No item bearing the Association name or emblem or the marks "Lions" or "Lions Club" or "Lions International" or "Lions Clubs International" may be sold or otherwise distributed to Lions or Lions Clubs or Districts or the public except upon express written permission of the General Counsel or the Club Supplies and Distribution Division.

(b) No Lion, Lions Club or Lions District may use the Association emblem on any item sold to Lions or to the pubic for fund raising purposes. A special "Lions Club Fund Raising Activity" seal has been created for this purpose and may be used only upon written permission granted by the General Counsel.

(c) No manufacturer, printer, producer, promoter, publisher, entrepreneur or enterprise in any form, be it profit or non-profit in nature, may employ the Association name, good will, trademarks, service marks, emblem, seal, insignia, the marks "Lions," "Lions Club," "Lions International" or "Lions Clubs International" or any indicia thereof in any manner whatsoever except upon license granted by the International Board of

Directors of the General Counsel or the Club Supplies and Distribution Division.

(d)   No Lions District or other group of Lions Clubs my use the Association name or emblem or the marks "Lions," "Lions Club," "Lions International" or "Lions Clubs International" in connection with any District or group project except upon express written license granted by the International Board of Directors. Applications for such use shall be submitted to the Board and shall be in the form attached hereto as Exhibit A: No such application shall be approved unless the proposed activity (in whatever legal form it may exist) is controlled by Lions Clubs or District or Districts involved and participation by Lions Clubs or Club members is on a strictly voluntary basis and without any necessity to contribute monies thereto in the form of dues or otherwise. (Revised April, 1978 *Exhibit "A" provided on request.)

There are two more pages with the above. If there are any questions, ask Lions Clubs International for a full set of these instructions and for help with your problem.

Code of Ethics

At the first International Convention in 1917, committees were appointed to take care of the many matters of great importance in the development of Lionism which would be acted on in subsequent conventions.

The committee appointed to prepare a statement of objects and principles included G.M. Cunningham, then Secretary of the Houston Lions Club. Although Lion Cunningham had missed the Dallas Convention, he wrote the first draft of the historical document which he submitted to Melvin Jones and, after gaving it careful consideration, Jones passed it on to R.E. Kleinschmidt and Walter Lybrand, attorneys of Oklahoma City, for a legal review.

It is said that Melvin Jones had made a study of every code known to history from Hammurabi of Babylon (2250 BC), through the Mosaic Commandments, the Justinian Codex, and the Code Napoleon. He found that they all had a common feature. They were filled with negative commands and had plenty of "Thou Shall Not...."

The committee thought that a code like that was outside our province, and what we finally got was what may be called a Leadership Code, with not one "Thou Shall Not...." in it. The points that Jones and the committee emphasized were that you must give the other fellow the benefit of the doubt, that friendship is an end, not a means, that a man must accept nothing that has a string tied to it. As the saying goes, "What we will, we are, and what we love, we yet will be."

In early 1918, copies of the Cunningham-Jones-Kleinschmidt-Lybrand code were distributed through the organization in a limited way for practice and discussion.

The second International Convention was held at St. Louis, in August 1918, and the Code of Ethics was presented to a committee to consider its merits. August J. Hirsch was appointed chairman of the committee, which included K.M. Warren, E.F. Hurst, Arlie J. Cripe and H.F. Endsley. After two late night sessions mulling over the Code, they recommended its adoption. The Delegates concurred and the Lions Code of Ethics was adopted and, with one single exception, it is the same Code which guides Lionism today.

Occasionally, efforts were made to change the Code. At the sixth International Convention in Hot Springs, Arkansas, in 1922, a heck of an uproar occurred when a delegate attempted to amend it.

Melvin Jones remarked that after reading it, there is little difficulty understanding why the members are proud of the Code of Ethics. It is simple, direct, unequivocal and a member can recite it without feeling like a Pharisee or a fool. Jones often told other Lions that he believed the most beautiful thought in the Code is in the Fourth Clause (or verse as he preferred to call it) where it discusses friendship.

"To hold Friendship as an end and not as a means," was his favorite line.

"This thought if put into action," he declared, "makes a man a real leader, a big man. For it makes him big enough, in questions of ethics, to resolve all his doubts against himself.

"This verse means to value friends not for what you can get out of them but for what they are–and this Code, which is for the individual Lions, has gone a long way toward making Lions International first among the service organizations of the world.

"Many students of ethics have stated that ours is one of the most thorough and yet most practical codes ever written and the greatest thing in the Code of Ethics–the really fundamental soul of the Code–is contained in the third paragraph where it says '...to be loyal to my clients or customers and true to myself,' for as Shakespeare puts it in Hamlet:

> To thine ownself be true,
> And it must follow, as the night the day,
> Thou canst not then be false to any man."

LIONS CODE OF ETHICS

TO SHOW *my faith in the worthiness of my vocation by industrious application to the end that I may merit a reputation for quality of service.*

TO SEEK *success and to demand all fair remuneration or profit as my just due, but to accept no profit or success at the price of my own self-respect lost because of unfair advantage taken or because of questionable acts on my part.*

TO REMEMBER *that in building up my business it is not necessary to tear down another's; to be loyal to my clients or customers and true to myself.*

WHENEVER *a doubt arises as to the right or ethics of my position or action toward my fellow men, to resolve such doubt against myself.*

TO HOLD *friendship as an end and not a means. To hold that true friendship exists not on account of the service performed by one to another, but that true friendship demands nothing but accepts service in the spirit in which it is given.*

ALWAYS *to bear in mind any obligations as a citizen to my nation, my state and my community and to give them my unanswering loyalty in word, act and deed. To give them freely of my time, labor and means.*

TO AID *my fellow men by giving my sympathy to those in distress, my aid to the weak and my substance to the needy*

TO BE CAREFUL *with my criticism and liberal with my praise; to build up and not destroy.*

Note:
In 1923, although warned by his doctors to stay home and rest, Lion G.M. Cunningham started on a long tour to spread the gospel of Lionism through the West. In Ogden, Utah, he dropped dead. Because of the great devotion of Cunningham, Melvin Jones's remarks were, "if there were such a thing as a book of Lionism's martyrs, this 'typical Texan' would have first place in it, for there is no doubt that his labors in behalf of the organization's philosophy cost him his life. He will be sorely missed."

Objects

The third International Convention was held in Chicago, in 1919. Here the members adopted the Objects.

The Objects, as well as the need of a slogan and a club emblem had been discussed at length at earlier conventions. The delegates knew what they wanted and the records show that everyone of them talked about it.

In those days, Lions International Conventions were small enough (in 1919, less than 30 clubs were represented) to permit the delegates to thresh things out on the floor. It was on the floor, with everybody having his say, and causing as much noise and confusion as the rules of order would permit, that these delegates pounded out a draft of the Objects to the Association which was good enough to stand unchanged for more than ten years.

The change came during the Fourteenth International Convention at Denver in 1930. The first paragraph was changed as a result of the oratory of Dr. Walter F. Dexter, International President in 1938-39, and at the insistence of a fellow Californian, Ray L. Riley, who was the International President at the time.

The Dexter address, a scholarly performance worthy of the distinguished educator who was superintendent of public instruction in his state, contained the words that since have led all the rest among the Objects to which all Lions are dedicated.

"We are here to create and foster a spirit of generous consideration among the peoples of the world through a study of the problems of international relationships from the standpoint of business and professional ethics." Lion Dexter said. "May we all go to our homes, put on a program of international idealism by inviting speakers of other countries to appear before our Lions Clubs, by passing resolutions of friendship and fellowship, and by disseminating our knowledge and our philosophy to the uttermost parts of the earth."

Every Lion, whether or not he stumbles over the latter parts of the litany, can roar confidently the text of Object 1: To create and foster a spirit of "generous consideration" among the peoples of the world through a study of the problems of international relationships.

Since they expressed too limited a view, the words, "from the standpoint of business and professional ethics," originally tacked to the end of this paragraph were deleted by constitutional amendment from the Objects.

Melvin Jones, in analyzing these Objects, pointed out: "Lions are fundamentally engaged in service work, and each of the six paragraphs comprising the formal expression of our Objects develops a separate but integral part of service work.

"The first paragraph refers to welfare at the international level, the second considers the national welfare, and the third, the welfare of the community, that great field in which most of the service of the Lions is performed.

"The next object deals with the personal relations of the members, one to another. Here we have the foundations of a Lions Club. There must be mutual understanding among the members, and there must be good fellowship in a Lions Club in order that it may function properly.

"Intelligence in action is a prerequisite to community service. Lions should have the advantage of all available information in order to determine the wisest course to follow. Therefore the fifth object...this (keeping informed) keeps the club alive to the needs of the community, and the problems of the state and nation. It provides for full discussion and knowledge on the part of all members, of the problems under consideration by the club...

"Because Lions Clubs take the initiative in community service, membership in a Lions Club must be made up of men of the highest qualifications. A man must be a credit to his business or profession before he can be an asset to the Lions Club. Therefore a Lions Club is interested in the preeminence of its members, and so we have the sixth and last object...

"The second clause of this object," and here Jones draws the distinction between the Lions and some of the *so-called* service clubs, "safeguards the service nature of a Lions Club. It keeps the club and the members from going out to prospective members and saying, *'Join our club and we will give you business.'* It puts the restriction in such a way that a man must join the club to serve. He must serve the club and the community and by serving he naturally develops himself.

"If a Lions Club follows out its Objects, it will have a full program. It will be interested in world affairs, in national problems, in the needs of its own local community, and in the welfare of the individual members."

The Objects set forth by Lions International are integrated with those listed in the constitution which is standard for every local Lions Club:

"1. To form a body of men thoroughly representative of the business and professional interests of the City of ...., to unite its members in the closest bonds of fellowship and to promote a closer business and social union among them.

"2. To encourage active participation in all things that have to do with commercial, civic and industrial betterment.

"3. To uphold the principles of good government.

"4. To assist in every honorable way of furthering the interests of its members and toward bringing about a better understanding among men.

"5. To teach that organization, cooperation, and reciprocity are better than rivalry, strife and destructive competition.

"6. To encourage the application of the highest ethical standards in business and endeavor, by the exchange of methods and ideas, to increase efficiency in all lines represented."

Lions International Objects

TO CREATE and foster a spirit of "generous consideration" among the peoples of the world through a study of the problems of international relationship.

TO PROMOTE the theory and practice of the principles of good government and good citizenship.

TO TAKE an active interest in the civic, social, and moral welfare of the community.

TO UNITE the members in the bonds of friendship, good fellowship and mutual understanding.

TO PROVIDE a forum for the full and free discussion of all matters of public interest, partisan politics and sectarian religion are alone excepted.

TO ENCOURAGE efficiency and promote high ethical standards in business and professions, provided that no club shall hold out as one of its objects financial benefits to its members.

Slogan

Being what they were, the Lions naturally had to have a rallying cry. But also, because of who they were–men of a thousand varying interests from hundreds of widely scattered and differing places–it was difficult to find one slogan that would arouse them all.

Because so many individual clubs were adopting slogans of their own, it was decided that there was a need for one slogan for all clubs. So all of these and many more were in the hopper when the Chicago Convention of 1919 undertook to select a slogan that should be the summation of Lionism. The choice of Objects for the official list had just been completed and was being given the finishing touches.

The selectors had their work cut out for them, as slogans have a way of becoming catch phrases that through endless repetition lose their inspiration, and rouse in the listener no emotion save a distaste for slogan makers. the Lions committee heard them all from "Twenty-three! Skiddoo!" to "Do it now!"

Some of the contributed war cries had been subjected to less wear and tear than these two samples. "Always faithful!" wasn't so bad, it seemed, if the U.S. Marines hadn't already been using it–in Latin. "At the Nation's right hand," was another that was fairly well received, and there was a pretty good percentage in favor of "We serve best."

Melvin Jones remarked that none of these seemed broad enough or deep enough for the purpose. A slogan is an inspiring message, the clarion call, the rallying cry. "We were groping to find some expression that would have the vitality of a rallying cry expressive of the purposes of Lionism"

He recalled that some consideration was given to the drafting of a creed. But he said no, a slogan was what was needed to bring the boys to their feet.

"A creed," he said, "is something you hang on a wall. Churches have creeds and more often than not, creeds have the effect of a fence, keeping men apart rather than drawing them together." After that, there was a long impasse.

Even though two years had passed since the name Lion was adopted and reaffirmed as the best possible choice, clubs that had sacrificed their own identities in the interest of unity would succumb to nostalgic regret. There would be mumbling in the cloak rooms, such as "the world was better when the Lions Club of Whooisburg had been the Parabola Club." Those were the days and soon another campaign would be afoot to make the Association of Lions Clubs into the Interplanetary Association of Parabola Clubs.

One of these moves was afoot in the Chicago Convention when Halsted Rittor, an eloquent member of the bar from Denver came onto the floor and made a speech which in the annals of Lionism has a rating something like the one that the history textbooks give to Daniel Webster's reply to Hayne.

"What an aggregation we have," exulted the orator from the Rockies as he warmed to his subject. "What a glorious meaning it has. Its name is more significant than any other. It spells not only the king of beasts, typifying all the qualities we love to extol; it stands not only for fraternity, good fellowship, strength of character and purpose; but above all, its combination of letters, L-I-O-N-S, heralds to the country the true meaning and basis of American citizenship–Liberty, Intelligence, Our Nation's Safety.

"Analyze carefully and behold the very cornerstone of our civilization. Liberty and Ignorance bring bloodshed, chaos, Bolshevism, anarchy and general ruin. Liberty and Intelligence signed the Declaration of Independence, gathered the Minute Men at Concord and won at Yorktown. They have preserved our nation in every crisis. An intelligent citizenry is the hope of democracy. It is the ideal of Lionism. In its promotion and protection is the opportunity we seek.

"The time is ripe for a new baptism of liberty and intelligence. We must all be immersed in the river of patriotism and shout our salvation and preach its reality. We must have reason for the faith that is within us. The River Yukon gathers to itself such a volume of pure water that when it flows into the sea it pushes the salty brine back from its mouth for ten miles. So should every Lions Club force a pure, clean stream of intelligent Americanism into its community life. In a few years, me thinks, with many such streams pouring into the nations' life, the muddy, murky and death-spreading waters of ignorance, disease and poverty will be cleansed and purified.

"Write it on your banners, Lions; inscribe it in your hearts; hold it high that everyone may see the magic, electrified letters:

Liberty, Intelligence, Our Nation's Safety."

And that did it. Lion Ritter, whose talents later were recognized in his elevation to the judicial bench, had every man in the auditorium with him as he concluded. Nothing further was heard from the dissenters. Everybody, it appeared, liked the acrostic idea. Earlier attempts to develop it had been somewhat strained, but Ritter had rung the bell.

"Liberty had been thought of as the first word in connection with the letter "l" in the Lions emblem," Jones recalls. "It seemed reasonable to everyone that liberty be coupled with education, judgment, consideration of the rights of others–in other words, intelligence. And since our slogan was not intended for the individual but for all and for every Lion country, it was altogether right to use the plural pronoun 'our' in speaking of the nation's safety. The slogan is so phrased as to be applicable to any nation represented in the International Association.

"So there we had a slogan durable enough to have stood the test of our first many years and, it is predicted that it will stand the test of many, many years to come."

Our Name

L - Liberty

I - Intelligence

O - Our

N - Nation's

S - Safety

Citizenship and Patriotism

In the 1930s, with increasing tension in the world, the Lions saw a need for a code that could be used by the citizenship and patriotism committees of the local clubs.

So, in 1939, a Citizenship and Patriotism Code for Lions International was copyrighted. It would meet a need of which the directorate had been conscious for some time. It was not developed in convention, nor submitted to a convention for approval. It was developed from a preliminary draft worked out in the International office in Chicago, from proposals submitted by many Lions Clubs and individuals.

The Secretary-General, Melvin Jones, acknowledged his indebtedness to the Reverend W. Murray Allan of Ames, Iowa for his aid in phrasing the final draft of the Code. Jones felt that the sentiments of patriotism and good citizenship that the Code was supposed to embody would be meaningless unless combined with religion or, as he put it, the soul. He immediately thought of "Bill" Allan, whose attractive Scottish burr, acquired at the Univeristy of Edinburgh, had made him popular with Lions audiences. Allan was a member of the International Board of Directors.

At Jones' request, he took time from his duties as pastor of Plymouth Congregational Church in Grand Forks, North Dakota to meet the Secretary-General in Minneapolis. The Lions "Citizenship and Patriotism Code," as subscribed to today, was completed as a result of this meeting.

A complication in the proper framing of the Code was that thought had to be given to institutions and customs in foreign countries. Lions having been truly international by this time, with clubs springing up on four continents, in addition to North America. The code of Citizenship and Patriotism in its final form is so phrased as to be applicable to any country professing to uphold democratic principles.

Lions Code of Citizenship and Patriotism

"To create by precept and example a civic and patriotic conscience by fostering an idealistic attitude toward my country, its historic past, its spiritual heritage, its free institutions, its boundless natural resources, its great men and women, its wonderful privileges, and its solemn responsibilities, that we may give it our full measure of devotion and love.

"To develop a greater knowledge and understanding of the principles of democratic government and the institutions which are the source of liberty, happiness, and freedom of thought and action; a respect and reverence of the flag; obedience to law and authority; and a sustained and intelligent interest in public affairs.

"To uphold the principles of democratic government by supporting such movements as seek to save a country from its own apathy; by awakening my fellow countrymen to their obligations of citizenship; by stimulating an interest in governmental policies on the part of future voters; by supporting Lions Of Age ceremonies; by encouraging and expediting naturalization of eligible aliens; by furnishing speakers and programs for patriotic events; and by observing patriotic holidays and displaying my country's flag.

"To perpetuate in the public memory historical episodes worthy of emphasis by aiding in the erection and maintenance of memorials, plaques, historical-site markers and other suitable evidences.

"To obtain suitable recognition for outstanding civic service by the presentation of awards and honors to those whose personal sacrifice and service on the field of battle and in the service of mankind in peace are worthy of the highest tribute.

"To reaffirm my belief in the government of a free people–whose inspiration is wisdom, whose greatest cause is justice, and whose noblest objects are peace and liberty–ever remembering our slogan: "Liberty, Intelligence, Our Nation's Safety!"

Growing Up

One of the obvious and important features of the growth of the Lions has been it entire freedom from hidebound restraint. Without precedent to guide them, Secretary-General Jones and his aides had to meet each new situation as it arose, and there were plenty of them. Even without thought of profits, such a rapidly expanding organization must presently become big business, with big business's numerous problems and headaches. In the early days, the leaders got little sleep, and Mrs. Jones considered the Lions Clubs as a growing concern with few differences from the business when–"the little *echippus* was deciding to be a horse." With work far into the night and emergency calls that took her husband to far places, the Lions made it impossible for her to make social engagements a week in advance or to plan for a Sunday dinner with her husband.

One day, during a stopover to get a change of shirts after one of his long absences, she asked, "Is this ever going to end?" He answered, "I don't know, there's never been anything like it before."

Nor had there been. The Lions, having decided what they were going to be and what they were going to do, then proceeded to plunge into what to the untutored eye looked like complete confusion. From the start, the voice of the Association as expressed in its conventions had been loud and vigorous. As more and more Lions crowded into these meetings, and more thousands of new Lions made their voices heard through the district officers, mere turmoil became bedlam, and bedlam began to resemble chaos. To outsiders, they might wonder why this great movement did not finish like the one it so closely approximated, the battle of the Kilkenny cats.

All of this may have come to pass if it hadn't been for the flexibility, stubbornness, and youthful energy of the skillful opportunists who sat in the front office. Their business operations were largely a matter of cut and try, but in the end, they evolved a lot of techniques that are still spectacular in a world of marvels. In those days, Melvin Jones, in a few seconds, could tell you the name of the latest Lion who joined up in Belle Fourche, South Dakota, or whether or not some member of a club in South America had paid his dues.

During the St. Louis convention in 1918, Melvin Jones persuaded the directors to apply for a charter in Illinois. This charter was granted on August 25, 1919, to The International Association of Lions Clubs, doing business as Lions International, (since changed to Lions Clubs International) and as a matter of convenience, the three names have become interchangeable in common usage. Lions Clubs International, except in legal documents, is more often used because of its brevity.

In their formative years, the Lions really got a lot done. The Code of Ethics, the Objects, and the Constitution were all adopted and the association acquired a basic coherence and unanimity of purpose.

The Constitution, in the earlier days, was accepted by the Lions in a carefree attitude and the average American is accustomed to thinking of a constitution–any constitution–as something contrived by the Medes and Persians, unchanging and unchangeable, the same today, tomorrow and forever, *saecula saeculorum*. As proof, one has only to cite the attempts of any party, faction or coalition to change the constitution of any state. But nothing was sacred to the Lions – not unless it worked.

So, with hardly any trouble at all, the 1917 constitution was turned in for a new model in 1918 which lasted no longer than 1919. The 1920 convention in Denver went through the same rigamarole. The constitution committee sweated it out in the accepted tradition in smoke-filled rooms in the Albany Hotel and on the floor of the convention at the Civic Auditorium. Bleary-eyed with panatella fumes and late hours, delegates and committee members – among them Kleinschmit and Lybrand, the able barristers who had helped formulate the Code of Ethics – continued to battle. The discussion even continued during a visit to the site of Buffalo Bill's grave after a convention trip had taken them to the top of Lookout Mountain. By the next morning, however, everybody seems to have been tired enough to compromise. There wasn't even an argument when the adoption of the revised and amended constitution was moved.

The weariness of the committee members doesn't seem to have been exceptional. After the vote had been taken and International President, Dr. C.C. Reid of Denver was about to move on to the next order of business, a delegate from Peoria, H.R. Armstrong, got to his feet. "I move," he said feelingly, "that this constitution be made permanent," and he was wildly cheered.

Despite the attitude of the rank and file, however, the perfectionists and parliamentarians continued their tinkering from year to year until, at San Francisco in 1926, another instrument was adopted that has since required only minor alternations.

Some of the changes included the addition of new general membership classifications and, in 1946, the article on membership was rephrased to define active members as "proprietors, partners, corporate officers or managers, or those substantially interested in the business or profession which they represent." Associate members were defined as the partners or associates of active members. Later came the Father-Son membership classification and the Member-at-Large classification which was created in Miami in 1927. To recognize those Lions who have been members for twenty-five years or more, the Pioneer Member classification was created at the Toronto Convention in 1942. Life membership in the Association was conferred on all retiring International Presidents in 1922; and in 1930, restrictions on Honorary Memberships were imposed.

Other changes involved changing the number of International Directors, the election of District Governors, the redistricting of districts into smaller sub-districts, the limitation of the number of delegates to an International Convention to one delegate for every twenty-five members, and to a District convention, one delegate for every ten members.

Later on, there were changes made when the Leos and Lionesses were organized and when women were permitted to become Lions.

Headquarters

In the early days, the Board of Directors delegated much of the administrative work of the International to committees, and then there were subcommittees reporting to committees, and so on *ad infinitum.* Problems did pop up, even with the Lions Committees, so the shift from the committee form of management to something tidier was accomplished as soon as Melvin Jones had the International Office sufficiently organized to take over.

An ad placed by Melvin Jones in the first copy of the *Lions Club Magazine* for November 1918, tells that the Melvin Jones Insurance Company was in Room 1625 of the Insurance Exchange Building at 175 W. Jackson Boulevard, Chicago. A notation at the bottom of the ad stated:

On Club matters, address Room 231, 175 W. Jackson Blvd., Phone Wabash 2020.

The *Lions Club Magazine* showed that it was from the office of the Secretary-Treasurer, 231 Insurance Exchange, Chicago, Illinois.

Cramped quarters plagued Jones as he struggled, (along with the experienced assistance of Mrs. Jones) to set up procedures for the mushrooming organization that wouldn't be outgrown before they could be put to use. He moved the International Office four times before April 15, 1921, when he settled into the McCormick Building on the corner of Michigan Avenue and Van Buren Street.

From then on, every so often, the seams would have to be let out, until in 1949, the floor space rented exceeded 24,000 square feet and the husband and wife team of Jones and Jones had grown to a complement of more than two hundred secretaries, clerks, auditors and executives. Until 1946, Melvin Jones had been the only salaried officer in the Lions organization. It was recognized that under his management Lions

International had grown in size and complexity to a point where he could use a few assistants to keep things going, so the convention that year authorized the appointment at headquarters of a paid Assistant Secretary-General, Secretary, Treasurer "and such other secretaries as may be designated by the Board of Directors."

Melvin Jones then started the departmentalization of the International business and organized sundry divisions of this office to act as information centers for the guidance of committees in the individual clubs, which relieved committees set up by the International Board of administrative detail which they were poorly equipped to handle.

Visitors were welcomed to the International Headquarters and the first thing they noticed as they stepped off the elevator on the third floor, was the large Lions emblem welcoming them to headquarters. They were reminded of the international aspect of the organization as they passed along the corridor flanked by the national flags of all the Lions countries. As they entered the reception hall, they were greeted with a smile and a sincere word of welcome by the receptionist who also served as one of the operators of the busy telephone switchboard. By the time they had signed their name in the visitors' register, the office manager was waiting to conduct them on a tour of the office. In the meantime, the receptionist was sending out a notice to their home Lions Club advising the Club of their visit so that they may be credited with the attendance make-up.

When Melvin Jones was at the office, just about every visiting Lion got to shake hands with him. Visitors were greatly pleased to find the jovial Secretary-General waiting at his office door, his hand extended. An air of unpretentious informality pervaded his book-lined office and visitors felt very much at ease chatting with this greatest Lion of them all. Many an average visitor blushed with embarrassment at not being able to recall some obscure event which occurred in his home club, perhaps years before, as Jones's remarkable memory unfolded minute details of the event.

Besides supervising the International Office, convention matters and matters of policy, the Secretary-General had established some twenty-eight departments at Chicago headquarters to handle all phases of Lions work. Among those which visitors usually found most interesting were: Club Activities Department, Club Service Department, Extension Department, Membership Department, Department of Accounts, District Administration Department, Magazine Department, the headquarters filing system, the supplies department and the merchandise department.

The _International Lions Magazine_ is published in eighteen languages–English, Spanish, Japanese, French, Swedish, Italian, German, Finnish, Flemish-French, Korean, Portuguese, Dutch, Danish, Chinese, Norwegian, Icelandic, Turkish and Greek and mailed to more than 1,344,660 members in 39,463 clubs in 665 districts and 166 nations and geographic areas of the world.

Literally tons of charts, folders and booklets which the International distributes to its 37,622-plus-clubs, are stacked at headquarters. Millions of pieces of mail are handled by the mailing room each year. Thousands of packages of various supplies, as well as awards, are shipped to the clubs. Merchandise ordered by clubs is handled on a nonprofit basis as a special service. Mailing lists are kept for more than 90,000 officers and committee chairmen so that a complete mailing can be made, if necessary, in one day.

Since the end of World War Two, the Lions had entertained intermittent hopes of putting up a building of their own. Finally in 1969, it was announced by Lions International President W.R. Bryan of Doylestown, Ohio that the International Headquarters of the World's largest humanitarian service organization, located in downtown Chicago for 53 years, was to be moved to Oak Brook, Illinois.

The decision to leave the Loop area came after two years of extensive, world-wide study to determine the most suitable location for the modern $4 million administrative office for the then 910,000-member organization. Although a professional research firm had recommended that the Lions relocate on the west coast, the International Board of Directors overwhelmingly voted in favor of remaining within the metropolitan area of Chicago. However, the move outside the city limits to the western suburb required a vote by the membership at the International Convention in Tokyo, Japan, July 5th, 1969.

Following this Convention, at the first Board of Directors meeting held in Spain, the board unanimously approved the purchase of 9.6 acres at the northeast corner of 22nd Street and York Road from the Oak Brook Development Company, a joint venture of Del E. Webb Properties, Inc. and Butler Properties, Inc., developers of the Oak Brook region.

Because of the tremendous expansion of the Lions Clubs throughout the world, averaging 1,300 additional clubs per year at that time, it was necessary for the Lions to sell their aging building and search for a site more adaptable to the extensive operations of the then 23,800 clubs. The new 108,000-square-foot building,designed by Chicago architects Holabird & Root, doubled the space available. In addition to offices, it housed a complete printing plant, 300-employee cafeteria and a large conference room for meetings of the International Board of Directors.

Before selecting the site, consideration was also given to an adequate labor market and to good living conditions for its more than 250 employees, as well as the international travel of the Lions Officers, Directors and some 3,000 global visitors each year.

The exterior of the building is of bronze tinted plate glass and pre-cast panels with quartz aggregate facing. Construction began in the spring of 1970 and was completed July 1, 1971, allowing the Lions to vacate their home of fourteen years and make way for new office and high rise apartment buildings.

On April 21, 1971, International President Dr. Robert D. McCullough of Tulsa, Oklahoma, along with Third Vice-President Tris Coffin of Montreal, Quebec, Canada, and Second Vice-President George Griendrichs of Annecy, France, unveiled the dedication plaque for the new International Headquarters building in Oak Brook, Illinois. Nearly 1,000 Lions, the International Board of Directors, guests and the International staff attended the dedication.

Penny Watching

That the Lions contrived to stay solvent during the first five or six years is not the least remarkable thing about them. There were no endowments or means of support except the money that came in from dues. Organization expenses ran above estimates, as they always do, and the no-assessment rule prevented sharing the burden among the members.

In forming the association, there was no income but there was a considerable outlay for travel, stenographic expenses and to entertain individuals and groups. Clubs that accepted the invitation into the affiliation began to pay dues after a constitution was adopted in which the amount that they should pay was stated–$1 per year. All this was worked out at the Dallas meeting in 1917 at which time it was also decided that Melvin Jones would be the Secretary-Treasurer of the Association and that the office of the Association would be in the city in which the Secretary-Treasurer was located.

So after the Secretary-Treasurer returned to Chicago, he opened an office in the Insurance Exchange Building and proceeded without funds or compensation. And on August 15, 1918 he reported to the St. Louis Convention that the total income from October 9, 1917 to August 15, 1918 had been $2,432,88.

(It has always been a contention that the St. Louis meeting, instead of being called the Second Annual Convention, should be called the First as, after all, the meeting in Dallas on October 8, 1917 was not actually a convention but was the completion of an organization. Nevertheless, the meeting in Chicago in 1919 got to be known as the Third Annual Convention and all conventions have been numbered from the Dallas meeting in 1917.)

At St. Louis, Jones reported that the Lions ended the year with

$488.20 to the good. At the end of the Third Convention in 1919 he reported a balance of $205.68 on hand with total expenses of $5,912.48, of which Melvin Jones received $4,050 in compensation. Of this amount he laughingly remarked, "As long as the insurance business is good, I would be glad to work for nothing and board myself." But in the early 1920s, the Board of Directors felt that he should be reimbursed for more of his time and voted him an annual salary of $4,000.

At this particular time there was considerable agitation about moving the office to Minneapolis or to Toronto, but Melvin Jones proceeded to lay out plans for an office in the McCormick Building. The Association stayed in Chicago until July 1, 1971 when it moved to new headquarters in Oak Brook, Illinois.

There was also a movement to reimburse Melvin Jones on the basis of one dollar per year per member and one dollar for every new member. The Board of Directors had voted to pay him on these basis, but Jones thought it over and refused to accept any such compensation on this basis. Accordingly, in 1921, the Convention created the position of Secretary-General, making it a full-time position and resolving that Melvin Jones be engaged for a period of five-and-one-half years at a salary of $7,200 per year, with the provision that the Board of Directors could increase his salary from time to time and as conditions warranted. In the Great Depression year of 1932, the headquarters staff accepted a 10 per cent salary cut, with the Secretary-Treasurer setting the example by voluntarily taking a 25 per cent cut.

After the Depression, the board restored Jones's yearly salary to $12,000. As time passed and over his objections, they raised it to $15,000 a year. In discussing his salary, he openly stated that he did not want to be rated as a cheap man because his salary was more or less than what others thought it should be. On the other hand, he did not get into the Association to make money out of it. If he wanted to make money he would have stayed where he was in the commercial field.

On one occasion he stated to a group that every Lion who joined the Association had to give some of his time voluntarily but he always backed the movement to reimburse the Board of Directors and District Governors for their actual expenses. The constitution provided that no officer except the Secretary-General should receive a salary. He felt that since the Directors and other officers were giving portions of their time and were being reimbursed only for their expenses, he also should make some contribution to the Association. However, he had to live and had home expenses to meet, so he felt that it was necessary for him to have some salary. Also, his co-workers in the office were not being paid in proportion to what others received in commercial lines and he felt that they too were giving to the Association because they believed in what the Association was doing and in its development and growth. Therefore, he never placed anyone in a position of authority unless he felt that the individual had the welfare of the Association at heart.

But, after all, some consideration must be given to those men who were devoting their entire time to the development of this Association. In answer to inquiries relative to his salary and the salaries of others, Jones replied by asking these questions: What is the value of a man? What is his worth? What would it be worth to you in your business to have a man or a group of men develop your business in such a way as the Association has been developed or built? What do you think he or they would be worth to you?

"In a sense," Jones continued, "the Lions are the owners of the Association. How much do you think they should pay a man or a group of men who have built it and what do you think they should pay to a man or group of men to run it? What do you think a man or a group of men are worth if they are able to build an Association up to what it is today? (By 1949, Lions Clubs International had grown to over 7,400 clubs with more than 380,000 members in 26 countries and had survived through the years of depression, war and inflation.)

Today there are those of us who lived during the Great Depression of the 1930s and those of us who have read or been told about it. It affected every business and organization, most of which were fighting to survive.

Survive the Lions Association did, thanks to the leadership of Melvin Jones. Not only was Jones an expert organizer, but he also proved to be a financial genius. Wilburn Wilson, one of the past Treasurers, who had worked closely with Jones for many years, pointed to the wisdom of Jones's management as basic to the continued success of the Association. The glum year of 1930 brought with it the double challenge of declining membership and finances.

The challenge was to prove to each man that he could not afford to relinquish his Lions Club membership.

New methods had to be devised to help the clubs and also the individual members who were paying dues. The details of the "Jones operations" towards these ends were immense. The effectiveness of his operations is reflected in the fact that only one year, 1930, passed in which a net loss in membership was recorded. After 1930, growth steadily continued. The CPA's financial statement for the year ending June 30, 1930 showed a net loss of $10,392.55, with accounts payable to trade creditors in the amount of $35,455.53, approximately that amount of assets on paper and only $1,417.89 in the bank. The accounts payable figure is proof enough that Jones had friends who believed in him and the organization. There were times when Jones would cash the employees' payroll checks out of his personal funds, holding them until there was sufficient money in the Association's coffers from which they could be cashed.

But Jones never became discouraged and by 1931 his "depression program" was grinding along in good style. The long hard hours he and his staff contributed paid off and the fiscal year of 1931 closed with a net excess of $2,442.15. The following few years were rough, but the young, aggressive organization surged forward. By the fiscal year ending June 30, 1940 the Lions showed a net worth of $4,358.34

After going through the financial difficulties of the 1930s Jones resolved that it would not happen again. His solution involved not only the funds of the International Association, but also those of the individual clubs. They were furnished with all the know how of a good financial program which helped them build up healthy reserves both in their administrative and activities funds, while still carrying on more and more worthwhile activities.

World War II called for a new type of planning that considered the uncertainty of wartime conditions, the inevitable inflation and other effects on individual clubs. It was definite that the war effort would need the help of strong Lions Clubs and Jones reasoned that building membership in existing clubs, increasing the organization of new clubs and continuing to suggest new ideas with respect to Association economy would more than offset the financial rigors of war and inflation. He had never been so right because this three-way program gave splendid support to the war effort, made Lions International the largest and most active service club organization in the world and made it possible to raise dues to $4.50 per year. By 1949, his program brought the total net worth and reserves for contingencies up to more than one half million dollars. Jones was indeed a wizard of finance and management who seemed to thrive on the challenges of depression, war and inflation.

Lions In Print

During the second convention of the Lions at St. Louis in 1918, the Delegates voted to establish an official monthly magazine and Melvin Jones found himself designated Editor and Publisher. There wasn't anything surprising about it, the delegates just naturally assumed that the multi-talented Secretary-General would be able to get out a magazine as he had learned to do so many other things in his spare time. Whatever Jones may have thought about it, he lived up to expectations and in two months after the convention, the first copy of *The Lions Club Magazine* went into the mail. The only change he had found necessary in his already jammed headquarters was a new sign on the door.

Jones had never been an editor, his only experience as a publisher had been confined to the production of insurance brochures. On the other hand, as he has frequently observed, experience is the cheapest thing a man can buy and the quickest delivered. Anyway, the first issue of the magazine made it apparent that Jones and whomever it was that he got to help him whitewash his fence, had ingenuity and resourcefulness, because the 28-page issue had a gratifying collection of advertisements, mostly from Chicago firms, along with pure reading matter consisting of timely discussions of the war, Liberty gardens, Spanish influenza and Lionism.

Lionism included a two-page spread of a picture taken at the St. Louis Convention which carried the caption: "Those who have been in touch with Lions Club activities will recognize many familiar faces in this group picture, although it shows only a portion of those who attended the convention at St. Louis, as it had been taken on the occasion of a delightful automobile sight-seeing trip tendered to Lions and their ladies on the afternoon of August 20, just preceding the formal banquet." That will give a general idea of the tone of the magazine at its inception. It was plain, unassuming, folksy, and somewhat haphazard in make-up. Certainly it looked little like the important, national slick-paper publication that it was presently to become, but the Lions loved it; with considerable reason too, since they looked upon Jones as a sort of magician for having produced it without any funds for that purpose.

In Chicago the next year, the Lions authorized the Board of Directors to name a committee on publications and their chief function was to look about for a new editor for the magazine. Through succeeding editorial regimes, however, the name of Jones remained on the masthead as editor and business manager. In what was undeniably an increase in pay, the Board confirmed his appointment to the editorial post in 1920 at a salary of a dollar a year.

The magazine acquired its present format–eight-and-one-half by eleven inches–with the issue of January, 1922 and the number of pages was increased to 48. As Lions multiplied, more space was needed to keep the individual clubs abreast of what the other clubs were doing. Art covers in two or three colors began to appear and the size of the magazine increased until it reached 64 pages.

Not until later would *The Lions Club Magazine* have its title changed to *The Lion – A Magazine for Lions*, and would it compete with great national publications for big name writers like Peter B. Kyne, Mary Roberts Rinehart, Ellis Parker Butler, James Oliver Curwood and Irvin S. Cobb and other contributors in the 1920's. By degrees it came to be understood that the principal function of the magazine was to print news items relative to the activities of the various clubs and articles of "such character as may be of interest and benefit primarily to members of the clubs."

A general directory of the clubs with names of presidents and secretaries, time and place of meeting and other information was at first included in the body of *The Lions Club Magazine.*

As early as 1922, Jones discouraged the idea of relying on advertising in a publication like *The Lions Club Magazine.* He discovered that the cost of printing more pages to carry ads just about equaled the income from advertisers. President Ewen Cameron agreed and said, "I haven't been able to see we were justified in having a lot of advertising we didn't get a good price for – I think we should keep a high standard of cost and, if an advertiser wants the back page, let him pay accordingly–let the advertiser pay so the magazine is not chock-full of advertising–we will get along just as well." He explained this idea quite simply: "The membership is paying for the magazine now, paying for the cost of it and it is financing itself, which practically no other magazine in the country is doing on subscriptions alone."

Lion John Noel, President in 1923-24 made a similar comment: "In one way, we are giving our membership that magazine. Don't send them a big magazine full of advertising. We want to give them the essence of Lionism."

In 1925, the Board decided that the magazine would accept no advertising in which the name of any individual Lion was mentioned and would print no professional cards as advertising. During the ensuing years paid contributions all but disappeared from the pages of *The Lion*. In 1939, the magazine had run over its budget, this in a year when Association finances generally were running low. In 1941, the Board looked for ways to increase revenues from the official publication.

The question of payment for editorial material was discussed and Jones declared that, with a subscription rate of one dollar a year, it would insure an annual deficit. Advertising manager and now managing editor Oscar Kurtz, explained the peculiar position of *The Lion* as an advertising medium. Agencies felt that if they used a publication of this type they would have to use others in the same category and they figured they could reach all *The Lion* readers more economically through general national magazines. After all the discussion, PIP Ray L. Riley burst out:"Well, *The Lion's* a dollar's worth, isn't it? If we go beyond the limitations of a club organ, we'll get in too deep."

One late summer day in 1932, Melvin Jones stormed into the magazine department and issued the ultimatum that the magazine had to be made more readable, that the contents be made livelier, "Even if you have to run crossword puzzles." It needed something to make the members drop what they were doing when the magazine was delivered each month and read it. In the weeks that followed many ideas were suggested and tested and some of the best were developed and used.

"Hm-m-m, 'Even if you have to run crossword puzzles,' I wonder," mused Oscar C. Kurtz when inspecting books of crossword puzzles in a store. "I wonder if I can make up a crossword puzzle." Well, he did. It was run in the November, 1932 issue of the magazine and the next one he prepared became a part of the December issue. Kurtz then reported that, except to introduce a new type of puzzle, he has not had to make up another one. "The fans kept us well supplied with excellent contributions." A very modest statement, because so many contributions rained on the magazine department that mimeographed supplements were issued "to use up the surplus puzzles." The supplements were mailed to members who had gotten on the puzzle-fan mailing list, but they only increased the flow of contributions. Supplements had to be issued monthly and, by the early part of 1949, 1,484 puzzles had been printed on the last page of the magazine, while 1,826 had appeared in the 68 supplements. And believe it or not, some of the puzzle fans solved nearly all of the 3,31 puzzles. Puzzle editor O'Casey issued pamphlets describing the various types and forms of puzzles and issued a lapel button as an award to those who solved at least ten puzzles.

In an editorial classified as definitive in the February, 1943 issue of *The Lion*, Director Charles J. Stevenson – Editor and Broadcaster – stated, "We've been in the publishing business a good many years and we think *The Lion* is a splendid job in every way, but it isn't a second *Saturday Evening Post* and the only fiction it carries are some reports from clubs in our neck of the woods. In short, some misguided individuals have somehow got the foolish idea that *The Lion* is a publication of general circulation instead of a fine specialty magazine which carries only materials pertinent to the Lion world. There probably are a few members of this great and growing organization who think the magazine should carry a 'How to Keep Well' column, a few choice recipes for making blackberry pie (or brandy), and a Dorothy Dix corner.

"Just how do they get that way? Aren't there enough magazines of general publication in the market to meet this demand? If you are looking for fiction, boys, we can recommend a number of bang-up publications, but don't expect any 'true confessions' to be printed in these pages.

Then we have a few blue bloods who whine because *The Readers Digest* doesn't reprint articles from *The Lion*. You don't happen to have seen any articles reprinted from any one of the hundred or more leading specialty magazines either, have you?...Our magazine is just for Lions..."

At the next Board of Directors meeting, International President Edward Paine reported that Lion Stevenson appears to have had the last word. He heard no further criticism of *The Lion*.

The extension of Lionism beyond the boundaries of the United States necessitated the publication of The Lion in several languages. In 1937, *El Leon* was published for the Spanish-speaking countries. It won wide and loyal readership among the many leading men of Latin America because it reflected their high ideals, public-spiritedness and ambition to serve. It was also a strong influence in stimulating the expansion and growth of Lionism throughout the Latin-American counties, thus linking them ever closer in friendship and mutual understanding, not only to each other, but also to their Lion neighbors to the north and across the seas. Through its word-and-picture reporting, world attention was focused on their activities, as object lessons of the constructive power of the Lions in behalf of their respective communities and nations.

Getting out *El Leon* made up only a fraction of the work of the editorial talent at headquarters. It was also required to keep district and club officers briefed with periodic reprintings of the Secretary-General's monthly letters–basic material on Lionism for all new officers, directors, committee chairmen and members. Each year they prepared a new edition of the directory as well as pamphlets published in the various languages.

Today the international magazine *The Lion* is printed in eighteen languages: the English issue was established in October 1918 and the first issue printed was dated, November 1918. The Spanish issue appeared in 1944; the German, French and Swedish issues in January 1957; the Finnish, Flemish and Italian issues in July 1957; the Japanese in July 1958; the Farsi in January 1962, the Portuguese in April 1963; and the Dutch in July 1964. Since then, issues have been printed in Chinese, Danish, Greek, Icelandic, Korean, Norwegian and Turkish. These issues are sent not just to the native home of the languages but to other countries where they are spoken.

The familiar purple-and gold highway signs and hotel lobby banners, wherever you go, show the way to the nearest Lions Club and are the organization's most familiar means of telling the world. And, the clubs rely on the local newspapers to print advance notices of their meetings, cover newsworthy programs and give an occasional friendly plug to their drives. Otherwise, the Lions ask few publicity favors and to the contrary, Lions International has a policy, unique among service organizations, of buying newspaper space to thank cities for hospitality extended at convention time. Individual clubs are urged to follow a simi-lar policy of buying space to render an account of the year's activities to the community.

Life Magazine once devoted its "Life Goes to a Party" pages to the annual Halloween Barn Dance of the Binghamton, New York, Lions Club. Publications devoted to recreation, library work and other phases of welfare work in which the clubs are interested periodically give the clubs their due. But by no possible stretch of the imagination could the Lions be called publicity grabbers. In fact, you are more likely to find the Lions promoting their community than their club to the general public. California had let itself go to the extent of an annual district-wide essay contest on the subject, "What the Lions Club Can Do For Our Community. After the Montrose, Colorado Lions read that Admiral William Halsey asserted that he would ride Japanese Emperor Hirohito's white horse down Tokyo's main drag, they arranged to furnish him with the finest saddle they could find. Halsey never did take his ride, but he did send the gear to the United States Naval Museum at Annapolis, Maryland. Lion Walter Allison, purveyor of saddles throughout the Colo-rado cow country and beyond, made the finest saddle he could turn out. Sixty-three local cattlemen chipped in $10 each to have their brands stamped into the leather work. Lion Allison also made the bridle and breast strap, then adorned them with cattle brands. The blanket, white with a red center field, was woven for the Lions by an old Indian who wove into one side, in blue, the words *Admiral Halsey*, and on the other *Montrose, Colorado* plus the word *Lions*.

In 1932, a representative of Chicago's Century of Progress Exposi-tion committee proposed that the Lions spend $10,000 to participate in the Fair for five months in 1933. Due to economic conditions, the amount had to be reduced to $1,000 for space in the Social Science Building on Northerly Island. When the Fair was extended into 1934, the Lions agreed to raise the ante and made registration at the Lions exhibit a make-up for club attendance. In 1939, the Lions had their special days at both the San Francisco and New York World Fairs. Mayor Fiorello LaGuardia and Fair President Grover Whelan welcomed 1,000 Lions who traveled to New York from the Pittsburgh convention. Another 4,000 Lions were honored at a special program at New York Fair's Trea-sure Island exhibit.

In 1966-67, the golden anniversary year of the Association, the Lions sponsored a worldwide essay contest entitled *Search For Peace*. The Lions of the world also raised $1 million to stock the cargo ship named *Lions-Care-Friendship* for the relief of the needy throughout the world. The ship was loaded with food, medical supplies, building equipment and school materials at Navy Pier in Chicago and left the dock after a brief program held during the Golden Anniversary Convention on July 4, 1967. It was a symbolic ship, since other ships were required to carry all the supplies that the Lions Clubs had donated to the project during the preceding twelve months. Special Golden Anniversary District Banquets were held in all 450 Lions Districts throughout the world on the same evening–January 14, 1967. Special Commemorative Postal Stamps were issued by the United States Post Office and many other countries around the world. Many clubs and Districts erected anniversary billboards throughout the state.

Winners Of The Peace Essay Contest in District 27 :

27-A Wisconsin - Christopher J. Rogers - Fort Atkinson
27-B Wisconsin - Colleen Casey - Manawa
27-C Wisconsin - *Susan Hinke - Marshfield
27-D Wisconsin - **Richard D. Wanke - Janesville
27-E Wisconsin - Mike Vinopal - Augusta

*Second place winner
**Multiple District winner

William Curry, age 17, Carrollton, Alabama, was the World Geographical Division Winner, representing the United States, Bermuda, Bahamas, and the Districts in United States and Canada.

A. Russell Wodell, of Cranbook, British Columbia, age 18, was the Grand Prize winner of the Lions International Peace Essay Contest.

Lions Clubs International also entered a float in the Parade of Roses in Pasadena, California.

217

Roar! You Lions!

Melvin Jones, whose strong resonant tenor was for many years a part of the offerings of the Apollo Club, Chicago's principal choral society, soon had the Lions singing like birds. Nobody was surprised.

"I introduced songs the first thing," he recalled. "It seemed to me that the meetings were pretty dead until we limbered them up with community song. Everybody talked business with his neighbor at the luncheon table and when that subject was exhausted, he shut up and kept his eyes on his plate. A few rounds of *Tipperary* and *I Want A Girl Just Like The Girl* ended all that. There's always some fellow in a club who can perform at the piano and someone to lead the singing."

Jones's sensing of the need to limber up with a song was reflected in *The Lions Magazine* in 1919. Under the heading "Not Roars but Music," the March issue carried the editorial:

> "He to whom the term 'lion' suggests roaring must be a non-member of our leonine fellowship, for where is the club that is not using the charm and power of music to enhance the pleasure and effectiveness of its gatherings?

"Such as the music is, such is the music of the commonwealth,' say an old Turkish proverb, as if anticipating the interest shown many centuries later by the commonwealth-uplifting groups that comprise our fellowship. As might be expected, patriotic music was much in evidence during the war years, but the termination of the great conflict has by no means brought a cessation of the singing. Worthy talent was always available among the club members and, on the occasional ladies nights, the wives and daughters provided variety. Clubs have had quartets or double quartets and one announcement referred to the next meeting as a "Sing Song."

"Some clubs enlivened the meetings with a series of short parodies of popular songs, written at the expense of the newly-elected officers. Indeed, the general absence of paid entertainers speaks well for our clubs and while enthusiasm may occasionally be vented in something akin to a yell or a roar, it looks as if our organization might acquire an quite enviable reputation as providers of good music."

From the singing of songs familiar to everyone, to the composing of tunes and lyrics exclusively for Lions was a logical progression. Sometimes the Tin-Pan Alley talent that supplied these compositions provided both the words and the music–sometimes only the words. Sixty-three of the 175 songs accepted for the 96-page official songbook are either adaptations or originals especially dedicated to Lionism. The copyrights for some of these are held in the name of The International Association of Lions Clubs and others are used by permission of the copyright holders.

First place in any Lion's book and heart obviously is held by "Don't You Hear Those Lions Roar?" for which Lion Joseph Thurston of Hartford, Connecticut contributed the words and Lion Robert Kellogg, of the same club, composed the music.

Without taking any polls it is apparent that *God Bless America* ranks first among the non-Lion songs heard everywhere Lions gather in the United Stated.

The evolution of the official *Songs for Lions* was slow and sometimes painful. In 1921, the International Board had begun prospecting for publication of a songbook. In 1925, International President Benjamin Jones informed the Board of Directors that "a questionnaire had been sent to all Lions Clubs for the purpose of ascertaining the most popular songs and arrangements were being made to obtain permission from publishers of popular music to use the words and music of certain song." And so, in 1926, after many delays, Lions International published an official songbook which has been reprinted many, many times.

After hearing these songs sung for over thirty years, I can say that they survived the test of time. I have heard some great renditions of these songs and I have heard some renditions which would curdle milk. There is one club which I was the Guiding Lion for–The Berlin-Hamburg Lions Club – which has a great group of singers. And, it does not come just from singing "ein Prosit."

Increase and Multiply

If you have needed any proof that unselfish service brings its re-wards, you need only look at the statistics. It is significant that of the millions or so men who have contracted the lunch-club habit in the United States and overseas, more than one-third are Lions. There are more Lions in the USA alone than the next largest luncheon-classifica-tion club can muster in the entire world. As of June 30, 1949, Lions International had 381,426 members in 7,427 clubs in twenty-six coun-tries on five continents.

The Lions International membership, estimated at 800 in 1917, had reached eight times 800 and extended to Canada by 1920. In 1921-22, International President Dr. C.C. Reid recognized that the growth was going to be something beyond all precedent and set their goal at "a new club every day." This goal was attained a few years later and passed in the forties. For the years 1946-1949, there was an average of more than 825 clubs organized each year.

A big factor in the vitality of the Lions membership structure is the seeming nonchalance with which the International will cancel out sub-standard clubs. Charters were summarily annulled at the discretion of the Directors for failure to meet financial and other obligations.

"If a club is persistently inactive, we'd better get rid of it and work with a new one, perhaps in the same community, frequently with some of the same membership," Melvin Jones explained. Yet, at all times Inter-national stood ready to administer first aid to ailing clubs – providing counselling, devising programs for weak clubs and reorganizing inac-tive ones. The Lions insist that their clubs be active.

During the Depression, 350 clubs were given tender nursing by never being billed, collections were a headache and the International was in the red. But as the Depression lifted, the Lions showed the flash of speed that put them permanently ahead of competitors for top rating in membership.

By 1923, they established the minimum charter membership requirements of at least 20 paid, active members before a charter would be granted. This varied as to the size of the community.

Lionism and other businessmen's clubs may have had their original impetus from the population drift from country to city that began in the 1890s. But a reversal is indicated in the directions in which Lionism has spread. The big cities and suburbs will probably always boast the biggest, richest clubs, but it is the small towns that set great store by the community leadership that Lionism can provide.

The small, independent businessman, backbone of the service club movement, has been absorbed in the personality of the big corporations in the cities. In the rural and semi-rural areas, small business still rates and it's a brash lot of city fathers who will lay down a piece of paving or set up a bandstand without first sounding out Lion sentiment–unless indeed, as frequently happens, the Lions Club and the city fathers are interchangeable.

So it has come about that the density of Lions Clubs, geographically speaking, often has been in inverse ratio to the density of population. A 1949 survey, taking in the entire service-club field, showed that 72 per cent of such clubs were in towns of under 25,000, 38 per cent in towns of less than 10,000 and 20 per cent in towns of less than 3,000.

At the time of the first International convention in Dallas in October of 1917, Lions Clubs were in business in 32 cities in ten States, which were: Waco, Austin, Beaumont, Fort Worth, Dallas, Houston, Wichita Falls, Texarkana, Paris, Abilene, Orange, Port Arthur, San Angelo, Temple and Greenville in Texas; Oklahoma City, Muskogee, Tulsa, Chickasha, El Reno, Okmulgee and Ardmore in Oklahoma; Pueblo, Denver and Colorado Springs in Colorado; Little Rock, Arkansas; Shreveport, Louisiana; Memphis, Tennessee; St. Louis, Missouri; Oakland, California; Chicago, Illinois; and St. Paul, Minnesota.

In 1941, Havana, Cuba had more than 900 members and became the largest service club in the world.

In 1920, the Windsor, Ontario, Lions became the first club to be chartered in Canada. It was also the first in the Dominion to introduce the white cane as a safety identification for blind persons.

Lionism spread to Canada in 1920; to Nuevo Laredo, Mexico in 1925; Tientsin, China, in 1925; Colombia, South America in 1936; Australia in 1947; Sweden in 1948; Each year, Lionism spread to new parts of the world. As of September 30, 1989, there were 1,344,660 members in 39,463 clubs in 665 districts in 166 nations and geographic areas. One of these clubs was chartered in the famous settlement for those suffering from Hanson's Disease at Kalaupapa, Molokai, Hawaii and more than half of the 31 chartered members of the Kalaupapa club were afflicted.

Lionism, as Jean-Paul Galland pointed out in the late 1940s, is "a window opening on the world." When he made this statement, the President of the Lions Club of Geneva, Switzerland was citing the predicament of his own country, "superorganized...with 1,800 to 2,000 associations...but still with a place for Lionism [which] presents a vehicle for larger participation in the affairs of the world." Through Lionism, Galland said, he hoped that his countrymen might overcome the national claustrophobia from which they had suffered as a result of being ringed in by Axis-occupied countries during World War II. Switzerland has long since overcome its claustrophobia and with help from its first Lions Club, chartered in 1948.

Happy Birthday

There is a wide choice of days in the calendar which might reasonably be celebrated as the birth date of Lionism.

There is October 8, 1917, when the first Lions convention was held in Dallas, and there is August 25, 1919, when the Illinois charter was granted. No wonder the perfectionists were thrown by this wealth of possibilities and only official convention action could end the confusion. "Conventions," as Melvin Jones said, "can do anything" and apparently this includes calendar tinkering.

In the summer of 1931, the fifteenth jubilee year of Lionism, the Convention decided that:

> **"Whereas, no birth date or Founders' Day has ever been designated or set aside for the proper observance by the members of this organization, on which might be held suitable celebrations and annual meetings, now therefore be it resolved, by the fifteenth annual convention of Lions International now assembled at Toronto, Canada, that January 13 be designated hereafter as Founder's Day and so established by the organization and that each club within the Association be requested to observe the same with suitable recognition and ceremony."**

There was nothing arbitrary about the convention's choice. It was Melvin Jones' birthday. Jones and Lionism were interchangeable in the minds of the delegates, so what could be more natural than to fix the founding of the one on the same day as the founding of the other?

Jones wasn't as used to demonstrations in his honor then as he was forced to become since his birthday became a semi-public holiday. In 1946, the flag that flew over the Capitol of the United States on the date of his sixty-sixth birthday was presented to him by the Southwest Harbor Lions Club of Washington, D.C. Jones was visiting Washington for the charter ceremony of the Southwest Harbor Lions Club, the 5,000th to be inducted into Lionism. Fifteen years earlier he had made only a modest beginning accumulating the honors that piled on him in later life. So he had been singularly moved when, several months before the Toronto Convention, the Lions Clubs of Cook County, Illinois, surprised him with a lot of rhetoric and a gold watch as he sat with other survivors of the Old Business Circle at a banquet in their honor.

"I use to think," the usually serene, white-maned Secretary-General responded shakily on that occasion, "that there couldn't be anything closer to a man's heart than Lionism. I find there is something that gets closer still–the friendship that Lionism brings us. It is when I stand here and look into the faces of the fellows who stood by me in 1916 and 1917 that I realize what friends there are among the Lions...No one man can build an organization. The whole gang stood by. One after another I've had to call on every one of these fellows at the table in times past when we got into a hole...I know you boys love me. I love you all. There is among us a friendship beyond understanding..."

The friendships Jones inspired in others are well exemplified in the many foreign decorations showered upon him and the scores of honors from national organizations.

While Jones deserved every honor he received, other veteran Lions were also recognized. They were designated as "Old Monarchs," and the second week of October, the anniversary of the Dallas Convention was dedicated to them. The idea was to bring back members who had strayed from their clubs. These men may well be typified by Rosa Bonheur's great painting, *The Monarch.* The Lion there is typical of the quiet strength, the supreme self-confidence, the serene tranquility, the hidden power which lies in every member of a Lions Club.

Old Monarchs – Lions with at least ten years' membership – wear chevrons on their special lapel pins signifying the number of years they have served. Charter Monarchs, Old Monarchs who, moreover, were in at the chartering of a club, are similarly decorated.

With the celebration of the first official Founder's Day in 1932, the birthday of Melvin Jones became Lionism's chief rallying time. The one day celebration soon stretched to a week and later became a month-long birthday celebration.

On the first Founder's Day the International Office in the McCormick Building was transformed into a bower of bloom and the telegraph messengers wore a path in the marble corridor outside. But the note of congratulation that meant the most to Jones was the one he couldn't read because it was written in Braille by the children of a sight-saving class sponsored by the Lions Club of Youngstown, Ohio.

Later, the Central Club of Chicago held its 1932 Founder's Day meeting in the Hotel LaSalle. Many of the old Business Circle crowd were still about and on behalf of the Club, International Director Joseph Adams presented Jones with a book with space for the autograph of every member of the Club.

In 1936, Director Lion Bob Lyles reported to the Board of a plan used by his home club in Austin, Texas. January used to be the month when Lions Club membership figures showed a seasonal drop, so when the Board agreed to accept the plan and named it the Melvin Jones Birthday and Founder's Program, Jones objected. A compromise was reached by just calling it the Birthday and Founder's Program, whereby each club could honor Melvin Jones during the month of his birth, but also the founders of their own club.

Chairman of the Board of Governors Melvin Wright, in 1948, wrote in a letter to all District Governors that, "Modern society places great emphasis on perpetuating itself by vigorous new generation. By the same token, the Officers and Directors of Lions International have, through the years, put emphasis on building, strengthening and enlarging the membership of individual clubs so that the clubs and the Association will perpetuate themselves. Through the Birthday and Founder's Program, Lions International has not only perpetuated itself but has taken its rightful place as the largest, most active and most useful service-club organization in the world. Lions International would not be where it is today had it not been for proper emphasis and attention to a well-organized plan for growth and self-perpetuation.

"I have come in contact with many clubs who do not wish to continually discuss membership at every meeting or very month during the year. They inform me they prefer to concentrate on membership development by a well-organized plan once a year whereby they can carefully choose their prospective members, concentrate on getting them into the club and properly induct them.

"It is true that every man who joins a Lions Club may not stay, regardless of when he joined...We just keep in mind that Lions clubs are made up of men – human beings – human beings who possess all the virtues and weaknesses inherited by the human race. Men drop out of the club because of many things – the rise and fall of their success, their health, their ages, their temperaments and all other things pertaining to human life."

January, 1937, saw 3,054 new Lions brought in as a result of the Birthday and Founder's Program, which showed increases, or good results each year thereafter.

Once a man becomes a lodge brother in most organizations, he is considered in good standing as long as he pays his dues. But, when he becomes a Lion member, he finds himself hooked for committee work, assorted community boosting and the regular meeting, whether it be an eatin' meetin,' or other. Forfeiture of membership can be the result of failure to pay dues, or for missing meetings.

In many groups, they "eat it and beat it," but as a Lion members, we can't just eat, sing and beat it as soon as we finish – we have to render actual service. That is why, although numbers are important, more stress is put on the character of a club than on the number of men in it. It has been proposed to have a "School of Lionism" to be conducted by two or three members for the briefing of the about-to-be-inducted. The committees on Lions information and on membership are very important, as they are to make the new member feel so completely at home that he will have no thought but to bat 100 per cent in attendance. The new member has come into the club under what is known as "The buddy system," with the sponsoring member. The President should have him introduced at a number of meetings and call on him to tell about himself. Show him that your club and members are interested in him and make him feel at home.

There are many ways in which a Lion member can make up lost attendance through absence from a regular meeting and these are listed on the back of his dues card.

Members who maintain perfect attendance records are issued awards by Lions Clubs International.

At the local level, the strategy of stimulating attendance is less formalized and more fun. The clubs have tried everything, from a point system with prizes and penalties used. Or like some clubs conniving with the cop on the beat to bring in the truants in irons. And another club chose up sides, with avoirdupois as equally distributed as possible and the side with the most "weight" at the meetings over the period of the contest took the prize. Or the "Pot of gold" drawings, with the pot accumulating from meeting to meeting and the members who played hookey out of luck if their names are drawn. Then there is the club whose Club Secretary sent the next meeting notices to the members' wives, along with the word that the weekly attendance prize would be sent directly to the wife of the winner. And were the boys in their seats at roll call!

Eatin' Meetin'

Tradition says Tuesday is the preferred day, when the Lion Tamer has presumably polished off the identification badges and members pick them off the rack as they file in for their meeting, meal, fun, frolic and up-lift. As Melvin Jones explained it, "A man had burrowed out from under the Monday mail by Tuesday and he has a bit of a breather before things begin piling up on him toward the end of the week."

However much the unbeliever may smile at the big badges blazoned with the member's nickname, their influence on American social custom can't be ignored. Prior to 1930, people were on stiffish "Mr." and "Mrs." terms for years before venturing to first-name each other. In by-passing the etiquette books and dropping formal titles outside the personal circle as well as in it, the service clubs of American started a practice so pleasant that it has been universally adopted.

The Lions Clubs have grown up in a Depression and have been tempered in the fires of war. Much of the exuberance of early meetings has been toned down. But so long as the Tail Twister flourishes and chairman's equipment includes a gavel and gong with which to choke off the long-winded, no Lions meeting can be completely dull.

The members are in the hands of the program committee and at the mercy of speakers who sometimes seem to have come out of a grab bag. Mediocrity of the average lunch-club speaker is not entirely the fault of the program committee which must take what it can get, a condition depending more on the geographic location of the club and the time of year than on the judgment of the committee.

One person who sympathized with the clubs post-luncheon sufferings, noted, first, there is the product of the rank novice who invites the prominent businessman of his own or some nearby city who takes a long time to deliver a ten-minute speech. Second, is other standard type, and just as bad, the "inspirational" address. But one thing the program chairman can do is to see that the meeting starts and ends on time.

Stunts that can be interspersed between the more serious program features are limited only by time and the ingenuity of the committee. One chairman invites everyone to stand up and stretch just after the committee reports and before the main event. He puts the crowd thorough some informal, upsetting exercises, then commands sharply, "Shake hands with the fellow behind you." Everyone turns, only to find the other fellow's back turned to him. At a Ladies Night, one club contrived a sprightly evening with a "fashion show." The show proceeds with three dummy, preferably headless, models borrowed from a department store. Three Lions are asked by the master of ceremonies to come to the platform and three ladies are asked to act as judges. The models are trotted out and presented, one to each of the men, who then are asked to dress them from boxes of clothing provided for the purpose. The man who turns out the best-dressed model gets a prize. All he would need to qualify would be to put the dress on neatly, but contestants invariably struggle with foundation garments and other odds and ends, adding considerably to the interest. A fashion magazine makes a nice prize.

Meetings can take place in the morning, at noon or in the evening and can be held on any day of the week, with Mondays being the most popular day. There are some clubs in Latin American which hold their meetings on Sunday. At one time, many of the clubs held weekly meetings, but now, for many varied reasons, meetings are twice a month as required by the Lions Clubs International.

Fun With Fines

And so we come to that once controversial figure in Lionism, the Tail Twister. The clowning of this character, circulating among the luncheon tables banging a gong which signifies that bald-headed Lion Joe Doakes has been fined a dime for not combing his hair, strikes the uninitiated as somewhat on the juvenile side.

But no Lions Club would dream of dispensing with its Tail Twister. Without the fines he industriously collects, the club's activities might be in a bad way. Without his merry what-next quips, many a meeting would bog down into dreary celery-chomping and fork-shoveling. The Tail Twister has proved his value to an extent where he has been given an honored place on the roster of club officers along with the lion tamer, or sergeant-at-arms.

As a matter of fact, the origin of his office is older than Lionism. Records of the clubs that flourished in 18th Century London contain rules such as:

> **"Every member shall fill his pipe out of his own box; if any member absents himself he shall forfeit a penny for the use of the club, unless in case of sickness or imprisonment; if any member tells stories in the club that are not true, he shall forfeit for every third lie a halfpenny; if any member's wife comes to fetch him, she shall speak to him without the door."**

The Lions have broken away from this precedent to the extent of holding an occasional Ladies' Night. Going to jail is no longer considered good enough form to serve as an acceptable excuse for absenteeism, but in the Tail Twister, tradition survives.

The Tail Twister has made good as an accepted institution in the face of skepticism and snide cracks and an abortive attempt at one time to foist on him the name of "spizzerinkter."

No lexicographer has successfully challenged the Lions' claim to having thought up, or dreamed up, this term all by themselves, and the best authority on its origin would seem to be the Lions' official magazine. In July, 1936, this erudite source said: "Some readers may be wondering about the word "spizzerinkter' used in conjunction with Tail Twister. Spizzerinkters began to pop up in clubs throughout the Association some months ago. They are close relatives of Tail Twisters–blood brothers, in fact and there is a definition–not by Webster–of their name. Here it is:

"Spizzerinkter, n.

1. A fire-eater; a live wire; a gouger; a snapper; a cutter; a pusher; a trail blazer; a wisecracker.

2. A Lion with the qualities of dynamite, pepper, ginger, great heat, T.N.T.

3. An official in a Lions club who is redheaded, sharp, witty, alive, awake, quick, sizzling, speedy, high-stepping, gate-crashing. Implies reckless partiality.

4. One who is in a state of perpetual eruption, as a volcano. One who has great zip.

"The spizzerinkter has also been variously described as worse than a revolution, more 'touching' than your most shiftless relative and about as subtle as an avalanche and as a new name for the old-fashioned affliction – Tail Twister."

But some way, the plain term of Tail Twister has out-lasted its more hifalutin' synonym and you hear more today of Tail Twisters than of spizzerinkters.

The first effort at innocent merriment in meeting took the form of pep committees supposed to prod members into the spirit of the occasion. A. D. Shaw, a field representative of the day, initiated this practice at the chartering of the downtown Detroit Club in 1920. The pep committees seem to have sifted down, as committees will, to a single energetic personality on each one, and presently these stalwarts came to be known – only Melvin Jones recalls exactly how – as Tail Twisters.

"Back in the early twenties we were trying to find some way to liven up Lion Meetings." Jones says. "For instance, after everyone was seated, with maybe five members of the pep committee at different parts of the table, one would say 'hummh!' Another committee member across the table would say 'hummh!' Then the third, fourth, fifth, members would repeat this grunting monosyllable. If no one noticed, they'd repeat. As a matter of fact, they'd repeat so often there'd be howls to take them out and choke them. Then the idea of fining was proposed. About this time, membership on the pep committees had begun to dwindle and the survivors got the idea that they should be the ones to do the fining.

"One Sunday afternoon three or four of us were discussing this matter of putting pep into the meeting. One fellow who had been born on a farm said that what we needed was to do what used to be done on the farm. When a cow refused to go through the gate, someone would grab her by the tail and twist. We all laughed, but one of the boys said, "Why isn't that a good name – Tail Twister?' We already had decided on the name 'lion tamer' for the sergeant-at-arms, so it seemed logical to confer the title of Tail Twister on the chairman of the pep committee."

The International Board, in a huff of offended dignity, issued an edict to the clubs against use of the low-comedy term. Melvin Jones remembers how the issue came to a head late in 1920 in Columbus. The Board was there for ceremonies at which fourteen clubs were being chartered and word came out from the Board-room that the term Tail Twister was prohibited. At that, the rank-and-file membership took matters into their own hands during luncheon by passing a motion in favor of tail twisting and the board agreed to reconsider. The question was batted about at Board meetings for years after that. Other names, to represent the same office, like spizzerinkter, were suggested, however, the consensus of the Board remained pretty much the same–that the terms Tail Twister, cub, lion tamer and den should be dropped from Lionism–until Ray Riley (International President, 1929-30) got up at a session in Washington one day and said they were taking themselves too seriously. Besides, he suspected the clubs were going to continue having Tail Twisters whether the Board liked it or not.

"Of all the novel and rich experiences which await the new Lion, none strikes him so forcibly as his introduction to that "Demon of the Dime," that "Debunker of Dignity," known as "The Spizzerinkter," or "Tail Twister."

"The Tail Twister, as we prefer to call him, is about the only absolute dictator we know who enjoys the affection of those whom he oppresses. The tolls he exacts profit him not, but find their way into his little bank, from which they eventually emerge to do some altruistic service.

"The novitiate often stands in red-necked and crest-fallen embarrassment when ordered by the Tail Twister to give explanation for his tardiness, his use of a formal address to a fellow Lion, or just for living. Or, for that matter, for anything which the fertile brain of the efficient Tail Twister can concoct that will serve as a "crime' and bring on the penalty...

"Of all the officers in the club, he alone has no rigid code, no well-defined plan of action. He must be a Lion of originality; a merciless prosecutor of friend and foe; one who stands not in awe of the unbending Lion or highest visiting dignitary."

Larry Taylor, a Weatherford, Texas Lion, put it more succinctly: "It is natural for men to have fun together but not so natural to start this fun on their own initiative for fear of seeming out of place."

So the game of forfeits goes on, providing not merely revenue but the spark that keeps the members interested and a Tail Twister with his heart in his work can be an indispensable officer of his club. He can find reasons enough to assess fines without resorting to fining for imaginary offenses, such as: tardiness, failure to wear a name badge or Lions button, failure to properly register guests, improper address to officers, plugging business, becoming a bridegroom or a papa, having a birthday, winning a golf prize, breaking into print, being promoted in business or elected to office, referring to another member a "Mister" or 'gentlemen,' singing too noisily or not noisily enough.

There is no appeal of the Tail Twister's fine, but the Tail Twister may not be fined himself except by unanimous vote of all present, including himself. Members are protected against triple jeopardy, i.e. being fined more than twice at the same meeting, and as a rule, only the most hardened offenders are nicked for more than a dime. One Tail Twister made a good thing out of renting advertising space on his receptacle for fines, setting up a sort of chain reaction, since advertising within the club is a fineable offense in itself. Some Tail Twisters find it profitable to toy with the no-advertising ban, giving a member's business a forbidden plug and then fining him for it.

Another Tail Twister got hold of members' business cards and placed them at each place at the luncheon tables with profitable results. At another club, the members were hauled into the "Soakum and Sockum" traffic court set up to make the club traffic-conscious. Warrants were issued for real traffic violations or, lacking those, for imaginary ones. Court sessions were held and fines assessed at regular meetings.

Oh yes, Tail Twisters know how to deal effectively with the absentees, as in Hugo, Oklahoma, where absent members were hauled to the club meeting in an ambulance, or Lakeview, Illinois, where they were carried in on stretchers, or in Tyler, Texas, where they were brought in irons and had to manage to eat with the bracelets still circling their wrists. But absenteeism was unknown in Owensville, Missouri after the Tail Twister there acquired a goat and sent the animal to board with any member who played hookey.

If you failed to show up wearing a Lions Lapel button, some clubs compelled the culprit to invest in another, or to buy an automobile decal, at a profit to the club. And who would think of having a roll call in which middle names are read off and fines dished out to members failing to recognize their middle names when called. Or those members of a club who preferred to forfeit a dime rather than get up and make a speech proving to the club that they were no fools. And there was one Tail Twister, smarting under criticism, who appointed his critic as his assistant. The assistant went into action by auctioning the clothes right off the Tail Twister's back, rolling up the sum of $60.81, for the activities fund.

What would it cost you if the Tail Twister conducted an impromptu quiz concerning items which have appeared in the very latest issue of the official Lions magazine? Even if you read it from cover to cover, you stand a little better than even chance of not being nicked for a dime, that is unless the Tail Twister pops up with a question he "just happened to dream up."

From which it may be judged that the Tail Twister is here not only to stay but to get away with murder. In Fort Worth, Texas, he has won recognition from the club poet laureate:

Tail Twister! Tail Twister!
I've known you of old;
You've robbed my poor pockets
of silver and gold;
You've kicked me and cuffed me,
you've been my downfall;
You've cheated and crooked me;
but I love you for all.

And this includes all Lions, Lioness and Leo Tail Twisters, Skirt Tail Twisters, or whatever you may call them to their face or under your breath.

The World's Biggest Doers

Who gives himself with his alms feeds three-
Himself, his hungering neighbor; and Me.
James Russell Lowell, *Vision of Sir Launfal*

> *This eagerness to serve,*
> *to be useful,*
> *to give of yourself—*
> *that is where Lionism*
> *gets its strength.*
> *For nothing unites men more closely*
> *than the sameness of purpose*
> *insofar as that purpose*
> *is inspired by high ideals and aims.*

Mariano Roca Gutierrez, in an address before the Lions Club of Santiago, Cuba.

Doers And Proud Of It

The man who joins a Lions Club in good faith presently is up to his belt in activities which, he may find, overlap at some points the welfare work of his church and the community boosting that is the *raison d'etre* of the Chamber of Commerce.

Not that there isn't enough of either to go around among them all, church and social agency workers have confessed to a frank envy of the efficiency of the Lions Clubs, which can commandeer the best business brains of the community when they want to get something done.

Lions Club presidents appoint committees to plan activities, but the carrying out of the plans is likely to be a whole-club activity. Melvin Jones once cited the example of an outstanding Lions Club, which held top places year after year. In handling projects, the Board of Directors of the club first went into a huddle, then at a later meeting, they invited into this huddle a third of the membership, later invited another third and still later the remaining third of the membership, until all of the members were in on the huddle and out of such conferences comes combined or organized leadership.

It is said that one of the strongest appeals of the service club to the busy executive, is that the club furnishes him a convenient channel through which to carry out his obligations as a citizen. On the other hand, the man who hasn't been overly conscious of such obligations is exposed to some concentrated education about them as soon as he bumps up against the club activities program. *The Lion* once reported an item about a member of a club who was delegated to investigate an appeal that had been made to the club to aid a young girl who had lost her sight. The upshot of the members' formal investigation was that he assumed full charge of the case, guaranteeing the girl – on behalf of the club – whatever care and means were needed to give her as normal a life as possible. That one instance is representative of a common pattern.

A Lion's participating in welfare activities through his club fulfills a two-sided purpose. It brings a program of service to those who need it and at the same time, it brings to the Lion a sense of well-being for having given of his time.

Once, a new Lion exulted, every pair of glasses we buy for an under-privileged child, every white cane we give to some blind person, or when we perform some other good deed, I get a feeling of joy out of it. And walking into the post office and seeing old blind Charley behind his cigar counter, it makes me feel good because our club made it possible for this poor fellow to give again – he is actually happy now. I have more respect for myself since I joined the Lions Club because our club is always doing something that gives a fellow a feeling that he is of some benefit to the world.

The International sums it up with this statement: "The activities program embraces every opportunity for community service, and the Lions Club presents an unrivaled medium through which every civic-minded, public-spirited individual may serve in the particular field in which he is most interested."

An annual report shows literally thousands of activities in the three major divisions of social welfare, community improvement and aid to business, of which close to one-half came under the heading–community betterment. And to describe what Lionism seeks to do in the fewest possible words might be said that its fundamental purpose is to make the club's home town a better place in which to live. This objective automatically puts the Lions into everything that goes on around town, which also points up a distinguishing characteristic of Lions – that no job is too small for them, which may explain why they have accomplished so many big ones.

Professionals in the welfare field have raised the point that Lions activity in this field is unplanned, that it meets only the immediate emergency – and the Lions' own record in doing just that, without smothering everyone concerned in red tape, is of course the best retort to this criticism.

Since the day they were founded, the Lions have been paying burial expenses for the elderly, sending coal to the shivering, and doctors to the sick, while other agencies were preparing case histories in triplicate. Lions are not above painting a fence or a home, repairing a pavement, or sitting with a baby if the circumstances are urgent. And over the years, the Lions have become used to many strange requests. Somebody has to do these things and Lions never have found a job too small for them if it is something that really needs doing.

A club embarking on a new phase of activity can almost certainly profit from the experience of some other club. Lions Clubs International through its activities file, most certainly can refer one club to another.

The International office also records club expenditures for activities, such as Community Betterment, Civic Improvements, Boys' and Girls' Activities, Health and Welfare. They also record how Lions participate in projects in cooperation with other agencies such as the Red Cross, March of Dimes, Community Chest, Boy Scouts, Salvation Army. Also in programs such as Juvenile Delinquency Prevention, Health and Education, Housing, Diabetes Education and Research and Drug Awareness. Each year sees new programs added and some may be dropped if no longer needed.

Let The Lions Do It

Service activities, once listed under ten committee divisions, now number twelve. Lions Clubs activities are a far-from-confining experience, as the activities have been divided and each committee must take part in welfare work, community service and – to a lesser extent – business promotion. The clubs turn in reports of activities under these headings:

> SightFirst
> Hearing and Speech Action and Work with the Deaf
> Youth Outreach
> Diabetes Awareness
> International Understanding and Cooperation
> Environmental Services
> Leo Clubs
> Lions Clubs International Foundation (LCIF)
> Journey For Sight
> Youth Exchange
> International Eye Banks
> International Youth Camps

Kind Hearts

Leaf through any monthly issue of *The Lion* and you'll find it packed with the sort of modest and moving little stories newspapers used to print in quantity until the brutal blow-by-blow report of a world trying to destroy itself pushed "human interest" out of the paper.

- *Provided needy family with groceries and paid part of a medical bill.*
- *Helped to furnish an orthopedic ward with a new wing.*
- *Furnished clothing and furniture for a family.*
- *Provided glasses for needy persons.*
- *Sponsored blood-donor services for hospitalized citizens.*
- *Equipped a junior hockey league.*
- *Paid expenses of crippled girl's day in camp.*
- *Helped to develop a community park.*
- *Held a Halloween party for children.*
- *Donated to a community center project.*
- *Paid to correct a boy's severe vision problem.*
- *Established a scholarship award for a needy university student.*
- *Purchased Christmas baskets for the needy.*
- *Rebuilt a home and provided furniture, food and fuel for a disaster-stricken family*
- *Purchased a machine for testing the eyes of school children.*

On and on this list could grow, as clubs and members help someone less fortunate.

Sometimes Lions have to try something new. Originality caused the Norfolk, Virginia Lions Club to become interested in a ten-year-old who caused quite a stir every time he came into juvenile court. Looking into his case and loosening some of the red tape, the court approved a sort of informal adoption by the club who scrubbed him up and sent him to a military school in a different part of the state. When he came home, he asked to attend a club meeting and thank the members in person for the chance they had given him. This "adoption" device spread and other clubs used it in various ways to help those less fortunate.

The Fredonia, Pennsylvania Lions helped a "newcomer farmer" who got burned out by lightning. With donated equipment, they helped cut, rake and baled nearly 55 tons of hay and arranged for a surplus for the young farmer after all expenses were paid. Another club helped harvest 7,000,000 bushels of wheat. Another 200 Lions helped harvest eight acres of potatoes in six hours when the farmer was injured in an accident. Another club turned out with scythes and rakes and tidied up a newly designated playground area of several acres.

Being human, Lions are more likely to glow over helping their neighbors than contributing to some remote cause. Like the club which installed a broom-making machine in the basement of a blind man, making him partially self-supporting, or the club which provided a sewing machine for a blind leather worker, or the members of another club who went to great lengths to break rules and incur the wrath of the Tail Twister until he had collected enough fines so the club could purchase a typewriter for a young girl who was crippled.

Each new issue of *The Lion* brings another list of service activities by the Lions, Lioness and Leo Clubs from throughout the world. Each service activity represents many hours of planning and work by many—all to add to the "miles of smiles" the Lions have created over the years.

Into Everything

In the darkest depths of the Depression, with other clubs folding right and left, Lions Clubs managed somehow to keep welfare programs moving. The greater the occasion, the easier it is to rise to it. During the 1932-1933 year, perhaps the Depression's worst, the records show:

- *3,987 children received eyeglasses.*
- *1,198 white canes were presented to blind adults.*
- *$16,697,27 was expended to supply milk to undernourished school children.*
- *475,318 free meals furnished to unemployed persons.*
- *12,617 Christmas dinner baskets were distributed.*
- *14,660 copies of the Moral Code for youth were presented to schools.*
- *Medical attention was given to 4,533 underprivileged children*
- *527 children received needed operations and 479 children received hospital attention.*
- *Summer camp vacations were provided to 2,034 underprivileged children.*
- *Throughout the country 44,117 trees were planted.*
- *1,960,000 baby fish were planted in lakes and streams.*
- *Clubs reported net profits of $118,427 from various community entertainments and events.*

The Lions Clubs continued to spread out into new areas of service: a home for convalescent children, Easter-egg hunts, child placement, circulating libraries in public schools, Community Christmas trees, encouraging fire departments into rehabilitating toys for children, a hospital ward for premature babies, iron lungs for polio victims and support of blood banks and cancer controls. One club put on an "Over 80" dinner with a corsage and a pearl necklace for older ladies in the community, others set up clinics for the prevention of blindness, bought eyeglasses by the bales, found jobs for the blind, set them up in business, sold their products, paid their tuition to special schools, provided them with white canes, Braille books and writers. Concern with the special equipment needed by the blind has led the Lions into bypaths of research that have contributed to the comfort and happiness of blind persons everywhere. The Lions were largely responsible for municipal ordinances penalizing motorists who ignored the stop-traffic signal of a white cane.

The credit for the invention of the white-cane device belongs to a Lion in Peoria, Illinois and to the Peoria Lions Club, the credit for the white-cane's universal recognition.

In 1924, a New York Lions Club underwrote publication of a large-type book for use of the partially blind. A Cincinnati Lions Club began experimenting in publication of a children's magazine in Braille. The Long Beach, California Lions club promoted a writing board for the blind. The Milwaukee Lions became interested in Braille city maps when Esther Fellows, the St. Paul woman who originated them, explained them to the club and obtained enough for all the city's sightless. In 1946, the San Diego Lions Club gleefully seized on the Banks pocket-Braille writer, a vest-pocket-size machine which enabled a blind person to write Braille at shorthand speed.

Another "first" in service to the blind to be chalked up to the Lions is the first Boy Scout troop composed entirely of blind boys. Camden, New Jersey, Lions set up blind men and women in newsstands throughout the city. The Tulsa, Oklahoma Club set up the blind in broom making, which became a flourishing business. The Detroit, Michigan Lions handed out "Talking Books" to the Blind. Many eye operations that were arranged and paid for by the Lions Clubs, were in turn paid for by the many letters received. Like one that said, "I am back in school, My eyes are well and oh, goody, they are straight. They look like other little girls' eyes now."

The way Lions felt about sight-saving was summed up in a plea for support for the Braille magazine. "We have all learned not to waste our time in the sentimental display of pity for blind children. The blind child of today, with our modern methods of training, does not need pity unless it leads to something constructive in the way of a chance to get on...

"Experience has shown that well-trained blind children can take their places in the modern social order and be creative and self-sustaining individuals. It has been found that great unfilled gaps in the lives of the younger blind, unfulfilled wants which approach mental starvation, terrible deserts of monotony which you and I have never known because we have our sight....If a blind child is brought up to be merely a machine with no mental background, you get machine-like results...

In addition to distributing the Braille magazine, Lions also distributed the "Moral Code for Youth." It was first issued by Collier's magazine, who held the copyright, permitted the Lions to distribute free copies which they furnished. The code reads:

In God We Trust

If I Want To Be a Happy, Useful Citizen I Must Have:

Courage and Hope

I must be brave. This means I must be brave enough and strong enough to control what I think, and what I say, and what I do,and I must always be hopeful because hope is power for improvement.

Wisdom

I must act wisely. In school, at home, playing, working, reading or talking, I must learn how to choose the good, and how to avoid the bad.

Industry and Good Habits

I must make my character strong. My character is what I am, if not in the eyes of others, then in the eyes of my own conscience. Good thoughts in my mind will keep out bad thoughts. When I am busy doing good I shall have no time to do evil. I can build my character by training myself in good habits.

Knowledge and Usefulness

I must make my mind strong. The better I know myself, my fellows and the world about me, the happier and more useful I shall be. I must always welcome useful knowledge in school, at home, everywhere.

Truth and Honesty

I must be truthful and honest. I must know what is true in order to do what is right. I must tell the truth without fear. I must be honest in all my dealings and in all my thoughts. Unless I am honest I cannot have self-respect.

Healthfulness and Cleanliness

I must make my body strong. My eyes, my teeth, my heart, my whole body must be healthful so that my mind can work properly. I must keep physically and morally clean.

Helpfulness and Unselfishness

I must use my strength to help others who need help–If I am strong I can help others, I can be kind, I can forgive those who hurt me, and I can help and protect the weak, the suffering, the young, and the old, and dumb animals.

Charity

I must love. I must love God, who created not only this earth but also all men of all race, nations, and creeds, who are my brothers. I must love my parents, my home, my neighbors, my country, and be loyal to all these.

Humility and Reverence

I must know that there are always more things to learn. What I may know is small compared to what can be known. I must respect all who have more wisdom than I, and have reverence for all that is good. And I must know how and whom to obey.

Faith and Responsibility

I must do all these things because I am accountable to God and humanity for how I live and how I can help my fellows and for the extent to which my fellows may trust and depend upon me.

After this code had been widely circulated, it was pointed out the need of some sort of follow-up – something which would make the principles laid down in the code come alive in the minds of boys and girls. The "Studies in Conduct" series was the result.

In Wisconsin, all the Lions, Lionesses and Leos can be very proud of our Foundation which runs the Lions Camp, Sight Projects, Hearing Projects and the Used Eye Glass program.

"What's Good For Business"

Outside the strictly philanthropic field, two key committees in every club reach out toward all the other activities demanded of the well-brought-up Lion. These are the committees dedicated to civic improvement and community betterment, or boasting. Their duties inevitably interlock. What's good for one is grist for the other. If the civic-improvement boys are on their toes in city planning, clean-up campaigns and such, the way of the community-betterment committee in attracting new business and tourist traffic is exceedingly pleasant. And vice versa.

Sustaining the efforts of the community-betterment and civic-improvement committees and even at times over-lapping with them in a friendly way, is the work of the committees on boys' and girls' activities, education, safety and agriculture. These committees, over the years, have been responsible for sponsoring athletic, camp, contest and hobby projects for "Y" and Scout groups of both sexes and similar juvenile and teen-age enterprises. Lions have cooperated with schools, libraries, churches and the PTA and sponsored book drives, public lectures, vocational guidance and hundreds of other activities of an educational nature. They've organized and equipped junior safety patrols, operated safety lanes and driving schools, removed traffic and fire hazards, engaged pool and beach lifeguards, conducted classes in first aid and lifesaving, run safety campaigns and contests in schools, factories, and offices, managed soil-conservation studies and conducted "Farmers Days" and "Home Products Days" as well as meetings and fiestas.

Some clubs conducted "Of-Age" ceremonies where they welcomed to citizenship young men and women of the community who attained voting age during the year.

Jewel Cave National Monument came into being through the effort of the Newcastle, Wyoming, Lions who explored and developed it to the point that the federal government was willing to take it over as one of the most beautiful spots of this nation.

Other clubs were responsible for cleaning up beaches, supplying luminous tape for kids' bikes, purchasing street lights, bringing about paved streets and good sidewalks, organizing a Chamber of Commerce and other city improvement efforts. One club raised the necessary funds to induce a factory to locate in its area which employed over 600 employees.

In 1932, Melvin Jones became a member of the White House Conference of business executives at the invitation of President Hoover and served as an advisor to Colonel Frank Knox whom Hoover had deputized to develop the recommendations of the conference.

Over the years, other Lions Clubs have found newer ways to help promote their communities. Smaller communities found that their local Lions Club also acted as their Chamber of Commerce and look to and rely on their Lions Club for this service. Each Club has added its paragraph or chapter to this story and will continue to do so over the years to come.

Each member can be very proud of his or her Club's accomplishments.

Nothing Shall Stay Them

From their earliest beginning, the Lions Clubs have been in the forefront of the relief drives that follow in the wake of depression, disaster and war. "Not so such for the money they have given from their own pockets, but because they always organize the community and get everybody to work and thus achieve immeasurably greater results, the Lions are among the most important agencies for relief, especially in the smaller communities," an astute observer once remarked.

The Association came into existence in time to participate in the tag end of the relief drives that accompanied World War I, shipping shoes and clothing to Belgium and the occupied areas of France and then providing the same relief when hard times came to the United States in the early 1920s. The clubs have been alerted in countless disasters–tornadoes in the Mississippi Valley, hurricanes in Florida, drought in the Dust Bowl, floods in the Ohio River Valley and hundreds of other catastrophes.

In 1947, the Friendship Train was organized to collect thousands of tons of foodstuffs for Europe and the Lions Clubs spear-headed the collection drive. They saw that the boxcars were loaded and waiting to be picked up in the various cities when the train passed through. When the Salinas, California Lions learned that the Friendship trains would not pass through their city, they collected canned milk and loaded 609 cases on the ship *Golden Bear* and sent it to Europe as a "good-will milk boat." The Texas Lions, also not on this Friendship Train route, organized a special section of the train from the Southwest.

During the 50th Anniversary Year, the Lions of the world loaded the "Care-Friendship-ship," which unloaded its cargo at various ports around the world.

During the Second World War, Lions Clubs again came up with new ideas how to help, either in Bond Drives, housing for servicemen on leave, aiding servicemen and their families and the bombed-out people of Europe.

Today, through the Lions Clubs International Foundation (LCIF), they have been the source of help in many different ways, in all parts of the world. When LCIF was founded in 1968, its capacity for service was necessarily quite limited. It took more than five years to accumulate enough assets to disburse just under $100,000 in 1972-73. Most grants that year were under $10,000 and nearly all were for disaster relief projects.

Now, both LCIF's capacity for service and its range of grants have expanded tremendously. In 1985-86, LCIF grants had climbed to more than $2.5 million for the year–a record for the Foundation–supporting a wide range of humanitarian projects with grants of up to $250,000 The 1989-90 grants exceeded $4,795,765. Grants for 1993-94 exceeded $36,695,389.

At the 1986 Lions Clubs International Convention in New Orleans, out-going President Joseph Wroblewski issued a challenge to the future of Lionism. The Lions Clubs International Foundation, he announced, had launched a progressive program to reach 20,000 Melvin Jones Fellows in honor of its 20th anniversary in 1988. That goal was reached and exceeded with more than 23,700 Melvin Jones Fellowships.

The Melvin Jones Fellowship is the highest honor bestowed by the Lions Clubs International Foundation. It recognizes deep commitment to LCIF's humanitarian programs through contributions of at least $1,000 to the Foundation.

Lions and the United Nations

In 1947, International President Fred W. Smith remarked, "It seems to me that in all the thirty years of Lions' service our widest opportunity as an international organization has occurred within the past three years or since that time, in the fall of 1944, when Lions were accorded the privilege of participating in the off-the-record discussion of the Dumbarton Oaks proposals."

"Following closely upon this participation came the invitation to the Lions to have a consultant and two associate consultants to the United States delegation at the United Nations Conference in San Francisco. The Lions were represented at the Peace Conference in Paris in September, 1946, by D.A. Skeen, (International President 1944-45) and Clifford Pierce, (International President 1946-47). Furthermore, ever since the opening days of the San Francisco Conference, the Lions have been active participants in the meetings of the UN's nongovernmental groups. In early 1949, the Lions were recognized by the United Nations as an organization with special competence and ability to represent peoples in many nations and thus were granted consultative status with the Economic and Social Council of the United Nations. This status, in my opinion, implies an obligation on the part of each Lion to develop a greater understanding of the multiplicity of the activities of the United Nations and particularly those relating to the Economic and Social Council. With this greater understanding by the individual Lion will come a greater opportunity for our Association to participate more fully in world affairs in the years ahead."

Up to that time, service clubs generally had shied away from taking a position on international political organizations. For example, after World War I the creation of the World Court was viewed as a partisan issue. The tinge of partisanship detected in a Lions Club meeting calls for prompt quarantine measures, the same as the appearance of measles. The reason for this caution is as obvious as the reason for the measles quarantine. You can't expect the members to attain that all-for-one-and-one-for-allness necessary to a going concern if they go around wearing their politics and their ideologies on their sleeves or on their shoulders.

Lions Club members always have been expected to check their deepest feelings in these matters with their hats before sitting down to the fruit cup. But in years after World War II, the Lions became acutely aware of the urgency of a world shrunk by A-bombs to altogether too cozy dimensions. How far the jolt propelled them as an organization into political action below the international level is a question that is still open. But they yield to no other group of comparable influence in all-out support of the United Nations.

As recently as 1937, the Lions, no more prophets than you or I or the prime ministers of Europe, conceived of international relations as something to be promoted by little visits back and forth and the exchange of postage stamps by school children.

However, by 1943, the International was plugging hemispheric solidarity by seeing that Lions Clubs in Latin American countries were supplied with material prepared by the speakers bureau of the federal Office of War Information.

At the International Convention held in Cleveland in 1943, the Lions wholeheartedly endorsed a resolution advocating "the adoption of the Ball-Burton-Hatch-Hill Resolution, the Fulbright Resolution, or some other resolution similar in effect and purpose." Both of these bills had to do with machinery for peace.

Late in 1944, the Lions were invited to send a representative to attend a meeting at the Department of State in Washington D.C., for "off-the-record" discussions of the Dumbarton Oaks proposals, from which the charter of the United Nations later came into being.

Reporting on these off-the-record discussions of the Dunbarton Oaks proposals, Past President Clifford Pierce of Memphis, Tennessee, then Second Vice-President and Lions International representative, told the Directors that he was quite impressed because we already had done the very things that the State Department hoped would be done. Our whole organization had developed means to get plans for the coming United Nations organizational conference before the people. He indicated that he thought we represented a cross section of business and professional thought in our Lions countries and that our program very definitely had been presented in such a way that we felt it was bringing results.

Thus began the years of Lions' participation in historic international strivings toward world peace.

In February, 1945, the Lions were again asked to send a representative to a meeting in Washington of national organizations, this time on the Bretton Woods agreement. Harold P. Nutter, President 1951-52, and Secretary-General Melvin Jones represented the Lions at that meeting, which was conducted by Secretary of the Treasury Henry Morgenthau, Jr. and Assistant Secretary of State Archibald MacLeish.

As a result of this particular meeting, Melvin Jones began to make plans for the Lions to take a more intensive part in the cause of world peace. Pamphlets containing the Dumbarton Oaks proposals had been mailed to all Lions Clubs and, on March 5, 1945, the Glenwood Springs, Colorado Lions Club adopted a resolution which was to have far-reaching effect. The resolution said:

> We believe the President of the United States, the State Department and the Senate should conclude, as soon as possible, agreements with our principal allies providing for the complete present and future demilitarization of Germany and Japan...We believe that the framework and the details of a World Organization must be worked out by the chosen leaders of the nations; that the document on which it is based must be elastic enough to expand to meet the needs which the future will dictate; that the document must be given life, growth and policies through the judgements of a final tribunal or assembly; and, finally that such judgements, when the necessity arises, must be carried out by force of arms contributed by signatory nations...We therefore endorse and urge a World Organization such as indicated in the broad basic principles agreed upon at Dumbarton Oaks, notwithstanding the fact that it is neither perfect nor complete.

Things were happening fast. The opening session of the San Francisco Conference was still several weeks away when, on March 28, Secretary William R. Bird left Chicago for San Francisco to take charge of the Lions office to be opened there for the duration of the conference. Bird was also furnished press credentials to represent *The Lion* and *El Leon* at the conference.

Early in April a letter went out from the International Office to all Lions Clubs asking them to celebrate the week of April 23-28 as United Nations Week and to hold a United Nations program in their club meeting during that opening week of the San Francisco Conference. With the letter went a program showing suggested procedure. The Glenwood Springs resolution was included in the program, as well as a suggestion that the clubs might wish to send a letter or a message of support to International President Skeen at Lions Conference Headquarters in the Sir Francis Drake Hotel, San Francisco.

On April 9, E.R. Stettinius, Jr.,–who had only a short time before been named Secretary of State–sent this telegram to the International Office, addressed to International President Skeen:

> I am happy to invite your organization to designate a representative to serve as a consultant to the American Delegation at the forthcoming Conference on International Organization to be held at San Francisco beginning April 25. The official American delegation consists of the eight Delegates appointed by the President and their professional and technical advertisers. Consultants representing organizations will be available for consultation at the request of the delegation and will be kept as closely informed of the work of the conference as possible. If you desire to appoint a consultant please wire the name of the person designated.

The Board of Directors of Lions International immediately acted to name President Skeen as the official Lions consultant. Later, when the Department of State authorized the appointment of associate consultants, the Board appointed Vice-President Fred W. Smith, President 1947-48, and Secretary-General Melvin Jones as associate consultants and all three were at the opening session of the San Francisco Conference and participated from time to time in the consultants' meetings.

On April 24, the evening before the conference opened, 1,200 Lions and guests took part in a pre-United Nations Conference rally at a huge banquet sponsored by the Lions in the Scottish Rite Temple in Oakland. Dr. Preston Bradley, pastor of the People's Church, Chicago, was the principal speakers of the evening and, reported *The Lion:*

"The audience was deeply moved by his eloquent and thrilling address. He took as his subject 'The World of Tomorrow' and his plea was for the success of the conference about to open. The size of the gathering, the deep – almost reverent – earnestness of the participants made a deep impression. The *Oakland Tribune* the following day ran a cut five columns wide showing part of the banquet scene, as well as a running story and other pictures of prominent Lions and interviews with some of them. It was made clear that Lions are backing to the full the endeavors of the conference to work out a plan for harmony among nations."

Bradley's talk, which was broadcast, was so well received that the station which put it on the air rebroadcast it the following evening and again on April 27.

The Lions had made their presence felt at the conference. They were to do so on more than one occasion in the days ahead. On May 8, President Skeen addressed a letter to the Secretary of State, assuring him the Lions were solidly in favor of what had been done in the conference to date, and telling him about the several thousands of messages which had poured into the Lions Conference Headquarters from Lions Clubs in many countries. All of these without exception indicated the enthusiasm these Lions felt because their organization had a place in the work of the conference. These messages of support came from every state in the United States, from Puerto Rico, Alaska, Hawaii, as from practically every province of Canada, from Cuba, Venezuela, Nicaragua, El Salvador, Guatemala and Honduras.

On May 1, the first of a series of Newsletters went out to the Lions Clubs from Conference Headquarters, to acquaint Lions everywhere with happenings of interest at San Francisco. The second letter dated May 10 informed the Lions that many worthwhile things were being accomplished at the consolation meetings, but with difficulty at times, as it was sometimes impossible to get all the American delegates together at all times, so a resolution was presented by President Skeen, which was passed, that they meet on a twice-a-week basis instead of daily.

The Lions, however, sensing the still restive outlook of some of the consultant group, sent informal invitations to all of them to attend a get-together dinner on the evening of May 22. As many of the consultants were preparing to leave for home, seventy-eight of them responded for this opportunity to get together informally before they left.

Nearly everyone present at the dinner was either at the head or near the head of organizations having great influence on American life. The guests were seated in typical Lions fashion and well-mixed–businessmen and labor leaders, farmers and industrialists, religious leaders and educators, representatives of organizations of business and professional men and women, all from the forty-two consultant groups. Speeches were limited and brief and each guest was asked to introduce the man or woman seated on their left, out of which grew much fun and fellowship, and the reserve and aloofness noticed in earlier meetings disappeared and complete unanimity, mutual understanding, good fellowship and cooperation became prominent in the month of consultants' meetings which followed and the Department of State was greatly elated over the new vigor attained by the consultants.

Before the conference concluded, the Lions Board of Directors, in order to stimulate further the work of their consultants in connection with the United Nations, held a board meeting in San Francisco. The Honorable Tom Connally, a leading member of the American delegation and chairman of the United States Senate Foreign Relations Committee, was the principal speaker at a banquet afterwards.

United States Secretary of State, Edward R. Stettinius, remarked at the conclusion of the conference, that he was delighted with the way in which the relationship with the consultants has worked out. "There is no question but that there are many things that you have helped us on of great importance and I think you will find that many specific things will have found their way into the United Nations charter as a result of this activity that might otherwise not have been in the final expression."

The Lions delegation left San Francisco inspired with zeal for its mission of keeping the country sold on the United Nations as the only feasible approach to world peace. At a later time, President Skeen remarked that the way to serve the cause of peace was to look toward the United Nations with faith and confidence rather than mere tolerance or, worse still, to search for a substitute organization. He bitterly criticized those who were talking against the United Nations.

In November, 1945, the Lions International headquarters asked all Lions Clubs to observe the week of December 2-8 as another Lions-United Nations Week, to study and discuss the Organization Plan, purpose and functions of the UN, so that all Lions would become familiar with some of the matters which would come up before the General Assembly and the Security Council when these two bodies met in London in 1946.

All Lions Clubs became active in United Nations programs and also arranged for community observance of United Nations Day on October 24 of each year. Later, the Board adopted a resolution proposing that one day be set aside each year for universal observance of peace.

In September 1946, President Pierce and Past President Skeen flew to Paris for the Peace Conference. When their plane arrived, they received a very warm reception. Later they presented a magnificent parchment scroll and gavel to the Secretary of State of the United States, the

Honorable James F. Byrnes, on behalf of the Lions of the World. Melvin Jones reported that it was recognized by all that the Lions were un-flinchingly united in a strong stand for a peace that ensured freedom and justice for all peoples and nations; that appeasement has been irre-vocably discarded; that there can be no temporizing where human val-ues and rights are concerned.

In January of 1947, Lions International staged a world conference of its own, when the International Relations Committee called a meet-ing of the Board to be held in Panama, the "crossroads of the world," to discuss intra-Lions international policy, with particular relation to the United Nations.

In March, 1947, Lions International was granted consultative status in the United Nations Economic and Social Council.

In October, 1947, the Lions celebrated their thirtieth anniversary in New York City in order to be close to the metropolitan home of the United Nations. Many officials of the United Nations were invited in order that both groups could become better acquainted with each other's viewpoints, procedures and objectives. At an elaborate banquet held at the Waldorf-Astoria Hotel, the Honorable Andrew W. Cordier, Executive Assistant to the Secretary-General of the United Nations, was the princi-pal speaker and he paid glowing tribute to the Lions for the energetic and vital part they had played from the very beginning in the support of the United Nations and in the cause of international understanding and cooperation, lasting world peace and human welfare.

Melvin Jones remarked that the Lions are doing a good work. "When we were in war, we worked assiduously for victory in war. We must work just as hard to win victory in peace. And not only should we work, but we should pray also. We should be calm in the face of emergencies, because only from calmness springs intelligent thought, courage and inspiration. Trials faced with confidence and a cheerful outlook are more than half won. We should have less doubt and more faith, less pessi-mism and more mental clarity."

The United Nations Conference on International Organization was convened at San Francisco, California on April 25, 1945, drafted the charter which was signed by 51 nations on June 26, 1945 and it entered into force October 24, 1945.

40 years later, membership had increased to 159 and the United

Nations continued to act as a buffer between disputing Nations, either in the United Nations Court, or with peace keeping units. During these years, the seams have bulged, but held – keeping the disputes to regional wars and name calling.

Lions International City

For one who by no possible twist of the definition could be called a visionary, Melvin Jones has had remarkable success looking into the future and translating dreams into tangible practicality.

He said Dreams are the fool ideas of day before yesterday that have become the commonplace miracles of today.

So it was hardly a surprise to anybody when the Lions celebrated the postwar era of prosperity and expansion with the announcement that they intended to have a city of their own–a real city with offices, homes, churches, memorials and transportation terminals all in the best traditions of Lionism.

Melvin Jones further remarked that this city was not any vision, when someone referred to it as a "dream city," as it got out of the dream stage long ago and it was always something more than a gleam in an architect's eye. The site had been selected by a committee of Lions and now belongs to the International. The plans have been completed in minute detail and the building of the physical city now depends only on the force and initiative of the Lions who have never been lacking in either.

The site for this community lies in the rolling woodlands just south of Chicago on US Highway 30 (Lincoln Highway)–beginning at US Highway 54 and extending east and south of the Illinois Central Railroad right of way to the Michigan Central Railroad. This site had good transportation service and such a community would certainly be without precedent in the archives of service clubs, if not in the history of the world. Its idea spans not only the time since Melvin Jones' first luncheon with the business Circle more than thirty years ago, but the whole gamut of human relationships.

Lions International City

To provide a permanent home for Lions International, buildings and other equipment necessary to take care of the headquarters' staff, which is constantly increasing in size and to make available homes for employees and other Lions who may want homes within the natural scope of a city;

To provide for the erection of a printing plant and storehouses for paper, supplies and other necessary material;

To provide for the printing of all publications issued by Lions International and for the distribution of supplies and materials to the thousands of Lions Clubs in the Association;

To provide for the installation of a post office, express and freight offices for dispatching the thousands of pieces of mail which go out of the International offices each day and switch tracks for loading and unloading;

To make provision for a hotel and parking facilities for visiting Lions and guests;

To make available facilities for the hospitalization and care of retired employees;

To provide for the establishment of a library, a house of worship, a Lions Museum, a memorial where busts or statues may permanently commemorate some of the eminent leaders of Lionism, a mausoleum, a chapel and a tower as a shrine to those Lions who have passed on, where visitors may offer up a prayer for those whom they wish to memorialize;

To provide for the establishment of schools and colleges, not only for educational purposes but also for the purpose of creating and fostering a spirit of generous consideration among the peoples of the world, to the end that through intelligence, forbearance, understanding, patience and diplomacy, statesmen of the world may "beat their swords into plowshares and their spears into pruning hooks, nation shall not lift up sword against nation, neither shall they learn war any more"; to promote the theory and practice of the principles of God, government and good citizenship; to hold "friendship as an end and not as a means" and "to be careful with my criticism and liberal with my praise; to be true to myself."

Lions Clubs International has advised the following:

"A track of land was acquired in south suburban Chicago as a proposed site of the 'Lions International City.' However, it appears that due to changing economic and cultural conditions, this dream of Melvin Jones was not able to be accomplished."

The dream vanished when the property was sold.

Demonstration of the Jones Law

The Lions are the fastest growing and most influential group of their kind in the world. Lionism grew out of the simple philosophy of the Melvin Jones Law - "you can't get very far without doing something for somebody else" - it follows that the truth of the law has been fairly well established. Melvin Jones, himself, was more than a little surprised at the results.

It was never his intention to set himself up as a spiritual leader or to make a religion out of the realistic creed that decency in business as well as in one's personal life brings a considerable return this side of the grave. He had been interested in friendship and abhorred loneliness and tried to bring kindred spirits together for the personal motive that he liked to meet people himself and in the instinctive realization that all men are gregarious. He would probably have liked to go through life as a sort of permanent entertainment committee, leading the band, giving verve to the chorus, lending most of his time to the promotion of gaiety. But his philosophy, his personal application of the golden rule, took him far into other fields. Whether he wanted to be or not, he had become a great spiritual force in the order he had founded.

He has been led to preach on a number of texts during the years, on interest in good government, aid to underprivileged children, pride in one's community, support of educational projects and active participation in all programs for the common good, but he never got very far from his fundamental idea of how human beings ought to behave. In all his public pronouncements the keynote was unselfishness. He spoke with complete confidence - not that he ever lacked it - and the inspirational knowledge that the Jones Law had become more than a theory.

Edwin Markham has expressed the essence of the Jones Law in his celebrated quatrain:

> *There is a destiny that makes us brothers;*
> *None goes his way alone;*
> *All that we send into the lives of others*
> *Comes back into our own.-*

David Lawrence, in an article, "I Saw America," in the *Saturday Evening Post,* gave wholehearted support to a proposition that Melvin Jones had been dingdonging into the ears of the world for better that thirty years:

"Are we developing leaders? I am sure that we are...I am more and more impressed, for example, with the work the service clubs are doing in the United States...I have attended service club luncheons from coast to coast in my journeys during the past quarter of a century. I find them the best instrument for the development of an awakened social responsibility that we have ever devised."

Mr. Lawrence was a little late in announcing his discovery, but Jones accepted his support uncritically and remarked that it doesn't make any difference who discovers truth so long as he discovers it and later remarked that truth has been in existence longer than anybody who goes out looking for it. And, he was quick to point out the immediate application of Lawrence's remarks, by saying that in this case, he has struck directly to the very core of Lionism, that Lions Clubs build leaders and Lions Clubs serve their communities.

It is not given to a great many men in the ordinary conduct of their lives to exercise leadership within a group yet every member of a Lions Club has this opportunity. Group action, the ability to live with others, is the basis of our civilization. By giving the business and professional men of the community the opportunity to lead their fellow businessmen toward accomplishments that rebound to the good of the entire community, Lionism is broadening and strengthening this basis. It is not an uncommon thing for a Lions Club to accomplish the complete transformation of a man from a misanthropic, selfish individual to a community benefactor. It is not uncommon for a Lions Club to effect the renovation of an entire community. Melvin Jones further told of being in more than one town where suspicion, personal ambition and greed were so dominant, so much the motivating factors in the public life, that they were obvious in the face of every businessman he met along Main Street. Nobody would speak well of a neighbor or cared a hoot for anybody else, yet in a few years, a Lions Club brought an entirely new atmosphere to the place. Lionism had demonstrated once more that what you give to humanity you get back, that bread cast upon the waters is something different from pie in the sky when you die.

David Lawrence saw the great need of trained community leaders whose vision is not confined to their own doorsteps but is as broad as the world itself. Lions Clubs are schooling such men.

In one of his letters, Melvin Jones asked, "Who owns this club?" Well I thought it was mine as much as anybody else's. But the way John has been carrying on you'd think he owned it all by himself. He's the first to greet distinguished visitors. He's the first to criticize all suggestions but his own. And then you've heard about Frank. Frank thinks he owns this club. He wants to make all the motions and do all the speaking all of the time. Or maybe somebody laments in your ear that Tom or Bob or Frank or Jim has been hogging all the club honors for himself. Well, who owns this club?

Melvin Jones then went on and told about the land he owned in a Chicago suburb and on which he paid taxes. During an April stroll, he ran across two garter snakes sunning themselves. He teasingly tossed his glove and they attacked it and the stick he used to retrieve his glove with, as they thought that they owned that ground, as did a noisy ground squirrel who chattered defiantly nearby, and so did a pair of bluebirds who fought off the sparrows who were trying to take the bird house. They too owned the place, as did the pair of robins who built their nest under the window and with the same independence, sang at their pleasure, stuck out their breast and hopped happily over the lawn. Later when Mr. Wren came, he picked out his home and this impudent, saucy little fellow drove away everyone who came near. And who would try to chase away the bees? But if you wanted to know who really owned the place, just come prowling around and let the dog see you. Yes, the dog, the birds, the bees, all claimed ownership of his home, the place he bought and paid taxes on–but during the winter, was lifeless without them. So say to them, what is mine is theirs, what is theirs is mine, together it is ours. It is our home and our home is my home.

"Now who owns the club–Tom? Jim? Frank? John? John likes to shake hands with everyone–Tom likes to sing–Harry likes to propose resolutions–Jim likes to be toastmaster–Frank likes to put on the boiled shirt and do the highbrow stuff. It's their club. I like to sit back and feel that I own the club too. So my club is their club and their club is my club and all together it is our club – and our club belongs to the community in which we live just as much as it belongs to us. Otherwise, it could have no purpose in existence."

The concomitant of unselfishness is, of course, friendship – a fact which Melvin Jones, apparently, foresaw from the very beginning. He may never have put into words his belief that friendship is the logical and unavoidable result of mutual association in the service of somebody else. But a complete understanding of that principle of psychology has motivated all his work for Lionism.

Jones wrote that he had often said that the Lions Club is a corporation of friends and has for its capital stock 'friendship.' Every member in a Lions Club is a friend of every other member and as the members of a club are linked together, so, also, are the clubs linked together in the Association. This means that every member in a club has as many friends as there are members in the Association. Members of the Association place a very high value on friendship, for they have incorporated in the Lions Code of Ethics the following:

"'To hold friendship as an end and not as a means, to hold that true friendship exists not on account of the service performed by one to another, but that true friendship demands nothing, but accepts service in the spirit in which it is given.'

"In other words, as a friend, I serve you. I demand nothing from you. It is my privilege and my pleasure to do so, because you are my friend. You, knowing that I am your friend, knowing as a friend that I demand nothing for my service and knowing that you cannot afford to accept service for which you cannot pay, other than from a friend, accept my service. I demand nothing; you owe nothing: I give; you accept in the spirit in which the service is rendered–the spirit of friendship.

"No one could express more beautifully or more effectively the reason for our being...We are primarily friends, friends to our Club, friends to our Association, friends to one another..Which today (1992), is approximately 1,400,000 loyal Lions, 1,400,000 friends, and yet not one to spare."

The words were Melvin Jones's, but represent the thoughts of Lions all over the world. Today, we sometimes wonder if the Lions of the World are aware of these words of Melvin Jones.

International Presidents

Dr. William Perry Woods, Evansville, Indiana, 1917-18

L.H. Lewis, Dallas, Texas, 1918-19

Jesse Robinson, Oakland, California, 1919-20

Dr. C.C. Reid, Denver, Colorado, 1920-21

Ewen W. Cameron, Minneapolis, Minnesota, 1921-22

Ed S. Vaught, Oklahoma City, Oklahoma, 1922-23

John S. Noel, Grand Rapids, Michigan, 1923-24

Harry A. Newman, Toronto, Ontario, Canada, 1924-25

Benjamin F. Jones, Newark, New Jersey, 1925-26

William A. Westfall, Mason City, Iowa, 1926-27

Irving L. Camp, Johnstown, Pennsylvania, 1927-28

Ben A. Ruffin, Richmond, Virginia, 1928-29

Ray L. Riley, San Francisco, California, 1929-30

Earle W. Hodges, New York, New York, 1930-31

Julien C. Hyer, Dallas, Texas, 1931-32

Charles H. Hatton, Wichita, Kansas, 1932-33

Roderick Beddow, Birmingham, Alabama, 1933-34

Vincent C. Hascall, Omaha, Nebraska, 1934-35

Richard J. Osenbaugh, Denver, Colorado, 1935-36

Edwin R. Kingsley, Parkersburg, West Virginia, 1936-37

Frank V. Birch, Milwaukee, Wisconsin, 1937-38

Walter F. Dexter, Sacramento, California, 1938-39

Alexander T. Wells, New York, New York, 1939-40

Karl M. Sorrick, Springport, Michigan, 1940-41

George R. Jordan, Dallas, Texas, 1941-42

Edward H. Paine, Michigan City, Indiana, 1942-43

Dr. E.G. Gill, Roanoke, Virginia, 1943-44

D. A. Skeen, Salt Lake City, Utah, 1944-45

Dr. Ramiro Collazo, Marianao, Cuba, 1945-46

Clifford D. Pierce, Memphis, Tennessee, 1946-47

Fred W. Smith, Ventura, California, 1947-48

Dr. Eugene S. Briggs, Oklahoma City, Oklahoma, 1948-49

Walter C. Fisher, St. Catharines, Ontario, Canada, 1949-50

H.C. Petry, Jr., Carrizo Springs, Texas, 1950-51

Harold P. Nutter, Camden, New Jersey, 1951-52

Edgar M. Elbert, Maywood, Illinois, 1952-53

S.A. Dodge, Bloomfield Hills, Michigan, 1953-54

Monroe L. Nute, Kennett Square, Pennsylvania, 1954-55

Humberto Valenzuela G. Santiago Chile, 1955-56

John L. Stickley, Charlotte, North Carolina, 1956-57

Edward G. Barry, Little Rock, Arkansas, 1957-58

Dudley L. Simms, Charleston, West Virginia, 1958-59

Clarence L. Sturm, Manawa, Wisconsin, 1959-60

Finis E. Davis, Louisville, Kentucky, 1960-61

Per Stahl, Eskilstuna, Sweden, 1961-62

Curtis D. Lovill, Gardner, Maine, 1962-63

Aubrey D. Green, York, Alabama, 1963-64

Claude M. De Vorss, Wichita, Kansas, 1964-65

Dr. Walter H. Campbell, Miami Beach, Florida, 1965-66

Edward M. Lindsey, Lawrenceburg, Tennessee, 1966-67

Jorge Bird, San Juan, Puerto Rico, 1967-68

David A. Evans, Houston, Texas, 1968-69

W.R. Bryan, Doylestown, Ohio, 1969-70

Robert D. McCullough, Tulsa, Oklahoma, 1970-71

Robert J. Uplinger, Syracuse, New York, 1971-72

George Friedrichs, Annecy, France, 1972-73

Tris Coffin, Rosemere, Quebec, Canada, 1973-74

Johnny Balbo, LaGrange, Illinois, 1974-75

Harry J. Aslan, Kingsburg, California, 1975-76

Joao Fernando Sobral, Sao Paulo, Brazil, 1976-77

Joseph M. McLoughlin, Stamford, Connecticut, 1977-78

Ralph A. Lynam, Alma, Michigan, 1978-79

Lloyd Morgan, Paraparaumu, New Zealand, 1979-80

William C. Chandler, Montgomery, Alabama, 1980-81

Kaoru "Kay" Murakami, Kyoto, Japan, 1981-82

Everett J. Grindstaff, Ballinger, Texas, 1982-83

Dr. James M. Fowler, Little Rock, Arkansas, 1983-84

Bert Mason, Donaghadee, Northern Ireland, 1984-85

Joseph L. Wroblewski, Forty Fort, Pennsylvania, 1985-86

Sten A. Akestan, Stockholm, Sweden, 1986-87

Judge Brian Stevenson, Calgary, Alberta, Canada, 1987-88

Austin P. Jennings, Woodburg, Tennessee, 1988-89

William L. Woolard, Charlotte North Carolina, 1989-90

William L. Biggs, Omaha, Nebraska, 1990-91

Donald Banker, Rolling Hills, California, 1991-92

Rohit C. Mehta, Ahmedabad, India, 1992-93

James T. Coffey, Toronto, Ohio, 1993-94

Prof. Dr. Giuseppe Grimaldi, Enna, Italy, 1994-95

International Convention Cities

1	1917	Dallas, Texas,	October 8-10
2	1918	St. Louis, Missouri,	August 19-21
3	1919	Chicago, Illinois,	July 9-11
4	1920	Denver, Colorado,	July 13-16
5	1921	Oakland, California,	July 19-22
6	1922	Hot Springs, Arkansas	June 19-24
7	1923	Atlantic City, New Jersey	June 26-29
8	1924	Omaha, Nebraska	June 23-26
9	1925	Cedar Point, Ohio	June 29-July 2
10	1926	San Francisco, California	July 21-24
11	1927	Miami, Florida	June 15-18
12	1928	Des Moines, Iowa	July 10-13
13	1929	Louisville, Kentucky	June 18-21
14	1930	Denver, Colorado	July 15-18
15	1931	Toronto, Canada	July 14-17
16	1932	Los Angeles, California	July 19-22
17	1933	St. Louis, Missouri	July 11-14
18	1934	Grand Rapids, Michigan	July 17-20
19	1935	Mexico City, Mexico	July 23-25
20	1936	Providence, Rhode Island	July 21-24
21	1937	Chicago, Illinois	July 20-23
22	1938	Oakland, California	July 19-22
23	1939	Pittsburgh, Pennsylvania	July 18-21
24	1940	Havana, Cuba	July 23-25
25	1941	New Orleans, Louisiana	July 22-25
26	1942	Toronto, Canada	July 21-24
27	1943	Cleveland, Ohio	July 20-22
28	1944	Chicago, Illinois	August 1-3
	1945	None Held	
29	1946	Philadelphia, Pennsylvania	July 16-19
30	1947	San Francisco, California	July 28-31
31	1948	New York, New York	July 26-29
32	1949	New York, New York	July 18-21
33	1950	Chicago, Illinois	July 16-20
34	1951	Atlantic City, New Jersey	June 24-28
35	1952	Mexico City, Mexico	June 25-28
36	1953	Chicago, Illinois	July 8-11
37	1954	New York, New York	July 7-10

38	1955	Atlantic City, New Jersey	June 22-25
39	1956	Miami, Florida	June 27-30
40	1957	San Francisco, California	June 26-29
41	1958	Chicago, Illinois	July 9-12
42	1959	New York, New York	June 30-July 3
43	1960	Chicago, Illinois	July 6-9
44	1961	Atlantic City, New Jersey	June 21-24
45	1962	Nice, France	June 20-23
46	1963	Miami, Florida	June 19-22
47	1964	Toronto, Canada	July 8-11
48	1965	Los Angeles, California	July 7-10
49	1966	New York, New York	July 6-9
50	1967	Chicago, Illinois	July 5-8
51	1968	Dallas, Texas	June 26-29
52	1969	Tokyo, Japan	July 2-5
53	1970	Atlantic City, New Jersey	July 1-4
54	1971	Las Vegas, Nevada	June 22-25
55	1972	Mexico City, Mexico	June 28-July 1
56	1973	Miami, Florida	June 27-30
57	1974	San Francisco, California	July 3-6
58	1975	Dallas, Texas	June 25-28
59	1976	Honolulu, Hawaii	June 23-26
60	1977	New Orleans, Louisana	June 29-July 2
61	1978	Tokyo, Japan	June 21-24
62	1979	Montreal, Quebec, Canada	June 20-23
63	1980	Chicago, Illinois	July 2-5
64	1981	Phoenix, Arizona	June 17-20
65	1982	Atlanta, Georgia	June 30-July 3
66	1983	Honolulu, Hawaii	June 22-25
67	1984	San Francisco, California	July 4-7
68	1985	Dallas, Texas	June 19-22
69	1986	New Orleans, Louisiana	July 9-12
70	1987	Taipei, Taiwan	July 1-4
71	1988	Denver, Colorado	June 29-July 2
72	1989	Miami, Florida	June 21-24
73	1990	St. Louis, Missouri	July 11-14
74	1991	Brisbane, Austrialia	June 18-21
75	1992	Hong Kong, China	June 22-26
76	1993	Minneapolis, Minnesota	July 6-9
77	1994	Pheonix, Arizona	July 12-15
78	1995	Seoul, Korea	July 4-7

Leos

Pennsylvania, our Keystone State, was the state where the idea of the Leo Clubs, a youth organization sponsored by and working with the Lions Clubs, was first implemented. In 1957, the Glenside Lions began with four purposes for the Abington High School Leo Club, the first Leo Club.

1. To serve the school by cooperating with the administration and faculty in the development of students for leadership, scholastic achievement, individual responsibility, honesty and respect for others.

2. To serve the community by responding to the needs of others.

3. To serve the nation by promoting the ideas of democracy and the principles of good government and citizenship.

4. To unite the members in bonds of friendship, and fellowship, and mutual understanding.

It was later corporately extended and fostered by District 14-K, Pennsylvania and later Leo Clubs were organized in New York State.

In 1968, when the International Board of Directors approved the sponsoring of a youth organization internationally, the states of Pennsylvania and New York then joined with Leo Clubs International.

These four purposes have since been extended to include all the Leos world wide, but service still ranks as a vital function of Leo clubs. Through Leo service activities, Leo members develop the elements of leadership, experience and opportunity. Activities are as varied as the number of Leo Clubs, including community beautification work, visiting and working with the handicapped and many other services.

Within a year after the program began, 200 Leo Clubs were organized in 18 countries. A year later, the number jumped to 918 in 48 countries and by 1974, the 2,000th club was established, with 50,000 Leos serving in 68 countries. It climbed to 4,000 in 99 countries in 1985 and as of February 28, 1995, there were 117,950 members in 4,718 clubs in 133 countries and geographic locations.

Today there are Leo Clubs in Wisconsin with over 100 members. They are located in Beloit, Caledonia, Fall Creek, Janesville, Madison, River Falls, Sherman Middle School and Sheboygan.

Lioness Clubs

In the early years of the history of our Lions Clubs, the women of Lion members formed their own clubs known by many different names: Lions Auxiliaries, Lionettes, Lionaides and Lion Helpers. They have a very impressive service record which dates back to at least 1935.

So, it was no wonder that in October of 1975 the Board of Directors of the International Association of Lions Clubs voted to give international recognition to women who had been serving in Lions auxiliaries all over the world. For the first time these women's clubs became united under one name, banner, emblem and constitution. The Mt. Pleasant Lioness Club in North Carolina was the first Lioness Club, and was certified into the new program in December 1975, By April 1977, the roster hit 1,000 clubs. Over one third of the current Lioness clubs were in existence as Lion Auxiliaries prior to the inception of the Lioness program, and some have given more than 40 years of service to Lionism.

Lioness Clubs assist their sponsoring Lions Clubs in a vast variety of service activities and they also plan and implement projects of their own in the community. Women's role in society, combined with their unique talents and capabilities, make Lioness Clubs an invaluable asset to Lionism's global effort to meet human needs. Among numerous activities performed by Lionesses are work with young adults, child care, health services, helping the aged, ecological concerns and vocational assistance.

As of January 3, 1990, there were 4,321 Lioness members in 166 Lioness Clubs in Wisconsin, 74,703 members in 2,683 Lioness Clubs in the United States and 145,624 Lioness in 5,633 Clubs world wide.

In the 1991-92 year, the International Board of Directors passed a resolution that has changed the status of the Lioness Clubs.

It is a shame, as these Lioness Clubs worked very closely with the

Lions and Leo clubs, besides doing their own thing in fund raisers and projects.

I have heard that this has changed the thinking of Lioness members and some plan to drop out, while others will become community groups and raise funds for local projects only.

Lioness Clubs continue to serve in Wisconsin as affiliates of the Lions Clubs. There are presently 150 clubs with over 3,700 members.

Women In Lions Clubs

For a number of years there had been a movement to open up the membership of all-male clubs to women Lions and at the 70th Lions Clubs International Convention held in Taipei, Taiwan on July 4th, 1987, the Lions of the world voted to amend the Constitution. The amendment removed the word "Male" as a requirement of membership in a Lions Club.

"BE IT RESOLVED, That Article III, Section 8, of the International Constitution be amended by deleting the word "male" as it appears in Line 2 of said Section and that a new sentence be added to the end of said Section to read as follows:

"Whenever the male gender or pronoun presently appear in the International constitution and bylaws, it shall be interpreted to mean both male and female persons."

As of December 30, 1989, there was a total of 26,203 women who were members of Lions Clubs. Of that total, 12,770 are from the United States and the State of Wisconsin had 155 Women in Lions Clubs.

In 1995 there are 80,533 women belonging to Lions Clubs across the world. In the United States, membership has reached 33,787 and in Wisconsin, 815.

Melvin Jones Memorial Shrine

Newspaper clippings and other records in the state of Arizona tell about some of the work and preparations that went into the ground work before the Melvin Jones Shrine could be erected.

A newspaper clipping dated January 11, 1955 tells that the Melvin Jones Memorial Foundation Inc. would receive a deed to land at old Fort Thomas as a site for a future Lions International Shrine dedicated to the memory of its founder. The deed was presented at the noon meeting of the Rincon Lions Club at Monte Vista Inn. The land was given by the Southern Pacific Railroad Company represented by their Superintendent of the Tucson Division, G.A. Bays. Arnold Grant, Chairman of the foundation and President of the Rincon Lions Club received the deed.

The article further tells that this parcel of land was located in the bounds of the old fort and they would have to remove an old building that was on that piece of property.

Another article dated October 20, 1955 tells that Melvin Jones would arrive in Tucson the next day in order to discuss plans for a Melvin Jones Memorial. He was met at the airport by Arnold Grant, State Chairman of the Melvin Jones Memorial Committee and officers from Tucson's five Lions Clubs at a dinner at the Pioneer Hotel. A 2:00 p.m. Sunday meeting was held at the Safford Inn in Safford and it was reported that the proposed memorial would be 25 feet high and 60 feet wide. It would be circular and partially constructed of flagstone. A large Lions plaque would be erected on top of the uppermost column and a bronze plaque placed on the others. On Jones' death, his body and his wife's body would be placed side by side at the base of the memorial. (This part of the plan was never carried out.)

In 1962 the Lions of Arizona had raised the necessary funds to start the construction of a 50-foot-high monument. It was completed and dedicated on June 27, 1965. These articles show that changes were made as the spire is fifty feet high with two shaped monuments on each side. The ceremonies were led by Edward M. Lindsey, of Lawrenceburg, Tennessee, 2nd Vice-President of Lions Clubs International.

The International Board of Directors, by proclamation in 1961, proclaimed the date of January 13, the birthday of Founder Melvin Jones, as a day of memory throughout the world of Lionism and that Founders and Rededication month traditionally observed in January, shall thereafter be designated as Melvin Jones Memorial Month.

Therefore, every year on the Saturday closest to the 13th of January, Lions throughout the State of Arizona gather at Fort Thomas to pay tribute to Melvin Jones. This is their tribute to a man who said, "Dreams are the fool ideas of the day before yesterday, that have become the commonplace miracles of today."

Each year near this date, the Lions of Arizona observe an annual Melvin Jones Day at the Melvin Jones Memorial with a very impressive program.

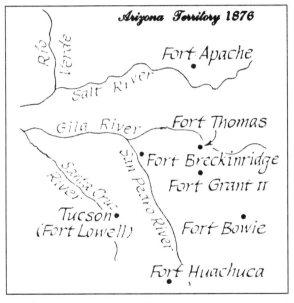

Future plans for the Melvin Jones Memorial site include the purchase of more land to expand the existing facilities for a more desirable place where Lions and visitors may stop and rest. It is hoped that by adding more land that they can have camping and picnic sites, ramadas, rest rooms and a building to house a museum where they can store and display the mementoes of Melvin Jones, other Lionistic mementoes and a caretaker residence.

Fort Thomas is located on State High 70, not far from Tucson. It is a very interesting historical site and it would be well worth your time to visit this area.

Fort Thomas

Fort Thomas, Arizona was first established as a military camp on August 12, 1876 and located three-quarters of a mile south of the Gila River on the site of the present town of Geronimo. Captain Clarence M. Bailey, 8th U.S. Infantry, established the camp on a site selected by Colonel August V. Kautz, 8th U.S. Infantry commanding the department. In 1878, the post was moved some five miles up the Gila to the site of the present town of Fort Thomas. This post was established in connection with the removal of the Chiricahua Apaches to the San Carlos Reservation, and to replace Camp Goodwin.

First called "New Post on the Gila," the name was changed to Camp Thomas in September, 1876. The post was designated a fort in 1881 and named for Brigadier General Lorenzo Thomas, who died on March 2, 1875. Abandoned on April 10, 1891, the military reservation was transferred to the Interior Department on December 3, 1892.

The initial garrison consisted of Troop F, 6th Cavalry, and Co. D, 8th. Infantry, commanded by Captain Clarence M. Bailey After it was moved to its present site, Captain May H. Stacey, 12th Infantry, assumed command. In August, 1880, Major David Perry, 6th Cavalry, assumed command. On May 12, 1882, Colonel Albert G. Brackett, 3rd Cavalry, assumed command of Fort Thomas and made it his regimental headquarters. In 1885, the 10th Cavalry relieved the 3rd.

During these years, many campaigns were made from this fort against Apache Indians who were led by Chiefs Natchez and Geronimo. After the Apache Indians fled into Mexico, these campaigns expanded into Mexico and many times the U.S. soldiers had gunfights with the Mexican soldiers.

On July 29th, 1886, about 100 miles below the Mexican border, Lieutenant Gatewood finally achieved a meeting with Natchez and

Geronimo and informed them of General Miles' terms of unconditional surrender and exile in Florida.

They agreed to the terms on the condition that Lt. Gatewood should march, eat and sleep with the hostiles until they reached Arizona. By so doing, he forestalled two attempts by the men of Troop B, Sixth Cavalry, to kill Geronimo in revenge for a defeat the year before.

On August 31, 1886, they reached Skeleton Canyon, in Arizona and on September 3rd, General Miles and escort arrived and went into camp. Shortly, Geronimo mounted a horse and presented himself at the tent of the American commander. After a long conference, which lasted the rest of that day and into the next, Natchez, the titular head of the Chirichua Apaches, formally surrendered his band. Thus ended the sixteen months of the Apache campaigns which required the entire forces of the regular army in Arizona, New Mexico and western Texas.

In June 1890, orders came to abandon Forts Thomas, Mojave, Verde and McDowell. In August, the orders affecting Fort Thomas were rescinded, but the reprieve did not last long. The final orders to discontinue the post were given by Major General John M. Schofield, Commander of the Army, on April 10, 1891.

The Camp Thomas Military reservation was declared May 18, 1877 in accordance with a survey made in January, 1877, by 1st Lieutenant E.D. Thomas, 5th Cavalry. The boundaries were announced in General Order No. 14 Department of Arizona June 11, 1877. The area embraced was 1,048 acres, 2 rods, 18 perches (51/2 yards) more or less. A portion of the Camp Goodwin reserve was included and the remainder surrendered to the Interior Department for disposition. July 22, 1884, Old Camp Goodwin, about 7 miles west of Fort Thomas was abandoned when the New Post was occupied on account of the unhealthy nature of the site.

A report describing the Fort shortly before it closed contains the following description.

The officers quarters are heated by means of stoves and fireplaces and heating the other buildings at the post by means of stoves. Soft wood is used as fuel.

There were 33 buildings including the commanding officer's quarter, officer's quarters, men's quarters, cellar, storeroom, office, sales and storehouse, ordnance storeroom, prison room and cells, Q.M. storehouse, blacksmith shop with shed for charcoal and coal, carpenter shop, library and reading room for the commanding officer, telegraph office, hospital, deadhouse, shed for hay and straw, quartermaster's corral, shed for cavalry corral, engine house for boiler and engine, and ice machine and tank, hospital, steward's quarters, commissary sergeants quarters, a well 48 feel deep, 10x12 feet square, and a water tank with a capacity of 22,000 gallons, which supplied the garrison by pipe. Water was excellent and supply sufficient. There is no system of sewerage at the post except natural surface drainage. All buildings are one storied. All buildings were of adobe with shingled roofs and were of various dimensions and this report listed their sizes even in some cases showing cubic feet.

Most buildings were built in 1876, except the telegraph office which was built in 1889, the hay and straw corral in 1877, engine house rebuilt in 1889-1890 and the hospital in 1888. (Another report told that Fort Thomas was a miserable outpost of badly made adobe buildings with dirt roofs that leaked during the rainy season. No doubt that this report was made before they shingled the building's roofs). There was a cemetery, (now abandoned), which was laid out in 1876, located on a narrow mesa overlooking the Gila Valley about one mile from the present town of Fort Thomas, which contained 47 graves of soldiers who died at the fort during its fourteen years as frontier outpost, and a number of marked and unmarked graves of civilians. The solders had erected a picket fence and gate that had enclosed the cemetery. Now all that remains are the marble markers, mounds, and some faded pieces of boards marking the graves of both, the good and the bad civilians.

During May 1892, George Edlridge of Thatcher, completed his government contract to exhume and transport the remains of the 47 soldiers buried there to Bowie Station for further transportation to, and for burial at the Arlington National Cemetery. It is recorded that there were a number of graves located along the road to the cemetery, but their locations are now lost.

During September 1986, on a trip through the western part of our country, we stopped at Fort Thomas, Arizona, and met Maurine and J.N. McEuen.

Maurine showed us what remained of the only building left from the old Fort Thomas, now part of another building in the village of Fort Thomas. Later she took us through a peach orchard, to the old cemetery.

Maurine served as the Postmaster at Fort Thomas, and J.N., who ran a store, told us stories of break-ins, shootings, and other interesting stories of the old days.

We also saw the memorial monument which the Arizona Lions erected in honor of Melvin Jones.

It is said, that of all the Indian tribes in North and Central America the Apaches were the most fierce. And, of the Apaches, the Chiricahua Band was considered the most fierce of them all. They made their living by farming, raiding and warfare.

When the Spaniards invaded the land, they brought horses along with them and eventually, the Apaches obtained some of the animals. They gave the Apache greater mobility for hunting and warfare.

The American army hired Indians as scouts. A scout would wear a white or colored piece of cloth around his head, a cotton shirt, a pair of pants, a breechcloth and moccasins. Certain tribes wore leggings made of deer, buffalo, or cowhide, and usually with excess leather folded a number of times on the top so if he needed a new pair of moccasins, he could just cut out a pair. The scout carried a rifle, a belt of ammunition slung over his shoulder, along with a rope of dried meat, to chew on while on the move. Thus equipped, he could outmarch a horse.

In addition to Indians, the army employed white civilians to act as scouts. Both the father and grandfather of Melvin Jones worked as scouts for the army at Fort Thomas. Melvin did not. By the time he was old enough to ride a horse, the frontier was at peace. As his mother knew, for a man to succeed in the 20th Century, he had to have an education and a job. She took her children back to the Midwest and prepared them for the new century. The Lions owe much to Mrs. Jones. For what would the Lions have become if Melvin Jones had been raised to be a muleskinner in Fort Thomas, Arizona?

Index